KU-208-611

HORSES

Authorised issue 2001 for
Mixing Medienproduktion GmbH, Neckarsulm, Germany
Translation: Rosetta International, London
Printed in Slovenia

HORSES

Faithful companions

Contents

Man's most

loyal friend

The horse in the world of humans

People owe more to the horse than to any other domestic animal

'The greatest happiness one can have on earth is found on the back of a horse'. More and more people are taking this ancient saying to heart and are discovering these large, elegant four-legged friends. Never before have so many young people wanted to learn to ride. For those who do it is the beginning of a long period full of pleasure to be shared with their horse. Those who succumb to the fascination of the horse usually remain fascinated for the rest of their lives. The horse is a harmonious combination of grace, strength, stamina and loyalty. An acquaintance with these beautiful animals arouses certain images, associations and ideas in almost everyone. Even today horses still play an indispensable role in our world and in our lives; they are part of us.

The fates of man and horse have been inextricably intertwined for many thousands of years. At first the prey of Stone-Age hunters, these big, powerful quadrupeds were domesticated 8000 years ago. We owe more to the horse than to any other domesticated animal - even the dog. The fact that they had so many uses enabled humans to develop rapidly. Stone-Age peoples would not have been able to make the transition from being nomads to being settled farmers without their hard-working, untiring horses. Then as humans learned to ride, horses' speed and stamina caused distances to shrink. The horse soon even began to play a role in the history of the world. Huns and Mongols reached Western Europe on their steppe ponies, and the outcome of many wars was decided by the use of horses. Empires were created and also destroyed with the help of horses. Innumerable noble beasts lost their lives in this way. Since the Industrial Revolution horses have become less and less important as working animals. Their tasks in agriculture, in the Army etc. have increasingly been taken over by machines and motor vehicles. Therefore contact with horses enriches the leisure-time of millions of people the world over – be it as riders or as spectators at one of the many equestrian sports events.

Being with horses has a positive effect on the character of young people

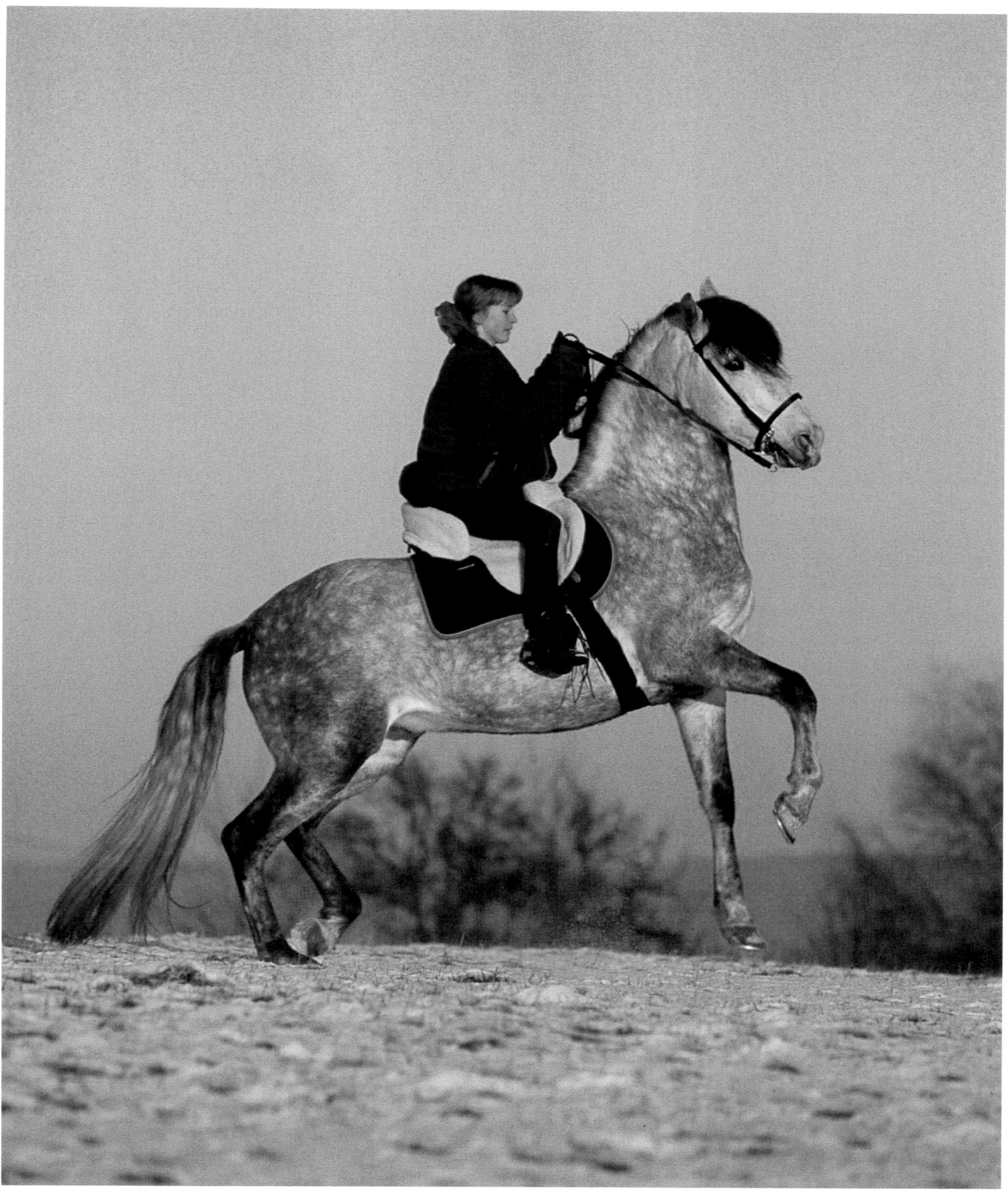

Millions of people all over the world are fascinated by horses

Horses and riding

Riding is a sport for people of any age. It is just as much fun for children put on a pony by their mother or father for the first time as for the many elderly people who retain their youth through riding. Seeing the world from the back of a horse is enjoyable both for the occasional leisure rider and for the ambitious competitive rider. Riding gives many people the strength to overcome the cares, demands and problems of their daily lives. A ride through woods, meadows or fields clears the mind. Discovering the beauties of nature in company with a horse is very special and beneficial experience. Working as a team with a motivated horse who is willing to learn and whom the rider is training for a specific purpose offers many wonderful moments. The horse's personality gives riding a special dimension that elevates it far above other hobbies and sports. It is essential, however, to understand the animal's character and to have a rapport with him. The rider must also understand all the little things a horse needs on a daily basis. The horse is not a piece of sports equipment to be used according to need and mood and otherwise put back in a cupboard, but a highly-sensitive living creature that deserves and needs the constant and full attention of its owner.

In many parts of the world the horse is still a major means of transport

Nearly everybody who has ever had anything to do with horses and has learned to ride develops the desire at some time or other to own their own horse. It is not, however, merely a matter of selecting one out of the more than 150 recognized breeds – a lot of thought must go into the decision! Buying a horse is also a very expensive business and involves a moral duty towards the animal. So before buying one the horse-lover must ask himself whether he can afford and has the facilities to house and feed a horse properly and whether he has the time to look after it.

Horses in sport

Happily the number of people owing horses is constantly increasing. But even without a horse of one's own there are countless ways of devoting oneself to these magnificent animals. Millions of people who don't ride still enjoy equestrian sports. They go to racecourses and exercise their 'understanding of horses' by betting. British successes in showjumping, dressage and three-day eventing, particularly in the Olympic Games, have also contributed to the enormous increase in people's interest in equestrian sports, as has our Royal Family's interest in horses.

A breath of adventure: a cowboy riding into the sunset

Horses still play a part in many ceremonial occasions, such as this procession of the Royal Canadian Mounted Police

The Horse in art

Horses have also always caught people's imagination. In Greek mythology there were the legendary Centaurs, creatures with horses' bodies and human heads. And horses have also often played a role in literature – what would Don Quixote be without his Rosinante, for instance! Horses have also always been a favourite subject of many artists. Prehistoric cave paintings show many horses, kings and princes liked to have their portraits painted on horseback, and many 20th-century artists were also fascinated by these wonderful animals. Horses still play a role even in more modern media such as film and television, be it in spectacular scenes in westerns or historical films or even as the main character such as in the film *Black Beauty* and the TV series *Champion the Wonder Horse*.

Thus today horses, with their elegance and beauty, but in particular their intelligence and loyalty, can be said to be man's best – if you know how to deal with them! This comprehensive book, illustrated with more than 200 fascinating colour photographs, contains detailed information on all aspects of the world of horses. It goes back to the time the ancestors of our noble four-legged friends evolved, shows how they have evolved up to the present day and introduces the reader to the 80 most important breeds of horse.

This book also gives practical and useful tips on how to buy, feed, house and look after horses. It offers the rider basic information about the various riding styles and techniques and the equipment required. All the varieties of equestrian sport are presented in detail. Finally an extensive glossary gives the meanings of the most important words and phrases in 'horse-speak'. Thus the book is a valuable and useful work of reference for any horse-lover.

Horses in art: **Mares and Foals in a Landscape** *by George Stubbs, the celebrated English animal painter*

The evolution

of the horse

The relatives of the horse

Its single hoof is one of the most striking features of the horse. Many horses are fitted with horseshoes which are renewed by the blacksmith

Within the class of mammals (Mammalia) today's horses belong to the order of odd-toed ungulates (Perissodactyla). This means that over time the whole of the animal's weight shifted onto the middle of the originally five toes. This toe then developed to such an extent that today the middle toe has become the hoof and all the other toes have shrunk. In contrast the hooves of even-toed ungulates always consist of two toes (cloven hooves) that developed more than the others, such as was the case with pigs, camels and cattle. Rhinoceroses and tapirs are the horse's most distant relatives amongst the odd-toed ungulates.

Within the order of the odd-toes ungulates horses belong to the once extensive suborder of the Hippomorpha. Today the Equidae is the only surviving family in this suborder, all the other representatives having become extinct. Yet apart from the genus Equus all the members of this family became extinct more than two million years ago. The genus Equus also includes such close relatives of the horse as the various species of zebra (Grevy's zebra, the mountain zebra and the quagga, this last only recently extinct), the Asian onager, the Asian wild ass, the African wild ass and the domesticated donkey

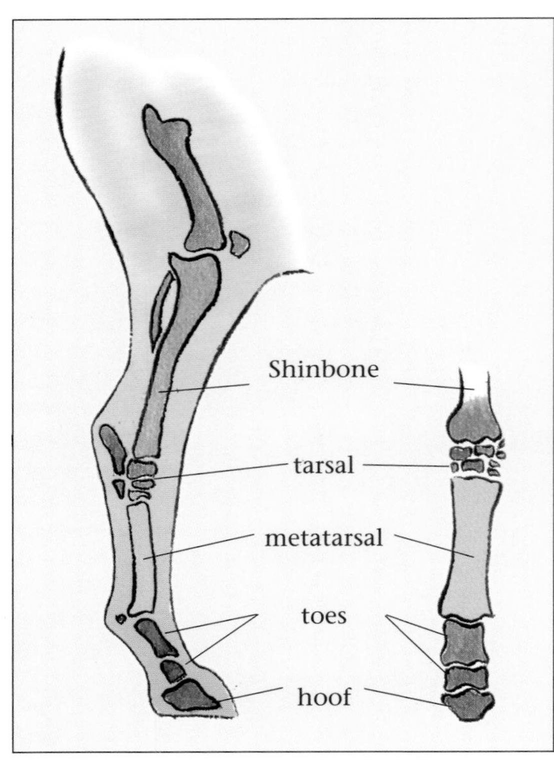

The middle toe of the horse's foot has developed into a hoof

The rhinoceros is another odd-toed ungulate

The ancestors of our horses

The dawn horse Eohippus or Hyracotherium is the oldest ancestor of the horse although there is now very little resemblance

Because of the numerous finds of bones and fossils the development of the horse and its distribution, originally extending over large areas of America, Asia, Europe and Africa, are today better researched than those of almost any other species of animal. So it is quite easy to trace their evolution back. But it is still very difficult to say much about what they looked like, the length and colour of the coat, the ears and the nose from bones several million years old, since the outer appearance of an animal cannot be judged accurately from the skeleton. However as each living creature is adapted to its environment comparisons of fossilized finds, teeth for example, with animals living today enable conclusions to be drawn about the plants growing at that time and what the ancestors of our horses ate. Thus the teeth of an animal living on the plains and eating grass are distinctly different from those of an animal living in woods and eating leaves. This is how we know a little about their habitat and can draw indirect conclusions about their appearance and way of life.

Today we know that while the Hippomorpha were evolving there were many different lines most of which, however, came to an end thousands of years ago. The oldest ancestors of our modern horses lived about 70 million years ago. They lived in huge forests of palm trees, which they shared with troupes of prosimians, primitive primates that included lemurs, tree shrews, lorises and tarsiers. Life at this time was dangerous: giant snakes lurked among the palm

The zebra is one of the closest relatives of the horse

trees, and huge crocodiles waited for prey at the waterholes. The existence of these species of animal is clearly proved by a large number of well-preserved finds from the famous pit at Messel near Frankfurt-am Main in Germany, the site of an Eocene lake in which soft sediment has preserved an exceptional number of fossils.

The first horse-like mammals originated in North America and Europe. For a long time they were given two different names. Those found in Europe were known as Hyracotherium and those found in America as Eohippus (Dawn Horse). However more recent investigations have shown that they are one and the same species, since the differences between them are so slight as to be insufficient to make them two separate species. These early horses looked nothing like today's horses. They were no bigger than a cat or a fox and with their low head carriage and their arched backs they looked more like tiny deer or small antelopes. Their long slender legs ended in paws, which had four toes in front and five behind. These early horses had still to develop real hooves and they walked on blunt nails. Yet the predisposition for the existence of a single hoof was already in place, since the middle toe was considerably stronger than the others. So this little early horse is considered to be the ancestor of all odd-toed ungulates and therefore of our horses.

The Hypohippus, a distant ancestor of the horse, has been extinct since primeval times

Evolution and extinction of the horse in America

About 40 million years ago these early horses suddenly became extinct in Europe but we still have no idea why. Early horses in North America, on the other hand, evolved further and gradually changed from being forest-dwellers and eating leaves to being plains-dwellers and eating grass. In the process, over millions of years, they lost the superfluous toes and for a while became three-toed, until about 15 million years ago the first single-toed animals evolved. At the same time they gradually became bigger, so by this time they were already the same size as a modern pony.

During the whole of this time larger and larger herds of these animals were migrating from North America into Asia and Europe (Eurasia). That was possible because at that time there was still dry land between Siberia and Alaska where the Bering Straits are today. This is how Anchitherium, Hypohippus and Hipparion reached Eurasia. Astonishingly none of these early types of horse in Eurasia evolved further but after a time died out completely.

When the North American ancestor of our horses had ceased to evolve, eleven million years ago, it had become Pliohippus, which already resembled modern horses so closely

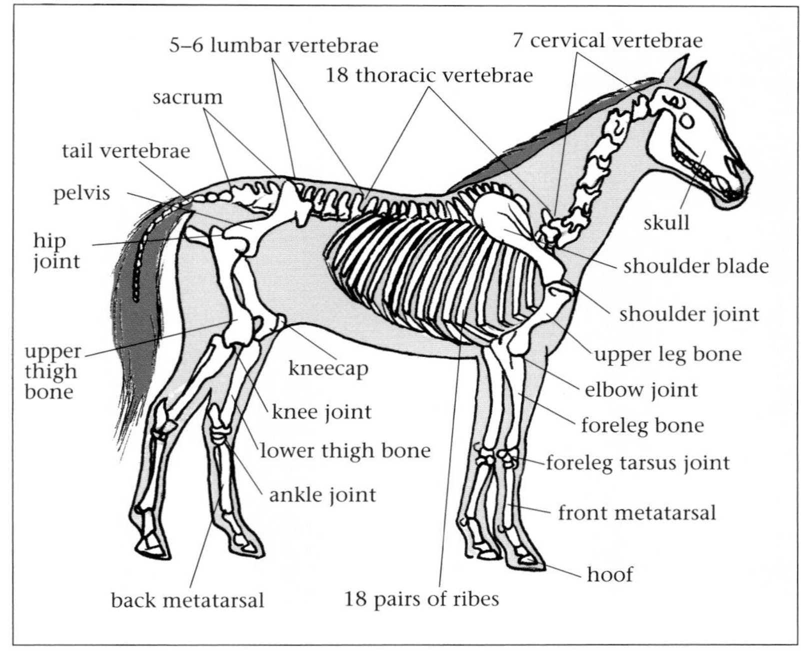

The skeleton of a horse

that later changes were only in small details. Its whole build had become adapted to its living conditions. Thus the teeth had become bigger than those of the earlier leaf-eaters in order to cope with the tough grass of the plains. As it ate only plants and had no effective method of defending itself against its deadly enemies, Pliohippus' only defence lay in swift flight. Therefore agility and stamina became essential. The chest became broader, the back longer and the whole body became altogether stronger. This prehistoric horse also migrated two million years ago over the Bering Bridge into Eurasia. As the first member of the horse family since Eohippus the descendants of Pliohippus in Europe and Asia apparently found the living conditions ideal, because they finally evolved splendidly into the actual Equus. However on the continent of America they evolved in precisely the opposite direction, until the last horses became extinct there about 10,000 years ago. The reasons for this are completely obscure, though it is presumed to be due to climate change caused by the last Ice Age and the resulting loss of habitat. Thus there is no longer a single wild representative of this species in the region where our horses actually originated. There were no more horses in America until the Spanish Conquistadores started to import them in a big way in the 16th century. Of by then they were fully domesticated.

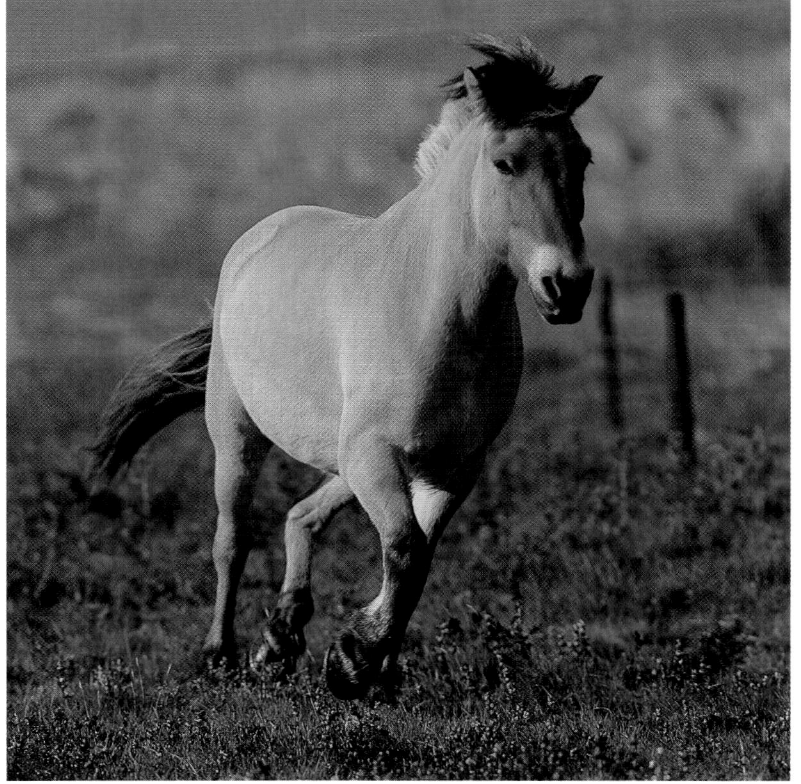

The horse is a 'flight animal' which can only escape from its enemy by fleeing. This is why it has a field of vision of 300°, so it can see danger coming from almost any direction

The Przewalski horse is the last wild horse on earth

The Tarpan and Przewalski's horse

More than a million years ago the immigrants from North America into Eurasia began to evolve into today's relatives of the horse. The common ancestor of the ass and the zebra developed. This line then split into asses and zebras. Both migrated to Africa, where they remain the only representatives of the horse family.

From the African wild ass Stone-Age peoples bred the African donkey, which in turn became the ancestor of the European donkey. The zebras split into many species, of which only two survive today, the mountain zebra and Grevy's zebra.

With the fluctuations in climate changes brought about by the Ice Ages the horses that had migrated into Europe changed. As it became colder and colder they became ever smaller, sturdier and stronger, with the result that many researchers consider them to be the ancestors of our ponies of today. However this theory is contradicted by the fact that after the end of the various cold periods these horses gradually became bigger again. Moreover all these animals became extinct at the end of the last Ice Age.

Today we are more inclined to the theory that all our domesticated horses can be traced back to only two species of wild horse, the Tarpan and Przewalski's horse. These two species were the only ones still in existence after the last Ice Age. The Tarpan, a small dun horse with a narrow head, lived in Eastern Europe. It was wiped out in the second half of the 19th century by Russian horse-breeders who

The African wild ass (right) and the domestic donkey which is descended from it (above) are close relatives of our horses

A distant relative of the horse: Grevy zebra mares form groups separate from the stallions, unlike other zebras which herd together

wanted to prevent wild stallions from breeding with their stud mares. They shot the huge herds of Tarpans mercilessly and thus wiped out the ancestor of the European domesticated horse. In the 1930s Professor T. Vetulani began to use the Polish Koniks belonging to Count Zamoyski to regenerate the Tarpan. Today's Tarpans are therefore not wild horses but feral domesticated horses that look like wild horses, since the process of domestication is irreversible owing to the very complicated biological changes that occur in wild animals when they are domesticated.

Przewalski's horse has a dun coat. Mane, tail and legs are dark. For a long time there was no proof that this inhabitant of the steppes of Central Asia had ever been domesticated. However this has now been proved by abundant finds of bones from prehistoric settlements in Mongolia. Today it is the last wild horse in existence. Apart from Mongolia Przewalski's Horse now lives only in zoos, where it is still bred pure.

So today, unfortunately, we have to say that the wild horse is a dying species, the culmination of the evolution of which is far in the past – sad as that may sound to those who love horses.

It is, therefore, all the more important to breed horses, which since the dawn of history have performed valuable services for us humans and have enriched our world with their beauty and noble nature.

The Tarpan was wiped out in the 19th century. It has been 'back bred' from the Polish Konik

Man and horse

in history

The horse as a prey animal

The history of the domestication of the horse can best be understood if one considers the changes that have taken places in the world in which man and horse have lived together for thousands of years. The relationship between man and horse dates right back to the Stone Age and at first was that of hunter and hunted. At that time people lived in groups of between 20 and 50. They lived from hunting and gathering wild fruits. Their delicate lightweight weapons – bow and arrow and light throwing spears – were used for hunting birds and small mammals. Heavy throwing spears, stone axes and stabbing spears were used to hunt and kill even large prey animals such as buffalo, red deer, roe deer and even horses. Often even whole herds of wild horses fell victim to large bands of hunters. The hunters were helped in this by the first dogs, which were the first animals to be domesticated 13,000 years ago. The dogs encircled the herds, which were gradually driven up onto a steep rocky plateau, with none of the horses being allowed to escape. When the animals finally got close to the drop they panicked and eventually fell from the cliff to their death. In southern France the remains of the bones of hundreds of wild horses have been found on the precipitous slopes of rocky plateaux. Hunters also trapped horses using pits and nets made from plant fibres.

Stone Age people recorded the most important things in their life with cave paintings. These tell us much about their way of life. Besides buffaloes, stags and roe deer, they also hunted horses

As the herds migrated over large areas, the hunters had to follow them constantly. Therefore they couldn't settle permanently in one place. People preferred to live in dwellings provided by nature, especially caves. One of Stone-Age man's greatest achievements, which tells us a lot about their way of life and hence their relationship with horses, is the invention of art. Splendid and elaborate cave paintings discovered in south-west France and in Spain tell us not only about their daily life and religion, but also about their hunting techniques and their favourite prey animals in particular. Stone-Age peoples also made lifelike engravings on stones and fashioned statues of people and animals from clay or ivory, many of which have

In the south of France wild horses were hunted in the rocky mountains. In their panic the animals would fall over the cliff edge

been found in caves.

When the hunters had to follow their prey on their migrations they set up camps and erected tents. The tents were round or oval with a diameter of up to eight metres and were usually built over shallow pits in the ground. They consisted of wooden frames covered with animals hides. Where the tents met the ground they were sealed with large stones or earth. Hearths have even been found in some tents. The largest camps discovered so far consisted of up to six tents. The archaeological finds from these camps show that even then there was division of labour. Some tents contained piles of parts of tools and fragments of stone. From this it is assumed that this is where specialists in the making of weapons and tools worked, whilst other members of the group specialized in hunting. Some researchers believe that the men went hunting whilst the women collected wild berries and fruits. However there is no historical proof of such division of labour between men and women.

The horse is domesticated

Man progressed ever more rapidly after the end of the last Ice Age, around 12,000 years ago. His environment changed considerably as the ice retreated. Huge forests grew, with an abundance of game. This meant that hunters did not need to go so far nor spend such a long time to find enough food. Man now made several discoveries that were so important that many historians refer to them as a revolution. He transferred his experience with domesticating dogs to other species such as goats, sheep, cattle and horses and thus discovered animal husbandry. At the same time he 'invented' agriculture by gradually breeding specific types of grain from wild grasses. Raising livestock and practising agriculture meant that man was now much better able to plan his life, since he was no longer so dependent on the whims of nature and the luck of the chase and no longer had to be constantly on the move in the search for prey or fruit. Soon he built the first permanent settlements, and even villages. Man had become settled!
The oldest fossilized remains

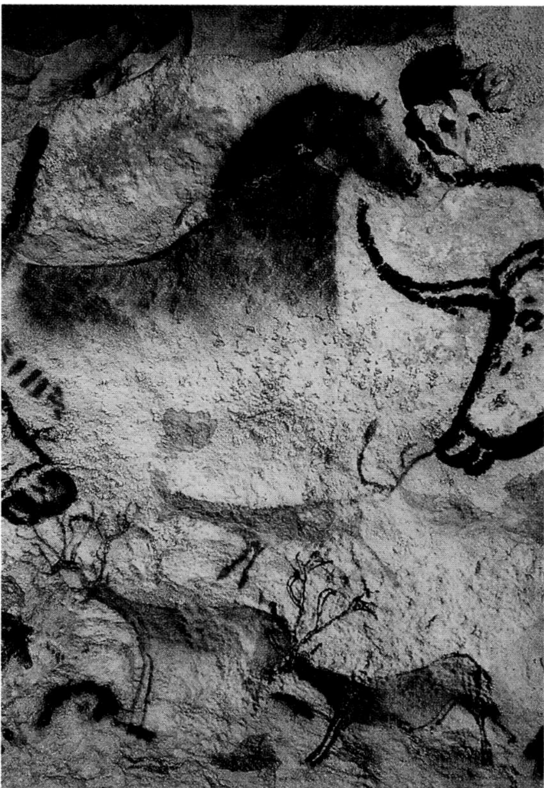

Picture of a wild horse (left) and of horses, buffaloes and stags in the Stone Age cave of Las in F

These Stone Age cave paintings have a breath-taking beauty

of domesticated horses were discovered in the Ukraine and are approximately 6000 years old. Reconstructions of these horses have shown that they were descended from the Tarpan. Remains of domesticated horses from this period have also been found in China. Because of their appearance scientist believe these are of the Przewalski type. However these discoveries do not prove that at that time domesticated horses existed only at the places where these finds were made. It is much more likely that as they became settled people domesticated horses wherever there were any.

When researching into the domestication of all animals historians have to do a lot speculating. There is a very widespread theory that at first the pregnant mares that were captured were allowed to live in order that there might be a store of meat from the young animals. Then the problem was how the mares would become pregnant again the following year without being set free. According to tradition in ancient times mares on heat were tied to trees to be served by wild stallions, which would support this theory. As the foals bred in this way grew, it was discovered that horses could be set to work. At first they were used as pack and draught animals – only later did people learn to ride them. 4,000 years ago, however, horses in ancient China were already pulling war chariots, and more than 3,000 years ago the first warriors rode on horseback. Since then the history of the horse is mainly a history of suffering in war right up to the Second world War in which they were still used mostly as draught animals.

The Great Wall of China was built to keep out the Mongolian nomads who were famous horsemen

The horsemen of the Steppes

The first people to base their way of life on riding horses lived in Mongolia in Central Asia, the home of Przewalski's horse. They were nomads and first tamed the wild horse for hunting, since they were so fast and had so much stamina that hardly any other animal could outrun them. These qualities, stamina and speed, meant that they were soon also used in battle against other tribes. After launching an attack the Mongols could escape so fast on their horses that they were practically invulnerable. Before their adversaries could gather to defend themselves the attackers had usually galloped off. In this way the riders of the Steppes conquered huge areas in eastern Asia. Finally the Chinese built the famous Great Wall of China to keep them out. However even this could not stop the nomads' constant raids, so the Chinese themselves soon formed mounted armies, which pursued the Mongols and drove them out of the country.

After their expulsion from China the riders of the Steppes then turned westwards. Thus it came about that 3,000 years ago hordes of Cimmerians and Scythians appeared out of southern Russia and rode their swift Steppe horses into Europe. They were able to do this because they were far superior to the peoples of Europe and the Orient who fought on foot with spears. The Cimmerians and Scythians brought the new fighting methods of the Steppes to Europe for the first time.

The horse conquers and destroys empires

In later history horses were decisive in the rise of many great empires. The Persians would never have been able to build up their empire without horses and huge mounted armies. And even Alexander the Great built up large mounted armies, which fought using completely novel tactics, before he set out to destroy the Persian empire.

The Roman empire collapsed under attacks from the Germanic tribes who were forced out of their lands when the Huns invaded Europe. The Huns wore light armour and fought their enemies with bow and arrow from the backs of their swift Steppe horses where they were perfectly at home. With these

Famous riders: Carlos, heir to the Spanish throne , and Napoleon Bonaparte

The horse created and destroyed world empires.

Here Alexander battles against the Persians

Indians too were excellent riders who used their horses more for hunting than fighting

long-range weapons the Huns were at first far superior to the Germanic tribes and the Romans, but were then annihilated when their method of waging war was used against them.

In the Middle Ages armour developed further. Great armies of knights, who fought wearing iron armour and carrying heavy lances, were formed. Their horses were correspondingly large and strong, which was of course at the expense of speed and agility. The skill of the riders of the Steppes thus fell by the wayside since a horse now had to carry not only its rider but also his armour and its own armour, a total weight of well over 16 stone. It was not until firearms were invented that this development came to an end, since speed and agility were now in demand once again. The cavalry came into being, and swiftly became the factor that decided the outcome of a battle.

At the Battle of Waterloo in 1815, in what was probably one of the largest battles in history in which cavalry was used, Europe liberated itself from Napoleon Bonaparte's rule.

In wars of the past – such as the American Civil War – many horses were killed as well as humans

The taming of the Wild West

After suddenly becoming extinct 10,000 years previously horses didn't reach America again until the Spanish Conquistadores brought them in the 16th century. Many Indian tribes soon based their way of life on them, but used them for hunting rather than as weapons. However they didn't breed them themselves but stole them from the Spanish. One exception was the Nez Percé Indians, whom we have to thank for the distinctive spotted horse, the Appaloosa. Later the Indians began to capture and tame Mustangs. Mustangs were the feral descendants of the horses the Spanish left behind. As huge numbers of Europeans began to migrate to North America they brought many horses with them over the Atlantic Ocean. In the 18th and 19th centuries they were used as cavalry horses but also as

draught and working animals, thus playing their part in the taming of the Wild West. They fought and suffered in the American Civil War, in which tens of thousands of them lost their lives. In fact the chances of survival in the increasingly-mechanized wars were reduced for both men and horses.

Industrialization also forced horses out of other roles that they had filled for thousands of years. In agriculture farm horses were replaced by traction engines and then tractors. The invention of the railway and the meteoric ascendancy of the car replaced the horse as a means of transport too. Today the horse, for a long time the fastest 'vehicle' and the one with the most staying power, is still the number one means of transport in only a few remote regions of the world. It has, however, conquered a new field - its partnership with man for leisure and competitive sports.

In the past the coach was the most important means of transport

The taming of the Wild West was only made possible by the use of horses. This picture shows a wagon train of settlers

Catalogue of

horse breeds

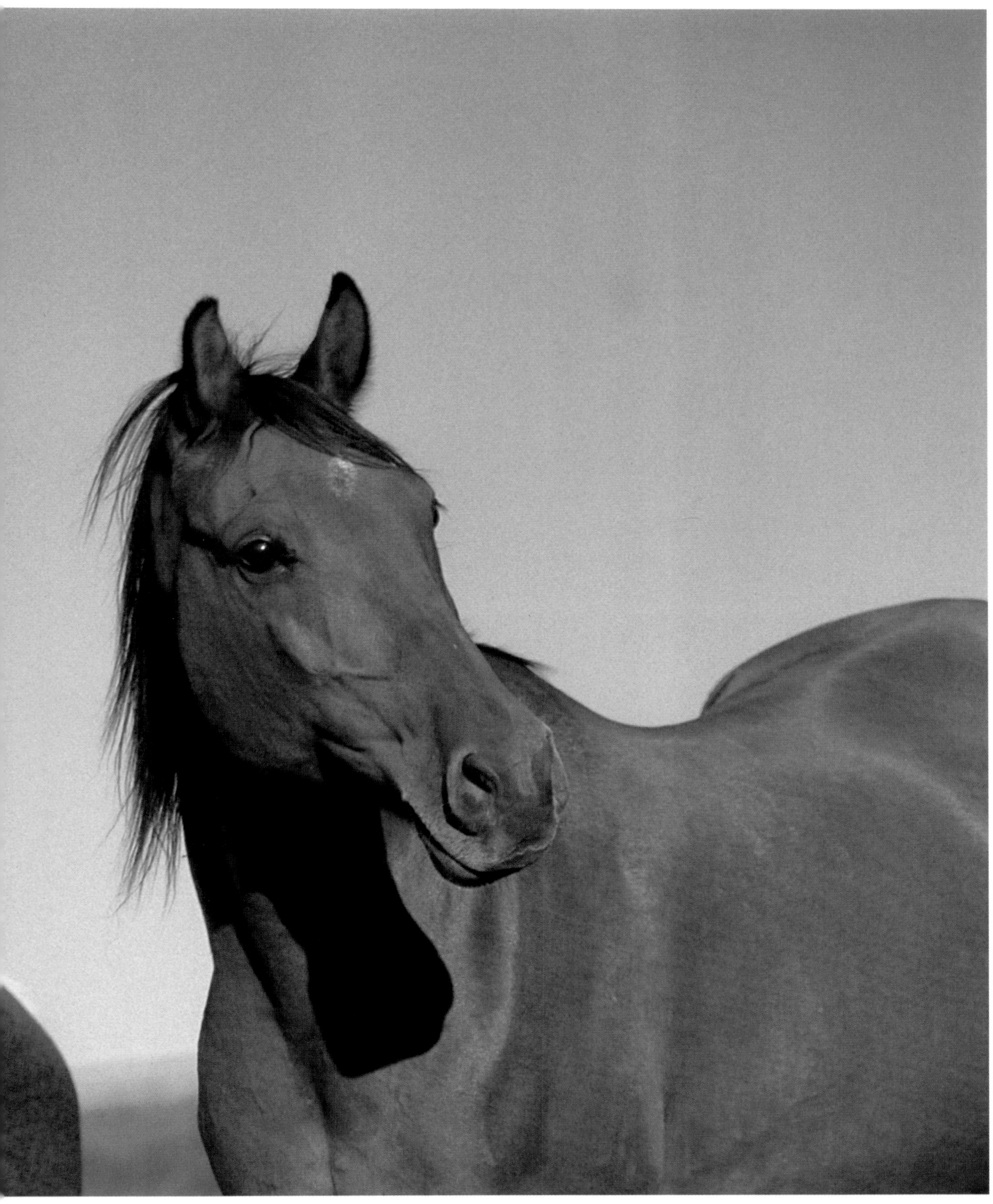

The start of breeding

It is rare nowadays that horses have to work as hard as these two

Even before horses were domesticated different natural environments meant that wild horses evolved into distinct types which even this early could be considered to be separate breeds. But real breeding did not begin until after domestication. Horses began to be deliberately selected and bred for specific purposes. Horses that were particularly strong and had a gentle nature were selected for heavy strenuous work such as pulling ploughs or heavy carts. Tribes who regarded horses as a favourite source of food preferred to breed heavy, meaty animals.

The first horses for riding and for use in war, however, were bred by crossing animals that were tame and swift and had staying power. In the Middle Ages the need was once again for very strong horses that could carry a knight plus his armour and also its own armour. Speed and agility were now longer so important. The various requirements and criteria for breeding resulted in numerous breeds of horse that were very different not only in

Norikers pulling logs.

Norwegian wild horses still have many of the characteristics which reflect their wild origin

appearance but also in temperament and character. However these different breeds do not differ from one another and from the original wild type as much as, for instance, the domesticated dog. As the Western world has become industrialized and mechanized horses have lost many of the jobs they used to do for us. In agriculture and forestry they have been largely replaced by tractors. As a means of transport the horse has been almost totally superseded by the car. Only a few breweries still use horse-drawn drays for advertising purposes. Horses are no longer even eaten very often in Western Europe. And in the army the horse's role is purely ceremonial. However this is not the

case everywhere in the world. In less-developed and very remote regions in Eastern Europe, Asia, Africa and South America horses are still very much used for working.

In Western Europe and North America the horse has changed roles and now is now overwhelmingly used for leisure and sport. This has, of course, also had an effect on horse-breeding. So it is not surprising that the breeds of horse most popular today are all bred predominantly for their kind and obliging nature and sporting ability. Almost all of them result from crosses, in varying proportions, with the oldest breed of all, the Arab. However this means that many breeds are becoming more and more similar to one another and hence more and difficult for the layperson to tell apart. The old breeds of heavy horse, on the other hand, are no longer in demand and for the most part continue to be bred only to prevent them from dying out and one of mankind's greatest achievements from being lost for ever.

Today, horses play an important part in people's leisure time activities

Most breeds of riding horses have been developed by crossing with Arabian thoroughbred stallions

The four basic types of modern horse

There are more than 150 recognised breeds of horse worldwide. However they can all be allocated to one of the four basic types. These are ponies, cold-bloods, warm-bloods and thoroughbreds. However the designations cold-blood and warm-blood have nothing to do with the animal's body temperature, which is the same in all healthy horses. They refer in fact to the horse's temperament.

English thoroughbred horses and Westphalian crossbred horses

The **thoroughbred** is a horse whose sire and dam are both descended from registered thoroughbreds. However there are relatively few of them, since there are only two breeds of thoroughbred, the Arab and the English thoroughbred. All race horses are thoroughbreds.

The designation **warm-blood** is applied to all horses that have some thoroughbred in them. However the proportion varies depending on the breed. Horses that have 75 percent thoroughbred blood are referred to as 'three-quarters bred'. Those that have only a small proportion of thoroughbred in them are more like the lighter breeds of the altogether sturdier cold-bloods both in temperament and in appearance.

The designation **cold-blood** or, more often, heavy or **draught horses**, is mainly used for older breeds that still look very much like their working forebears. They are mostly big, solid, powerful animals. Some are real giants strong enough to be able to shift weights of several tons. These heavy horses are those that are today bred only for the reasons mentioned above, to prevent their becoming extinct.

This giant Shire Horse is a heavy draught-horse.

The Haflinger-Ponys are popular with children

Ponies differ very much from one another in appearance. Depending on the breed they may be a miniature version of a thoroughbred, like a small, dainty warm-blood, but they may also look like a sturdy little cold-blood. In fact the only difference between a pony and a horse is the size. All horses measuring 14.2 hh (147 cm/58 in) or less are ponies. The only exception is the Falabella, which, despite its small size, is always referred to as a horse.

Their different colours do not stand in the way of friendship. A white horse and a black horse with a star-shaped marking

Colours and markings

Within a breed individual horses may look very different from one another owing to their different colours and markings. However the colour of an animal does not affect its other qualities and characteristics. A smart pure-bred Arab will always be temperamental and a Shire always good-natured and strong – irrespective of their colour. Nevertheless there are many breeds in which a particular colour of coat predominates and is therefore typical of the breed. This is mainly due to horses with that particular colour of coat being used for breeding more than the others. In addition there are some colours that are breeds in themselves, such as the North American Palomino,

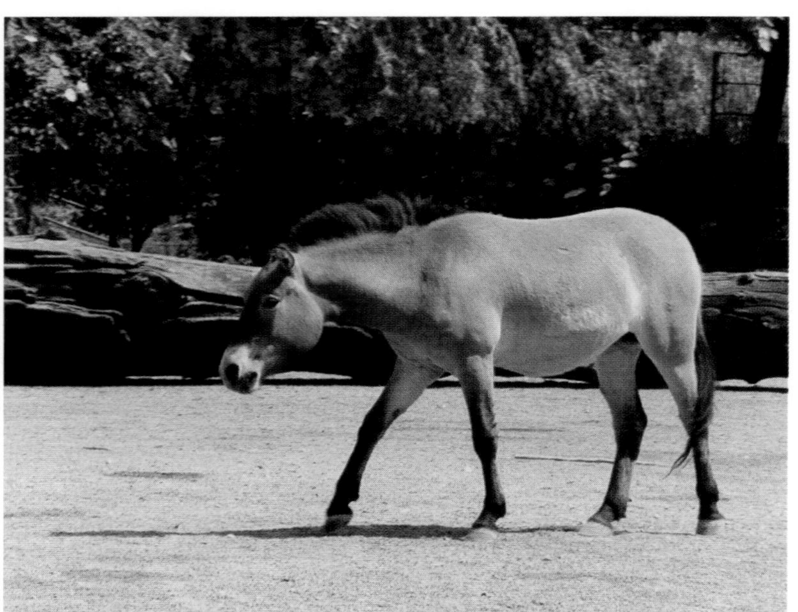

The Przewalski horse or Mongolian wild horse is the last original wild horse in the world. Its yellowish to mouse-grey coat , dark mane and tail and distinctive withers are characteristic features of the wild horse

with its coat ranging from cream to dark gold, but always with a silvery-white mane and tail. Animals of a breed that is also a colour are often very variable in build and size, since the only criterion for belonging to the breed is the right colour.

The many colours of today's horses are the result of domestication and selective breeding. The original wild horses all had yellowish to mousy-grey coats as Przewalski's horse still has. However the individual hairs were not evenly coloured but lighter at the root than at the end. Wild horses had a dark stripe along their backs, known as an eel stripe, and some native breeds still have one.

The principal colours of a horse's coat are known as black, chestnut, brown, bay and grey. **Blacks** must have coat, mane and tail completely black. White markings are allowed on the face and legs, but if there are any brown hairs anywhere on the body then such horses are referred to not as black but as dark

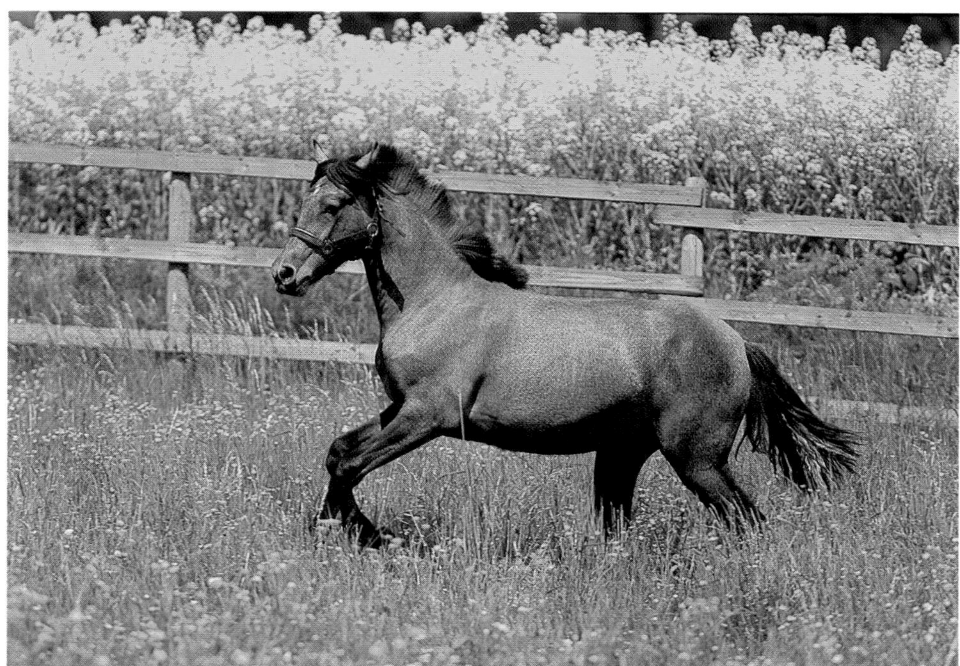

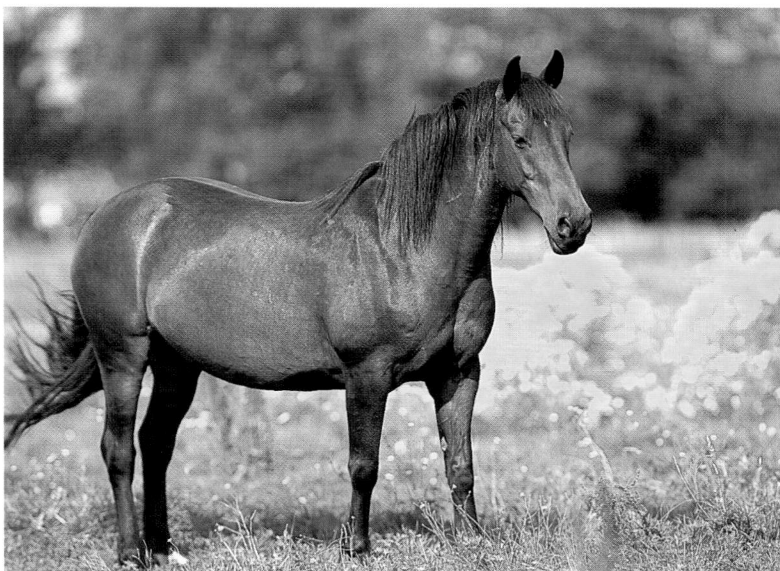

The basic colours: an Andalusian black horse, a brown English thoroughbred and a chestnut Trakehner

A beautiful piebald Quarter Horse

bay. **Chestnuts** may range from very dark (liver chestnut) to very light (golden chestnut). However the coat, mane and tail must be also be chestnut, though it may be a lighter or darker shade. **Browns** must not have any black hairs, otherwise they are known as **bays. Greys** may be grey, but in fact white horses are also always referred to as greys. Both are born dark and become gradually lighter over a period of up to ten years. Some retain dark marks on the body. Depending on the shape and size of these marks the horses are known as flea-bitten greys or dapple greys. Horses born white lack natural pigmentation and are known as **albinos**.

Apart from these basic colours there are others. **Creams** have a creamy-golden coat with the mane and tail the same colour or lighter, even white. **Palominos** have a golden coat with a lighter mane and tail. **Duns** are the closest in colour to wild horses. They are a greyish-yellow with black mane and tail. Like wild horses they have a distinct eel stripe. Like bays, the legs are often black. **Piebalds** and **skewbalds** are covered in irregular patches of a different colour or colours. If they are black and white they are called piebalds, but otherwise, that is if they are black, brown and white or brown and white, they are known as skewbalds. Even more distinctive is the colouring of the Appaloosa, whose coat is grey or strawberry roan superimposed with darker spots. The hindquarters are usually lighter-coloured with a profusion of spots, giving a very striking effect.

Opposite page: a dapple grey Shagya Arab

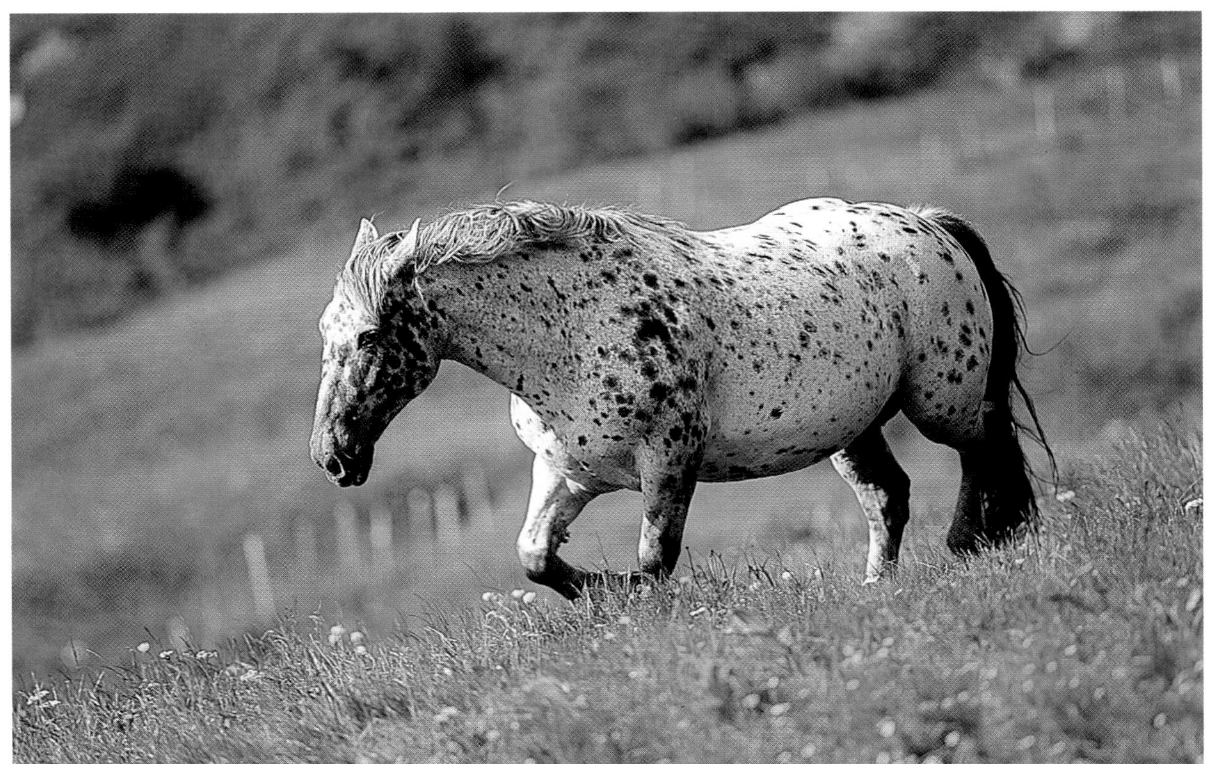

Norikers are often piebald

A brown Holstein with as star marking

Apart from the various colours of coat horses can also be distinguished by white markings on the head and legs. These markings do not alter with age, and as they can therefore be used to identify the individual animal they are described in detail in stud books and on registration certificates. White marks on other parts of the body are not considered to be markings and are usually the result of old wounds that have healed, since the skin often

Horse markings. Top row (from left): snip, white muzzle, star, strip (blaze if wider), white face Bottom row (from left): pastern, sock, coronet, fetlock, stocking

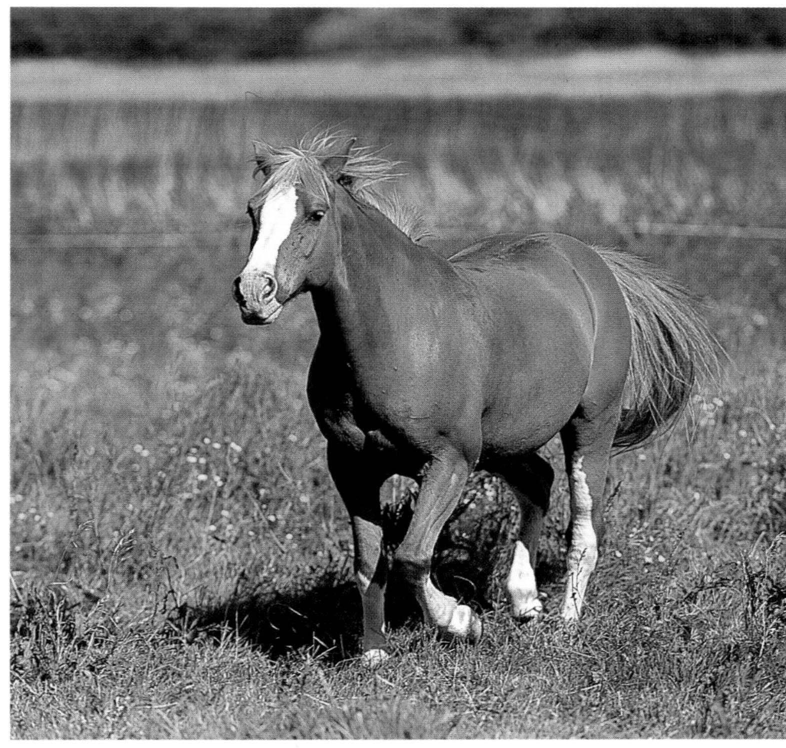

Groninger with blaze and stocking markings.

Shire Horse with strip and sock markings

lacks pigment at these points.

The terms for these markings are as follows. A small white mark on a horse's forehead is called a **star**. However if the mark is on the nose, just between the nostrils, it is called a **snip**. If, however, the white covers both lips and extends to the nostrils, this is known as **white muzzle**. A **strip** is a narrow white stripe from the horse's forehead to between the nostrils. If it is wider, covering almost the whole width of the forehead between the eyes, it is known as a **blaze**. If the whole face is white the horse is described as having a **white face**.

A horse's legs may also carry markings. These are often referred to as **socks**, or **stockings** if they extend above the knee or hock, but for identification purposes the markings should be described accurately. For instance, 'white to half pastern' or 'white to below the fetlock'.

Catalogue of horse breeds

Akhal-Tekké

Origin: The Akhal-Tekké is mainly bred in its country of origin, Turkmenistan.
Size and colour: These animals usually stand between 14.2 and 15 hh (147–152 cm/58–60 in). The usual colours are bay, light bay and chestnut and an unusual feature is that the coat often has a wonderful metallic sheen.
Conformation and character: The conformation of this elegant horse is somewhere between the English Thoroughbred and the Arab. This remarkable horse's great ability to withstand thirst and heat is almost legendary. Its hardiness, stamina and athletic ability make it an ideal horse for showing-jumping and dressage. However they are also very sensitive and highly-strung and therefore not easy to handle. The Akhal-Tekké has a narrow frame, a small head and long clean legs. Also typical are sloping shoulders and high withers.

Almost all American pure-bred horses are descended from the noble Andalusian. Here is a white Andalusian at full trot

Altér Real

Origin: The Altér Real is a Portuguese breed.
Size and colour: The usual size is between 14.3 and 15.1 hh (150–155 cm/59–61 in). The main colours are bay, brown and black.
Conformation and character: These high-spirited horses were bred for the Portuguese court from 300 Andalusian mares imported from Spain in 1747. Attempts to reverse the harm done by the sacking of the stud at Vila de Portel during the Peninsular War by outcrossing with foreign and Arab horses did not have the desired effect, so at the beginning of the 20th century further Andalusians were obtained to reinforce the breed's original characteristics. Like the Andalusian the Altér Real is also especially suitable for dressage. It has a small head, a short but well-arched neck, muscular hindquarters and clean legs.

American Saddlebred

Origin: The American Saddlebred is mainly bred in the states of Kentucky and Virginia.
Size and colour: It stands between 14.3 and 16.1 hh (150–165 cm/59–65 in) and comes in all the basic colours.
Conformation and character: With its long, slim, arched neck, small, noble, clean head, short back, high withers and strong, sinewy legs the American Saddlebred gives the general impression of good breeding. Yet it is not just its appearance and elegant paces that make it a star. It is principally its unusual gaits such as the slow gait (a slow trot in which the legs on each side follow each other instead of diagonally as in the normal trot) and the rack (a very fast trot in which the legs come down singly instead of in pairs) that have earned this intelligent, tough and highly-

strung horse its place in the show ring. Whether this 'career change', from being used on plantations and as a cavalry horse to being a show attraction, is a good thing is a moot point. Not only must the animal perform unnatural and strenuous gaits but the tail is often tied up or even operated on for cosmetic reasons.

Andalusian

Origin: As the name suggests, this elegant breed has its origins in the southern Spanish province of Andalusia. The main centres for breeding are Jérez de la Frontera, Seville and Córdoba.
Size and colour: Andalusians stand between 15.1 and 16.1 hh (155–165 cm/61–65 in). They are usually grey.
Conformation and character: It is not surprising that this spirited yet obedient and very elegant horse is the ancestor of so many popular breeds, including the Lipizzaner, the Kladruber, the Altér Real and most of the American breeds. The Andalusian itself was bred from native Iberian horses and the Barbs brought by the Moslem invaders in the 8th century. Its appearance is characterized by flat withers, a short, strong back, well-rounded hindquarters, strong, clean legs and a fairly large head with a dished face. They make good showjumpers and are particular popular for dressage.

Anglo-Arab

Origin: The Anglo-Arab is mainly bred in south-west France.
Size and appearance: It stands between 15.2 and 16.2 hh (156–168 cm/61½–66 in) and comes in all the basic colours.
Conformation and character: The Anglo-Arab is a cross between the English Thoroughbred and the Arab or is descended from Anglo-Arabs, but the proportion of Arab blood must be at least 25 per cent. Its stamina and speed make this elegant animal ideal for riding and showjumping, and it is less highly-strung than the Thoroughbred. It is the shape and carriage of the head in particular that show this horse's good breeding. It has well-rounded hindquarters, sloping shoulders and small hooves and carries its tail well.

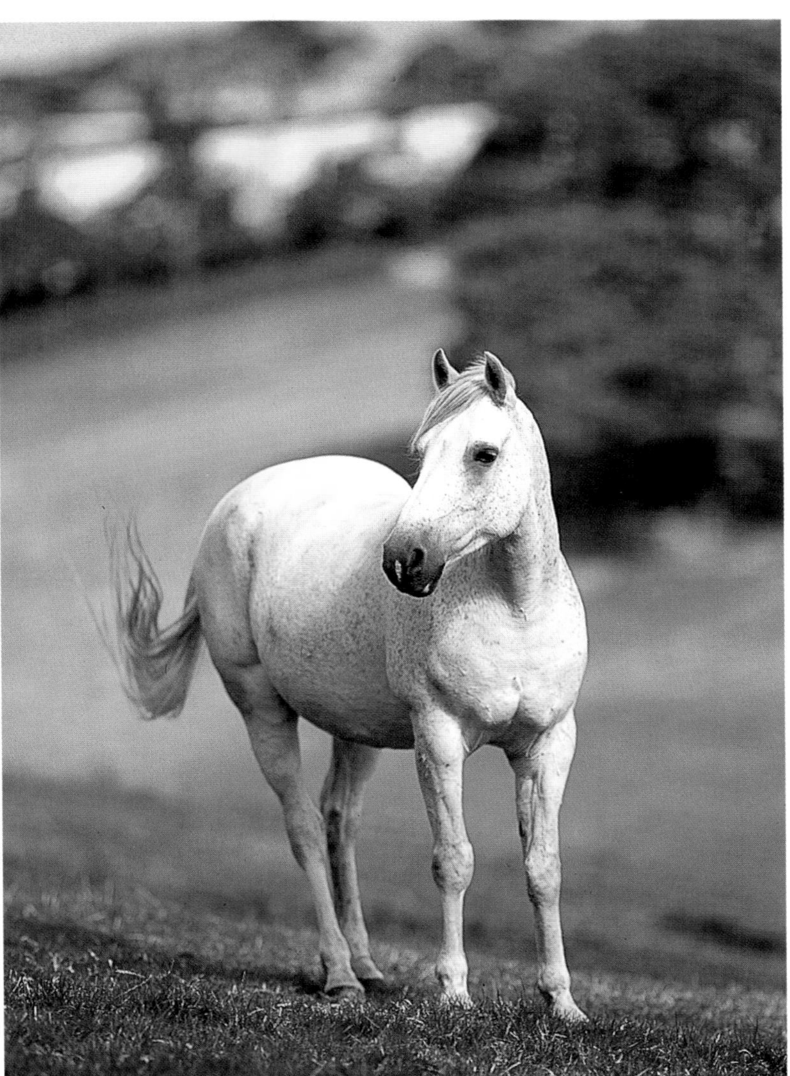

There is a lot of thoroughbred blood flowing in the veins of the Anglo-Arab horse because it is descended from English and Arab thoroughbreds

Anglo-Norman

The Anglo-Norman breed was almost extinct when breeders became aware of it again

Origin: The home of both types of Anglo-Norman is Normandy in northern France.
Size and colour: The Selle Français stands between 15.3 and 16.1 hh (160–165 cm/63–65 in), the Norman Cob between 14.3 and 15.1 hh (150–155 cm/59–61 in). The predominant colour of the Anglo-Norman is bay.

Conformation and character: The Anglo-Norman has a long but varied ancestry. Normans were bred as war-horses almost a thousand years ago though by the 19th century they were threatened with extinction. However they were then crossed with the English Thoroughbred, the Arab and the Norfolk Trotter to produce this athletic, good-natured and spirited horse. Two types of this breed are distinguished. The Selle Français used to be a popular carriage horse but has since proved to be an athletic riding horse. It has a long neck and very strong legs. The Norman Cob is a small, powerful and relatively light and agile working horse. It has a fine head and short, sturdy legs.

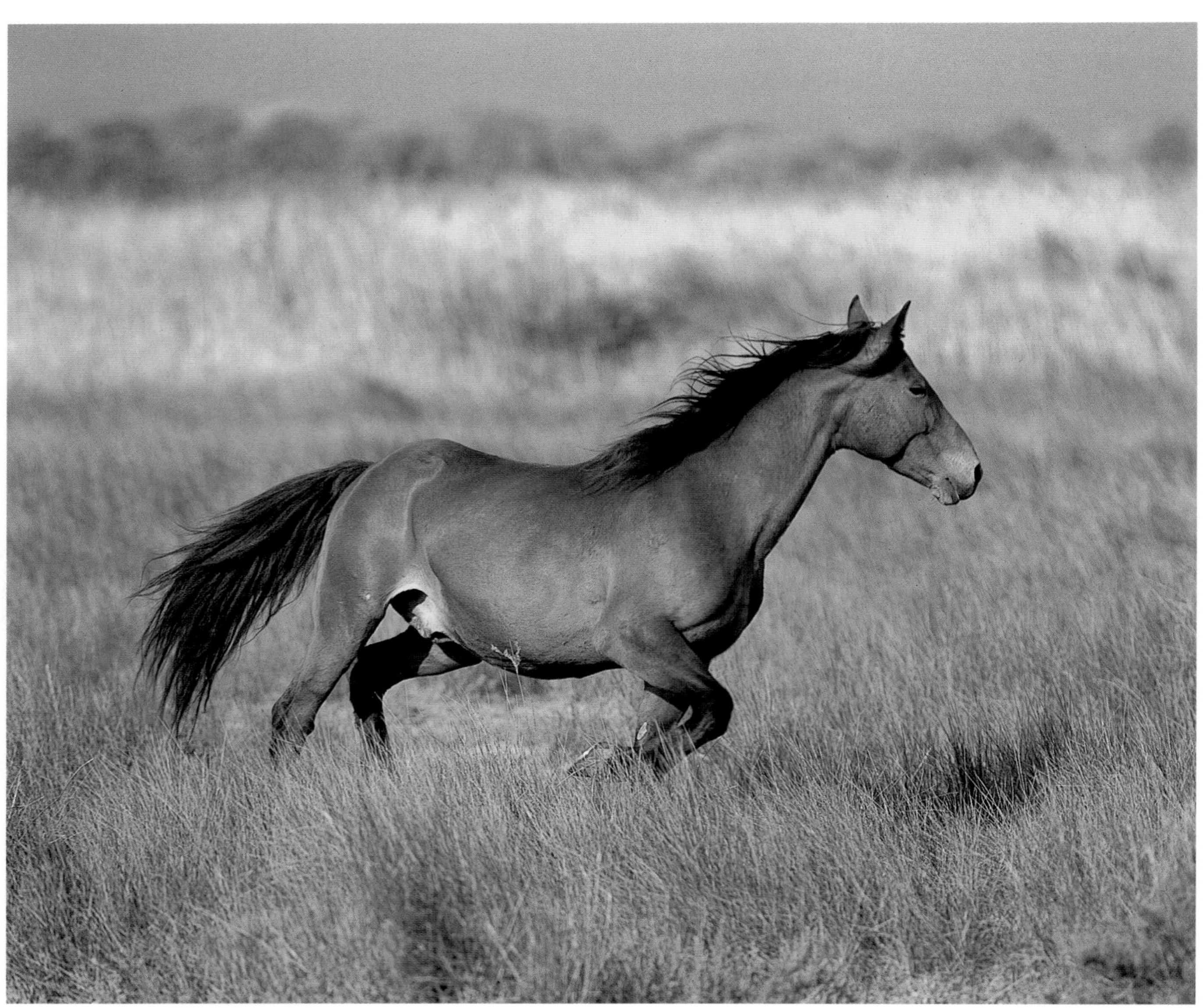

Appaloosa

Origin: The Appaloosa was first bred by the Nez Percé Indians in the Palouse Valley of Idaho, North America.
Size and colour: It stands between 15.1 and 16 hh (154 –162 cm/60½–64 in). The most eye-catching characteristic of this breed is its spotted coat.
Conformation and character: The breeding of the strikingly-marked Appaloosa was an exception amongst the Indian tribes, since they did not normally breed horses at all. The Nez Percé Indians bred them from the horses brought to America by the Spanish. The tribe was annihilated in the bloody wars at the end of the 19th century and its horses were taken over by US soldiers. Settlers continued to breed the Appaloosa here and there. The Appaloosa Horse Club was founded in 1938 in Moscow, Idaho, and devoted itself to maintaining the breed. There are seven different types of coat marking in this breed - Blanket, Blanket with Spots, Varnish Roan, Leopard, Spots, Roan Blanket and Roan Blanket with Spots. It is not only the unusual coat that marks the Appaloosa out; they also have a straight head, a well-balanced neck , sloping shoulders, clean legs and very small, hard hooves. Also typical are flat withers and powerful, well-rounded hindquarters. Appaloosas' toughness, speed and stamina make them ideal cow ponies. They also have a reputation for being particularly good-natured, which makes them especially popular as riding horses for the whole family.

The Appaloosa is one of the most beautiful American pure-bred horses. Its most striking feature is its spotted coat which occurs in many variations

Arab

Origin: Today the Arab is bred all over the world and is used to refine other breeds. Particular credit must go to it as one of the ancestors of the English Thoroughbred.
Size and colour: Arabs stand between 14.3 and 15.1 hh (150–155 cm/59–61 in) and come in all the basic colours.
Conformation and character: As the noblest and, as far as horse-breeding in general is concerned, the most important breed, the Arab is considered to be the king of horses. Its origin is correspondingly legendary. No less a person than the Prophet Mohammed is said to have founded the breed. One day he led a herd of his mares, which had had nothing to drink for several days, to the water trough. But he had also arranged for the trumpet to be blown for battle at the same time. Most of the thirsty animals took no notice but began to drink greedily. However five mares turned round at the signal without having quenched their agonizing thirst, ready to follow their master without question. These five exceptional animals were the foundation for the Arab breed, and it is said that all Arab horses are descendants of these five legendary mares. The breed's unequalled qualities can be put down to the remoteness of the region in which they were bred, Mohammed's instructions on horse-breeding and the harshness of life in the Arabian desert. Courage, tenacity, stamina and high spirits are just as

An Arab mare with its foal

Page opposite: the Arab thoroughbred is recognised by many horse-lovers as the quintessential breed

typical of this splendid creature as its gentleness and fidelity. It is a real beauty. It has a very fine, clean head with the proverbial dished face, broad nostrils and big expressive eyes, a beautifully-arched neck, fairly level hindquarters, wonderfully slim, clean, sinewy legs and small, hard hooves.

Ardennes

Origin: Bred in the mountainous region that straddles the French - Belgian border and after which it is named, the Ardennes is one of the oldest breeds of heavy horse.
Size and colour: It never grows to more than 15.1 hh (156 cm/61½ in). Most Ardennes are grey or roan.
Conformation and character: This powerful, hardy horse is said to have been very popular with the Romans. Its ancestors were probably descendants of horses living in southern France in prehistoric times. At the beginning of the 19th century this originally rather dainty animal was crossed with Arabs, Percherons, and Boulonnais. Today this compact, study cold-blood is often crossed with other breeds in order to improve their bloodlines. The Ardennes is a good-natured and obedient horse with a calm disposition, able to withstand a harsh climate, and is usually used in agriculture and forestry. Its appearance is characterized by a long, heavy neck, a head with a low, flat forehead, protuberant eyes, a very muscular body, a short back and very short, strong legs with a lot of feather. Unlike many other heavy breeds, the withers on the Ardennes are not on the same level as the point of croup but somewhat lower.

An Ardennes mare galloping round the paddock

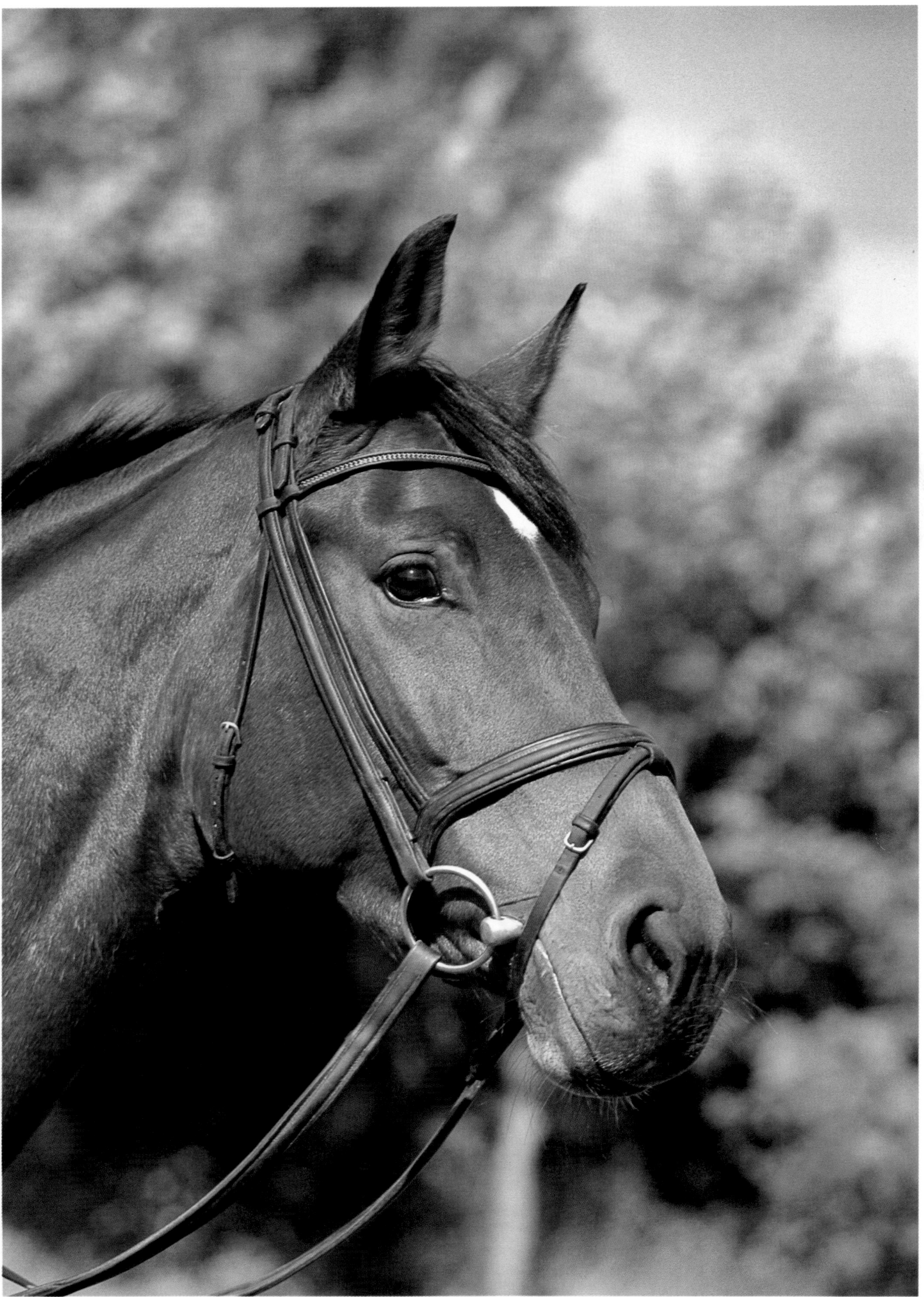

Bavarian

Origin: The Bavarian originates from Lower Bavaria, Germany.
Size and colour: It stands around 15.3 hh (160 cm/63 in). They are very often chestnut but light bay and bay are also quite common.
Conformation and character: This elegant horse was used for riding as long ago as the time of the Crusades. It attained the athletic build it has today by being crossed with Cleveland Bays and the French Anglo-Normans. Its strength, stamina, athleticism and even temperament make the Bavarian an excellent horse for riding. It is also occasionally still used on the land. The special features of the Bavarian are its powerful build, pretty head and clean legs. Also typical are a medium-length neck, upright shoulders and prominent withers.

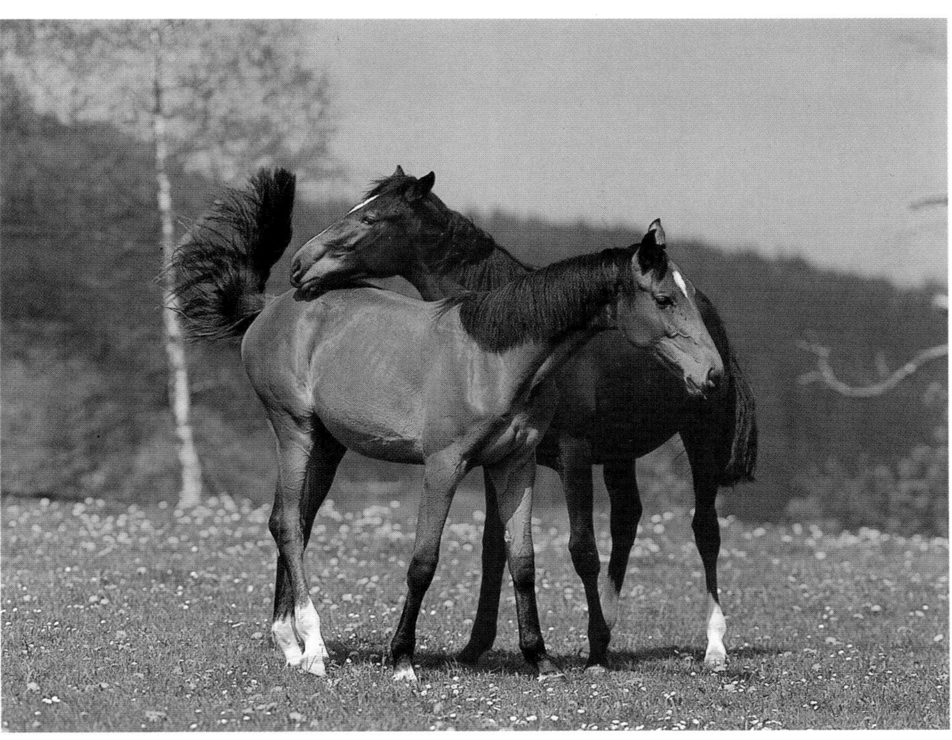

Above and page opposite: Bavarians
Below: Two Belgian heavy draughts

Belgian Heavy Draught

Origin: The powerful Belgian Heavy Draught (also known as the Brabant) comes from the Belgian province of Brabant and is the only breed of horse of Belgian origin.
Size and colour: The Belgian Heavy Draught can reach 17.1 hh (175 cm/69 in). Red roan with black points is the predominant colour.
Conformation and character: Itself cross-bred for over 100 years with the Ardennes, the Belgian Heavy Draught had a strong influence on the breeding of the Shire. Like the Ardennes the powerful, energetic but good-natured Belgian Heavy Draught also makes a very good worker. It has a relatively small head, a short, strong but elegantly-carried neck and a short back with long hindquarters, and its hooves are usually large and flat.

Barb

Origin: This elegant creature is bred mainly in Algeria, Morocco, Libya and Tunisia.
Size and colour: Standing 13.3–14.3 hh (140–150 cm/55–59 in) the Barb is not a nig horse. It may be any of the basic colours.
Conformation and character: The very attractive appearance of the Barb is characterized by a long, beautifully-carried neck, a fine, slightly-dished face with a broad forehead and lovely eyes, and a medium-length body with upright shoulders and powerful, sinewy legs. But it is not only its appearance and elegant paces that make it a remarkable horse. Its spirited temperament, its speed and its stamina have made this intelligent, tough horse a favourite for riding. It was this ancient breed that the Carthaginians rode into battle in their wars against the Romans more than 2,000 years ago. After the Arabs had conquered North Africa in the 8th century the Barb was changed by being crossed with Arab stallions. Today it is used to lighten most of the warm-blood breeds.

The Barb is particularly attractive cross-breed horse. This one has very unusual markings

Breton

Origin: Today there are two types of heavy horse from Brittany - the Draught Breton, a compact, heavily-built draught horse which has Ardennes, Percheron and Boulonnais ancestry, and the lighter Postier Breton, which has the blood of Norfolk Trotters and Hackneys in its veins.
Size and colour: The main colours in this breed are chestnut, bay, grey and, in particular, red roan. The Postier Breton stands about 14.3 hh (150 cm/59 in) and the Draught Breton about 15.3 hh (160 cm/63 in).
Conformation and character: The Breton has a broad, powerful, muscular body, a short, very strong neck and short legs with very little feather. The overall impression is one of a powerful, short-coupled and sturdy horse. However this rather cumbersome appearance is deceptive, for it can manage a fair turn of speed, especially when trotting, and is quite agile. Both types of this breed are used as draught animals and the Postier is also very popular for driving. The Breton is a good-natured, lively and athletic horse.

Camargue

Origin: The Camargue takes its name from the marshy region in the delta of the Rhône in south-eastern France where it runs wild.
Size and colour: They stand between 12.3 and 14.1 hh (130–145 cm/51–57 in). They are usually grey, but occasionally other colours do occur.
Conformation and character: These tough, fearless animals, who thrive on even the poorest grazing, are especially popular with the many tourists that visit the Camargue. Ponies that have been caught and broken-in can be hired and taken on long rides through the love-

Camargues are the famous wild horses which live in the marshes of the Camargue, a region situated in the Rhone delta in the south of France

ly countryside where, apart from the famous black bulls, white horses and huge flocks of pink flamingos, many other sorts of creature can be observed. The origin of the Camargue pony is still unknown. They are characterized by upright shoulders, a short, powerful back, a short rump and strong, clean legs. The head is straight and long, with small ears and large eyes. Sometimes the face is slightly dished.

Cleveland Bay

Origin: The Cleveland Bay is of British origin and is mainly bred in the Cleveland Hills of north-east Yorkshire.

Size and colour: Standing between 16.1 and 16.3 hh (165–170 cm/65–67 in) this is one of the larger breeds of horse. Colours range from light to dark bay, and the legs have zebra marks.

Conformation and character: The Cleveland Bay was popular as a coach horse because it was hardy, long-lived and a frugal eater. Crossing with Arabs and English Thoroughbreds made the breed rather highly-strung, but today a return has been made to breeding pure. It is an attractive horse and played a part in the development of the German Oldenburg and Holstein. It is powerful with a large head, a long neck and well-developed shoulders. The back is long and strong, the legs are short and muscular. It is popular for driving, not least with HRH The Duke of Edinburgh who drives Cleveland Bays for the British team in Combined Driving competitions.

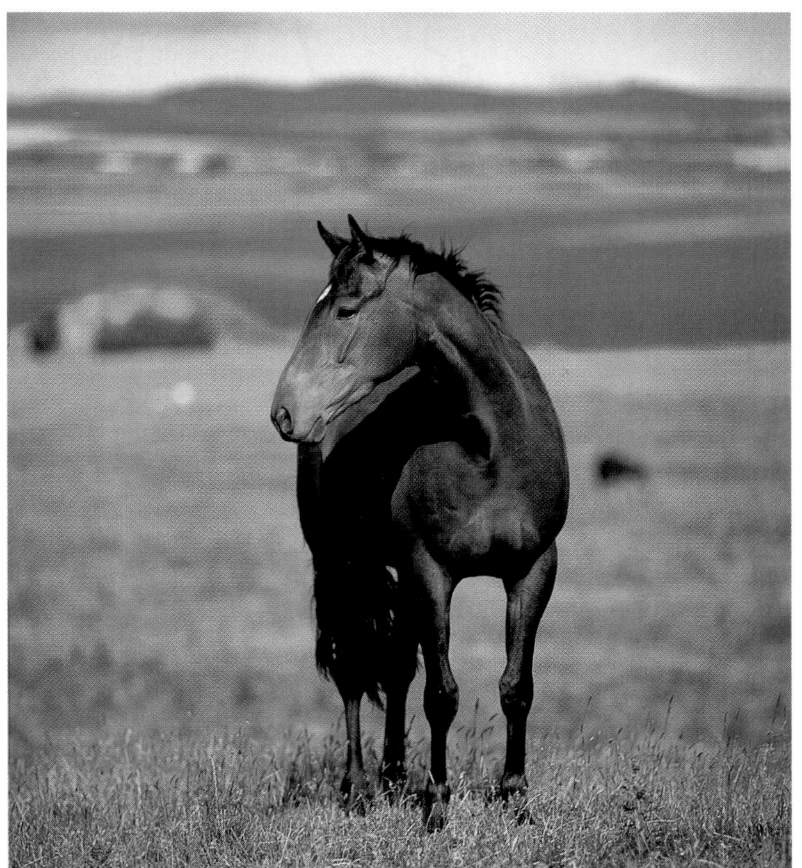

The Cleveland Bay is known for its resistance and placid temperament

The Clydesdale is a strong, lively, good-natured breed

Clydesdale

Origin: The Clydesdale was first bred in the valley of the Clyde in the Scottish county of Lanarkshire.
Size and colour: It is a very big horse, standing at up to 16.3 hh (170 cm/67 in). The Clydesdale is almost exclusively bay, brown or black and often has particularly attractive markings on the head and legs.
Conformation and character: In the mid-18th century the native breed was crossed with Flemish stallions to produce this big, strong, lively and good-natured horse. The Clydesdale is very versatile. It can be ridden, but is also strong enough for heavy draught work. They are often cross-bred with Thoroughbreds to produce heavyweight hunters and showjumpers. It has a long, well-arched neck and powerful legs with a lot of feather. The animal's head is characterized by having a broad forehead, large nostrils and very bright eyes. The shoulders of the Clydesdale are muscular and the back is short and strong.

Cob

Origin: The Cob is in fact not a breed but a type and is mainly bred in England and France. It is often the result of crossing a hunter with an animal with some Thoroughbred blood.
Size and colour: Standing up to 15 hh (153 cm/60 in) the Cob is a small horse and may be of any colour.
Conformation and character: A strong, well-arched neck, a small head, a powerful back and short legs typify the appearance of this type of horse. It may have its mane hogged. With its powerful hindquarters and its calm, reliable nature it can be used for nervous and inexperienced riders and is therefore popular in riding schools and trekking centres.

Connemara Pony

Origin: The Connemara is descended from the Celtic pony and is the only breed of pony native to Ireland.
Size and colour: It stands

Connemara mare at full gallop

between 12.3 and 14 hh (130–142 cm/51–56 in). The predominant colour is grey but black, bay, brown and dun also occur. Chestnuts, on the other hand, are very rare.
Conformation and character: During the course of its history the Connemara Pony has been repeatedly crossed with Arabs, Andalusians and English Thoroughbreds. It often runs wild and has a delicate head carried well on the neck and powerful, sloping shoulders. The legs are clean with very small, hard hooves. The long, powerful body and the muscular, often strongly-sloping hindquarters are typical. Its toughness, stamina and speed make the Connemara an ideal children's pony. It has a lovely temperament and a wonderful character.

Criollo

Origin: The Criollo is bred exclusively in Argentina. It is descended from Spanish horses brought to South America in the 16th century and set free after Buenos Aires was destroyed by Indians.
Size and colour: Criollos are not very big, in fact standing between 13.3 and 14.3 (between 140 and 150 cm) they are one of the smaller breeds of horse. They are usually dun.
Conformation and character: The Criollo is very hardy, has a lot of stamina and can survive on poor grazing. It had a reputation amongst the settlers who used to capture it and break it in for never being ill. By the end of the 19th century, after being crossed with European and North American stallions, the Criollo had become an elegant and fast horse. However in the process it had lost its original qualities and was becoming more and more sensitive and prone to illness, so it was soon bred true again. The Criollo is a powerful, sturdy horse with strong legs and a large, wedge-shaped head on a muscular neck. The back is short and strong and ends in a long croup. Despite its small size the Criollo makes a good riding and draught horse. It is also used for ranch work and is crossed with the Thoroughbred to produce polo ponies.

Dales Pony

Origin: The Dales Pony is closely related to its smaller neighbour, the Fell Pony. For centuries it has been bred in north-east England, where it used to be used mainly as a pack-pony, in particular for carrying lead ingots down the Dales to the ports. In the 19th century the legendary Welsh Cob Comet, a very fast trotter stallion, was brought to northern England and crossed with Dales mares, thus becoming the most influential ancestor of this breed.

The tough Criollo makes an excellent riding horse. It is used in breeding polo ponies

Size and colour: The Dales Pony stands around 14 hh (142 cm/56 in). Many are completely black, but bay and brown are also common colours.
Conformation and character: Largely usurped on farms by the internal combustion engine, these loveable creatures are now much in demand in the tourism industry. Their amiable nature and even temper make them especially suitable for use in trekking centres. The Dales Pony is characterized by its small, pretty head, intelligent eyes, strong back and powerful legs with a lot of fine hair on the heels.

English Dartmoor ponies make ideal riding horses for children. Here is a mare with its foal

Dartmoor Pony

Origin: The Dartmoor Pony originates on the heather-covered heights of Dartmoor in Devon, in the extreme southwest of England.
Size and colour: It does not exceed 12.3 hh (130 cm/51 in). Brown, bay and black are the predominant colours.
Conformation and character: Dartmoor mares have been crossed with English Thoroughbred stallions to produce a noble and elegant animal. The Thoroughbred influence can still be seen today although for a long time now the purity of the breed has been stringently regulated by the Dartmoor Pony Society. Its head should be delicate, narrow and well set-on with very small, alert ears. The back should be strong and the hindquarters well muscled. With its thick mane and tail the Dartmoor Pony is especially popular with children. These sensitive, good-natured and sure-footed animals are ideal children's riding ponies and being good at jumping are very suitable for gymkhanas.

Dülmen

Origin: The Dülmen is the last breed of pony running wild in Germany. For more than 600 years they have belonged to the Dukes of Croy and live on a reserve near Münster in Westphalia.
Size and colour: The ponies stand between 11.3 and 13.1 hh (120–135 cm/47–53 in). The predominant colours are dun, brown and black.
Conformation and character: Dülmens are versatile, lively and intelligent ponies. They are often used as light draught animals but being fast and good jumpers also make excellent riding ponies for children. These ponies are characterized by their medium build, small head with alert ears and bright eyes, and clean legs with small, hard hooves. Also typical are good shoulders, an attractive neck, a strong back and a low-set tail.

Einsiedler

Origin: The Einsiedler was originally bred in the eleventh century by monks at Einsiedeln in Switzerland but became much less common

when the cavalry was disbanded.
Size and colour: It stands 15.3 hh (160 cm/63 in). It may be any of the basic colours.
Conformation and character: The Einsiedler is a particularly fine-looking horse with Norman ancestors. It used to be used mainly by the Swiss Army as a cavalry horse. It is medium-sized and powerful, with a finely-chiselled head well set on a long neck, prominent withers and a large ribcage. The shoulders are muscular, the back short and flat and the hindquarters sloping and well muscled. The legs are of medium length and powerful and end in small, hard hooves. Today its great stamina and athleticism mean that it is mainly used for general riding and as a competition horse.

English Thoroughbred

Origin: The extremely spirited Thoroughbred was first bred in England in the late 17th and early 18th century. Today the English Thoroughbred is bred the world over.
Size and Colour: These noble animals stand between 14.3 and 16.3 hh (150–170 cm/59–67 in). They occur in the basic colours but brown and bay predominate.

Dülmeners have lived wild for 600 years in the Merfelder Bruch near Dülmen in Westphalia

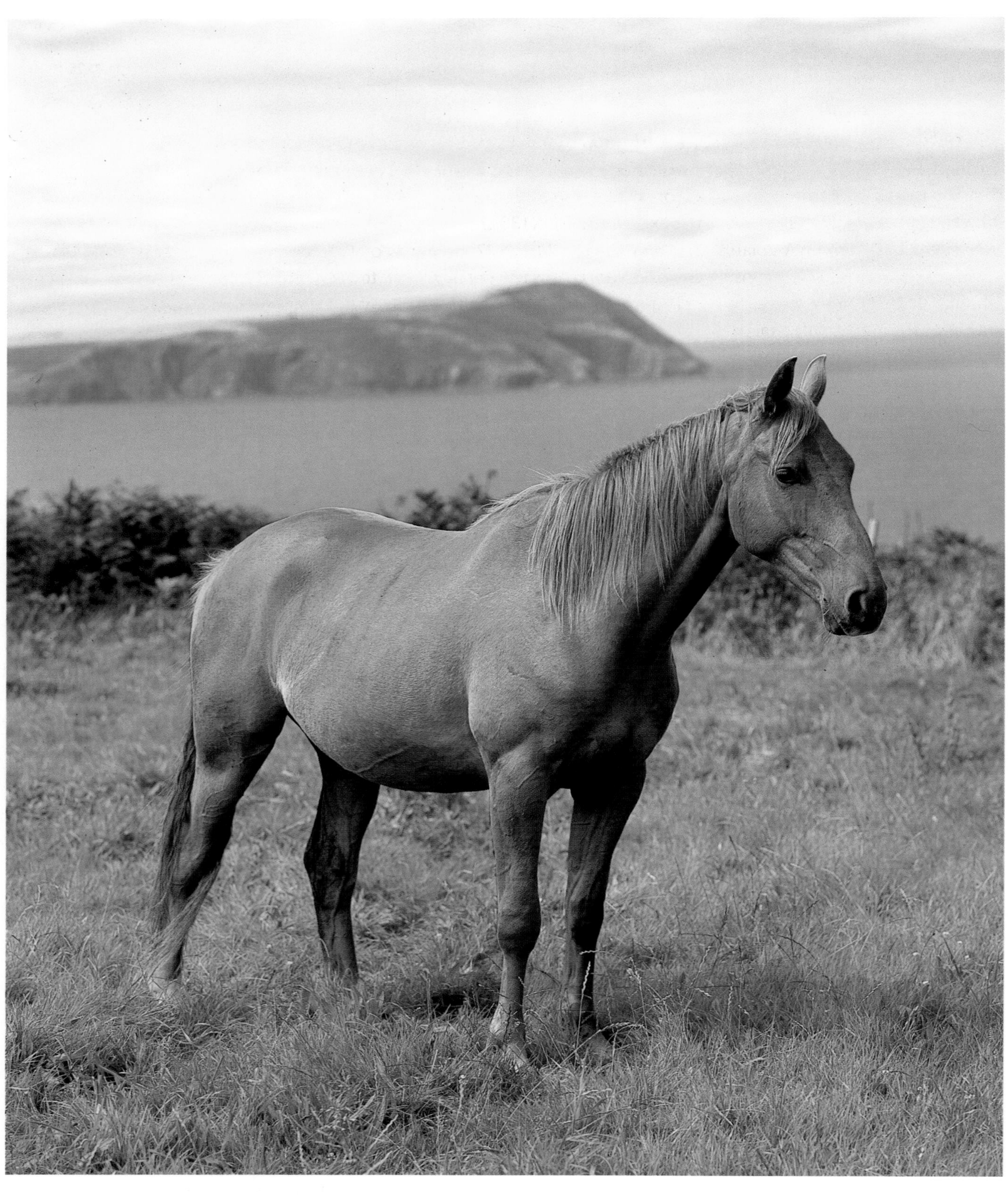

A fine English Thoroughbred

Conformation and character: The English Thoroughbred was a product of the English passion for racing horses and betting on the result. Native ponies had been raced against one another from time immemorial. The winners were used for breeding, with the result that over time racehorses became ever swifter and stronger. Then by cross-breeding the racehorse gradually gained in size and elegance. In the late 17th and early 18th centuries three Arab stallions were imported into England, the Byerley Turk, the Darley Arabian and the Godolphin Barb. Almost all their progeny proved to be exceptionally successful as racehorses. Therefore the decision was made to allow breeding only from descendants of these three Arab stallions, and the result was the English Thoroughbred. However as the English Thoroughbred is the result of much inbreeding breeders have to be constantly aware of the need to choose sire and dam carefully in order to avoid degeneration. The English Thoroughbred is one of the most elegant horses in the world. It is slim and long-legged and is considered to have the perfect build. The head is refined with large, bright eyes and small, pointed ears. The long, slender neck ends in prominent withers. The broad chest is an indication of strength and stamina, the powerful back is short and ends in muscular sloping hindquarters. This highly-strung, courageous but sensitive creature with its tenacity, stamina and speed it needs an experienced and capable rider. Almost all the finest breeds in the world have a considerable amount of English Thoroughbred in them.

Exmoor Pony

Origin: The original home of this pony is Exmoor in the south-west of England.

Size and Colour: The Exmoor Pony stands 12 hh (123 cm/48½ in) on average. Stallions should not exceed 12.3 hh (130 cm/51 in) and mares 12.2 hh (127 cm/50 in). Its coat is usually bay or brown but may be dun with black points. Its distinguishing features are the lighter circle of hair round the eyes and the lighter-coloured muzzle, known as a *mealy muzzle*.

Conformation and character: This pony has existed in its present form for several thousand years and is therefore considered to be the oldest breed of horse. Descended from the native British wild horse, it may have been used by the Celts to pull their chariots. It still runs wild on the moors of west Somerset and north Devon. It is strong for its size, has a fairly large head and short legs and grows a shaggy coat in the winter. It is resilient and healthy and can survive on a poor diet, surviving the harsh climate and living conditions in its native area. Its speed, sure-footedness and good nature make it an ideal children's pony for general riding and gymkhanas.

The Falabella pony is a 'toy horse' which is only 7.2 hh (76 cm/30 in) high

Falabella

Origin: The Falabella was originally bred in Argentina. It is always known as a horse, not a pony.

Size and colour: Standing at the most 7.2 hh (76 cm/30 in), the Falabella is the smallest breed of horse in the world. Its coat may be any of the basic colours.

Conformation and character: Named after the family that bred it, the Falabella was based on the

Shetland Pony, crossed with the smallest of other breeds. Only the smallest are used for breeding. Little bigger than an Alsatian dog, this good-natured 'toy' horse is seen in circuses and zoos.

Fell Pony

Origin: The Fell Pony's original home is the western slopes of the northern Pennines, and is the equivalent of the Dales Pony on the eastern slopes. The two breeds have a common origin but diverged during the late 19th century. Small herds of Fell ponies are still a common sight in the Howgills, the high rounded hills between the Lake District and Wensleydale.

Size and colour: The Fell Pony stands around 13.1 hh (135 cm/53 in). The most usual colour is black, but brown, bay, dun and grey also occur.

Conformation and character: The Fell Pony has a long history. It is thought that when the Romans reached northern England they crossed them with Friesians in order to obtain bigger animals. Like its close relative, the Dales Pony, the Fell Pony was also for a long time used in agriculture and as a pack pony for carrying lead ingots and also like its cousin this robust, sure-footed, courageous, active and good-natured animal is now very popular, especially in trekking centres. The Fell Pony also makes an ideal ride-and-drive pony. It has a small, pretty head, sloping shoulders, prominent withers, a good depth of girth and powerful hindquarters. There is some feathering on the legs but the hair is fine.

The French Traber is a particularly elegant and beautiful horse

French Trotter

Origin: It originated in France.

Size and colour: French Trotters stand about 16.2 hh (168 cm/66 in). They occur in all colours and often have pretty markings. **Conformation and character:** The French Trotter was developed for racing by deliberately selecting the most successful animals for breeding. Its ancestors were Anglo-Normans and English cross-breed stallions. More than half of all French Trotters can be traced back to a single ancestor, the English stallion Young Rattler. In France trotting races are run not only in harness but also under the saddle, which is why the French Trotter is somewhat larger than other trotters. It is well-proportioned with straight head and neck are and pronounced withers . The strong back shows the power and stamina of this beautiful animal.

Frederiksborg

Origin: Originally bred at the royal stud of King Frederik II in the 16th century, it is thus the oldest Danish breed of horse. **Size and colour:** They stand between 15 hh and 16 hh (153–163 cm/60–64 in). By far the commonest colour is chestnut.
Conformation and character: Frederiksborgs have a good neck, strong legs and a short back. Flat withers and a flat croup are also typical. Their upright shoulders make them more suitable for driving than riding. They have a reputation for being spirited and affable. Their attractive, powerful appearance made them very popular in Europe in the 17th, 18th and early 19th centuries and they were often used to refine other breeds. For instance the Frederiksborg stallion Pluto helped to found the Lipizzaner breed.

Freiberger

Origin: Switzerland.
Size and colour: They stand 15.2 hh (157 cm/62 in) on average. The original colour was chestnut but they now come in all the basic colours, though predominantly brown.
Conformation and character: The Freiberger is a light draught horse. A few years ago attempts began to turn it into a lighter saddle horse by huge infusions of Arab blood. Thus it is one of the few heavy horses also suitable for riding. It is a powerful, well-proportioned horse with a small pretty head on a high neck. The back is strong, and the sturdy legs indicate what it was originally used for. The

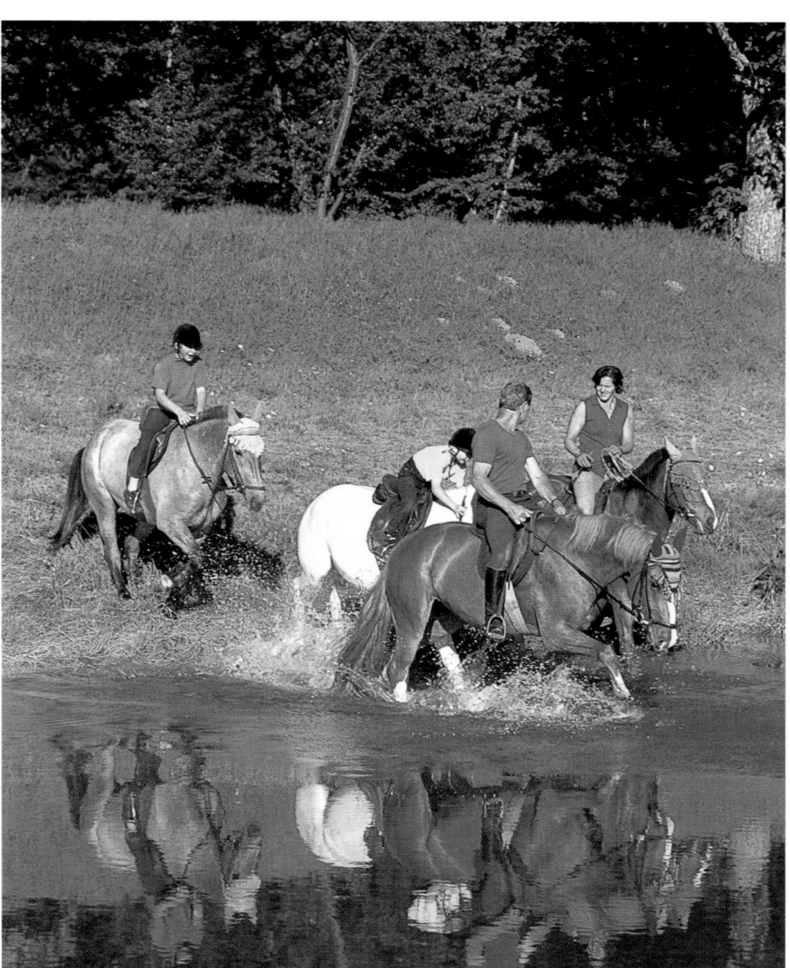

The Freiberger is one of the few heavy draught horses which is also suitable for riding

Freiberger still has sufficient stamina to be used as a draught and working animal.

Friesian

Origin: The Friesian probably has the same origin as the Oldenburg and today is bred in the Netherlands.

Size and colour: It stands between 15.1 and 15.3 hh (155–160 cm/61–65 in) and is therefore of medium size for a heavy horse. Friesian horses are always black.

Conformation and character: The Friesian is a powerful heavy horse with a good nature. It has a very pretty, long, straight head with large, gentle eyes and an elegant neck. The mane is thick and slightly wavy, the back flat with sloping hindquarters and a low-set tail. Apart from its traditional use as a coach and draught horse it has so much energy and spirit that it is also popular for riding.

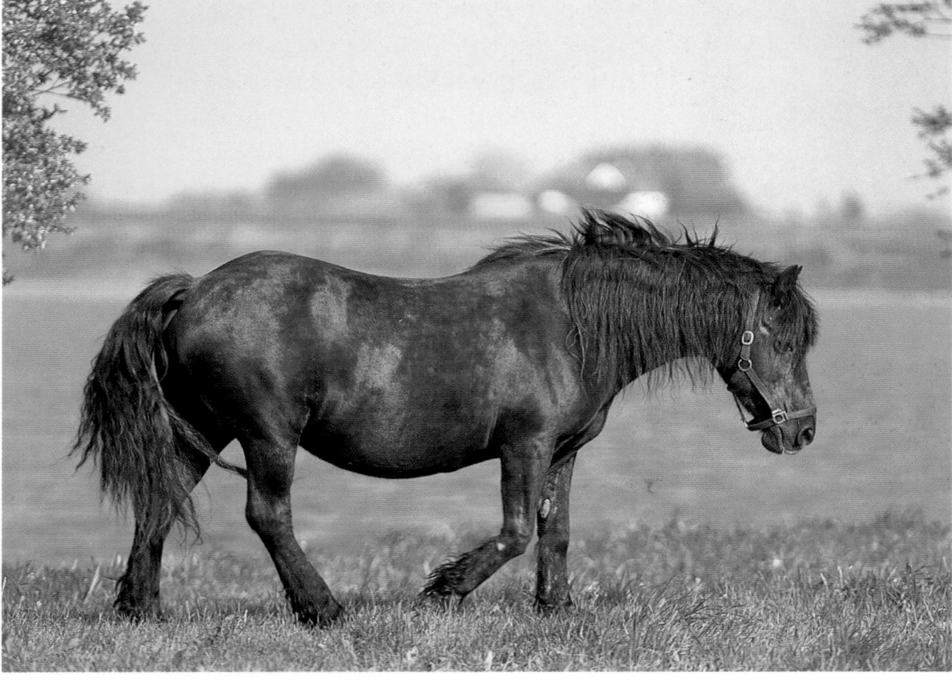

Friesians only come in one colour, black

Furioso

Origin: The Furioso comes from Hungary. The breed owes its name to its foundation sire, a Thoroughbred stallion imported from England in the mid-nineteenth century to serve local mares, but it also has some Arab blood.

Size and colour: It stands between 15.1 and 16.0 hh (155–163 cm/61–64 in). Although the main colours are black and dark bay, the Furioso also occurs in other colours.

Conformation and character: The conformation of this elegant horse is somewhere between the English Thoroughbred and the Arab. Its ability to withstand thirst and great heat is almost legendary. Its hardiness, stamina and athleticism make it very good for both riding and driving. It performs well in dressage and showjumping and is also very popular for military use and as a hunter. The Furioso is characterized by its slim build and its very small but long head with large expressive eyes. The neck is long and muscular, the back narrow but nevertheless strong. Also typical are its long legs with small, hard hooves.

Gelderland

Origin: As the name suggests, this breed comes from the Dutch province of Gelderland.

Size and colour: The Gelderland stands between 15.1 and 16.0 hh (155–163 cm/61–64 in). Most are chestnut, bay or grey, and they often have attractive markings.

Conformation and character: The Gelderland is one of the heavy warm-bloods. Though not particularly elegant it is strong and has a lovely nature. The head is very big and has a slightly Roman nose, and the back is long with a flat croup. Its excellent paces make the Gelderland a very good light carriage horse but it is also still used for light agricultural work. However it is also popular for riding and can be a sur-

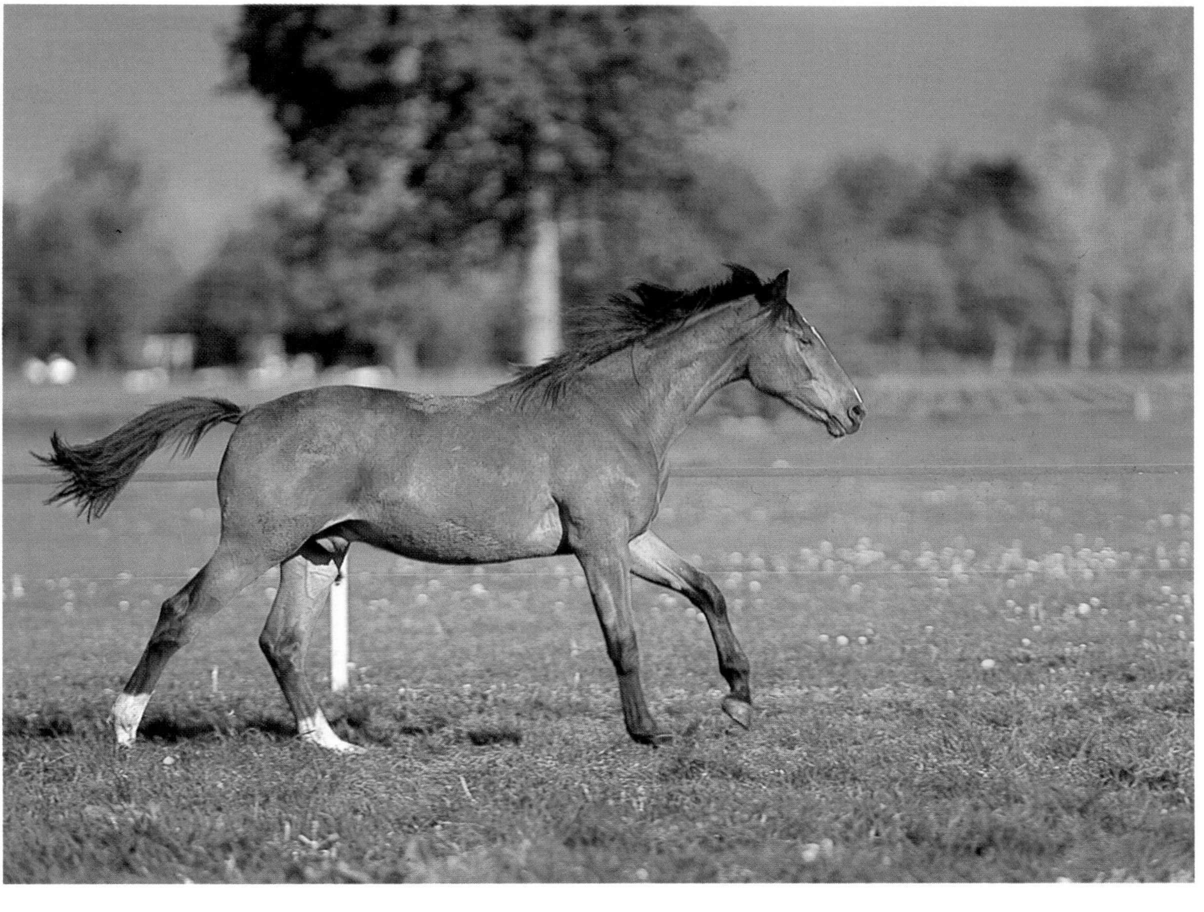

Gelderländ cross-breed horses are very robust and strong. They are occasionally used as work horses

prisingly good jumper. It is therefore often used as a competition horse.

Groningen

Origin: It comes from the Dutch province of the same name.

Size and colour: It stands between 14.3 and 16.1 hh (150–165 cm/59–65 in). Colours are black, bay or dark brown and they often have attractive markings.

Conformation and character: Like the Gelderland to which it is closely related, the Groningen is classified as a heavy warm-blood. The head is finely chiselled and set on a powerful neck. The shoulders are well-set. Its broad chest gives an indication of the strength that makes the Groningen a first-class carriage and working horse. However with its long energetic paces it is also a reliable riding horse and occasionally it even shows genuine sporting ability.

The Groninger is closely related to the Gelderländ and can be used for a variety of purposes

A striking show talent: the Hackney

Hackney

Origin: The eye-catching Hackney is an ancient British breed.
Size and colour: It stands a maximum of 15.3 hh (160 cm/63 in). The usual colours are brown, bay, black and chestnut, often with very attractive markings, but other colours are not rare.
Conformation and character: The Hackney is the showman amongst British horses. It is an extremely elegant horse whose appearance is strongly reminiscent of the Thoroughbred. It is very attractive to look at, with its very delicate, refined head and its famously dished face and big expressive eyes. It has a very short but well-arched neck and muscular, rather upright shoulders. The hindquarters are powerful with strong hocks. The tail is set rather deep but is carried very high. The Hackney was bred from the Norfolk Trotter, a breed known since the 12th c. but which became extinct with the advent of the railway. It made a very smart carriage horse but today is used almost exclusively for showing.

Because of their beauty and sweet nature Haflinger ponies are particularly popular with children

Haflinger

Origin: The Haflinger comes originally from the South Tyrol region of the Italian Alps, more specifically from the area around Bolzano and Merano. However today it is over the border in Austria that it is most popular and widespread.
Size and colour: These ponies stand between 13.1 and 14.1 hh (135–145 cm/53–57 in). They are always chestnut with flaxen main and tail.
Conformation and character: These pretty mountain ponies are the outcome of crossing Arab stallions with local mares. The result was a powerfully-built, sure-footed and frugal animal with an abundance of stamina and tenacity. Haflingers have a lively temperament but are also exceptionally good-natured and willing. They have a rather small finely-chiselled head with expressive eyes, large nostrils and small, lively ears. The neck is powerful and is carried well. The Haflinger's back is broad and strong and the shoulders rather upright. The clean legs end in small, hard hooves. The Haflinger makes an excellent children's riding pony or light driving pony. Because of its sure-footedness it is also used in difficult terrain by mountain troops.

Hanoverian

Origin: This breed dates back to 1735 when George II, Prince of Hanover and King of England, founded the state stud at Celle in the German region of Lower Saxony. Originally it was mainly used as a carriage horse but by being crossed with Thoroughbreds it has become lighter and more elegant and today it is mainly used as a competition horse.
Size and colour: It stands between 15.3 and 17.1 hh (160–175 cm/63–69 in) and occurs in all the basic colours.
Conformation and character: The Hanoverian is considered to be the most important German breed of horse and has made an international name for itself in the sports of dressage and showjumping. Intelligence, consistency and common sense are just as typical of it as athleticism and reliability. They are powerful and elegant in appearance, having a fine, expressive, medium-sized head, a very long, well-carried neck, excellent shoulders, a strong body and a high-set tail. Legs and hindquarters are well muscled.

Hessen

Origin: This horse was based on the Oldenburg and East Friesian horses of northern Germany and the Netherlands and refined after the Second world War by crossing with Hanoverians and Trakehners.
Size and colour: The Hessen occurs in all the basic colours and stands between 16.1 and 17.1 hh (165–175 cm/65–69 in).
Conformation and character: It is an intelligent, sensitive, good-natured animal with a quiet temperament. The Hessen gives the impression of strength and is characterized by its expressive head, sloping shoulders, slim, clean limbs and prominent withers. It is a good horse for both general riding and showjumping.

Highland Pony

Origin: The Scottish Highland Pony, also known as the Garron, is descended from the Celtic pony. It owes its present appearance to being crossed with Arabs, Clydesdales, Norwegian Ponies and American trotters. The breed was founded by the Dukes of Atholl and the ancestor of the breed was their elegant stallion Herd Laddie.
Size and colour: This breed is quite often dun with variable shading and an eel stripe, light-coloured mane and tail and black legs. However some are brown, and grey is very common. They stand around 14.1 hh (145 cm/57 in). A height limit of 15 hh (152 cm/60 in) is imposed by the Highland Pony Society.
Conformation and character: The powerful Highland Pony has for long been used by stalkers in the Scottish Highlands. Steep hillsides pose no problem for this sure-footed animal, which is used to carry the bodies of the deer. However it is also popular for riding, being extremely good-natured and eager to learn. It is very compact, with a powerful but not particularly short neck with a good crest and an especially attractive flowing mane of very long, fine hair. Also typical are flat withers, a short, broad head with open nostrils, bright, kind eyes and very small ears. The legs are short and powerful and have a fair amount of feather.

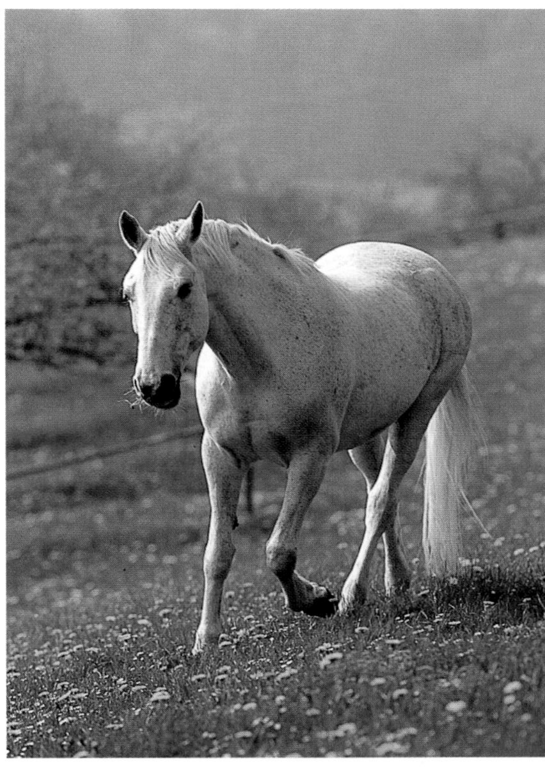

The Hanoverian is the most important German cross-breed because of its great competition qualities

Holstein

Origin: The Holstein has been bred since the 13th century. It is from the former dukedom of Holstein in northern Germany.
Size and Colour: It stands between 15.3 and 17 hh (160–172 cm/63–68 in). All the basic colours occur.
Conformation and character: The Holstein is a big, heavy warm-blood. It is nevertheless a very elegant creature, which expresses its character in particular in its unusually graceful paces and considerable jumping ability. The Holstein has an expressive head with large, bright eyes, broad nostrils and small, lively ears. The neck is long and elegant, the back long and sometimes quite strong. The very muscular hindquarters, the broad chest, the well-set shoulders and the clean powerful legs show its aristocratic breeding. It used to be crossed with Neapolitans and Cleveland Bays, mainly in order to produce a draught and coach horse. However today the introduction of Thoroughbred blood has led to its being a horse that is remarkably versatile, winning Olympic medals for dressage, show-jumping and eventing.

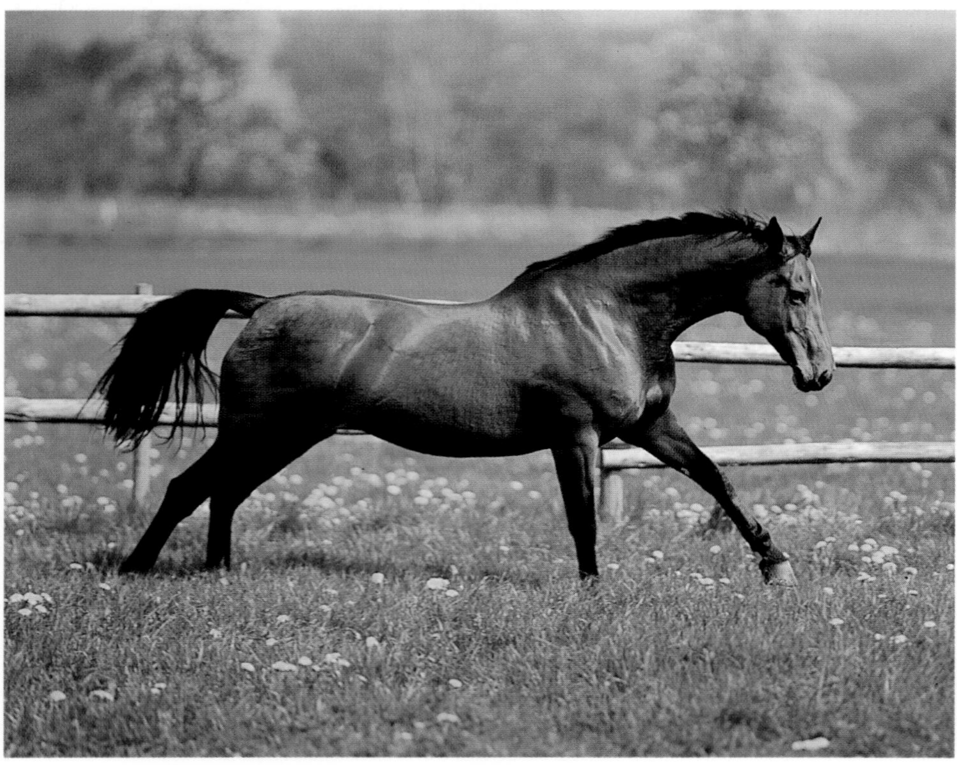

The Holstein is a very old breed

Irish Cob

Origin: The Irish Cob is bred from Connemara or Irish Draught mares and English Thoroughbred stallions. So like the Irish Hunter it is not actually a breed but a type of horse.
Size and colour: The Irish Cob occurs in all the basic colours and stands between 14.2 and 16.0 hh (148–163 cm/58–64 in).
Conformation and character: The appearance of this sturdy horse is characterized by a rather common head with a Roman nose, a powerful neck, powerful shoulders, very hard legs and large, round hooves. The energetic, very powerful and tireless Irish Cob makes a good ride-and-drive horse.

Irish Draught

Origin: It is thought that the Irish Draught is descended from the Connemara Pony. In any case the ancestors of today's Irish Draught were popular with Irish farmers, who did not need heavy horses on their small farms but a single utility horse that they could use for work on the land, driving and riding.
Size and colour: The Irish Draught stands between 15 hh and 16.3 hh (153–170 cm/60–67 in). Colours are bay, brown, chestnut and grey.
Conformation and character: Not only is this gentle, sensitive animal an excellent worker but it also has courage, stamina and considerable jumping ability. By crossing with the English Thoroughbred first-class hunters and showjumpers have been bred. The Irish Draught has a small head, clean limbs

with very little or no feather, large, round hooves, a deep chest and a high-set tail.

Irish Hunter

Origin: The Irish Hunter is not actually a separate breed of horse but a type. It is bred by crossing Irish Draught or Cleveland Bay mares with English Thoroughbred stallions.
Size and colour: The Irish Hunter usually stands between 16.0 and 16.1 hh (163–166 cm/64–65 in). It is bred in all the basic colours.
Conformation and character: This bold, sensitive horse is known for its stamina, intelligence and generally attractive appearance. Its close relationship to the English Thoroughbred can be seen from its head. The Irish Hunter has hard legs, good hooves, excellent, well-set-on shoulders and slightly-sloping hindquarters. It is very often used for showjumping.

Icelandic Pony

Origin: The Icelandic Pony was brought to the island more than 1000 years ago by Viking immigrants and ever since has been bred pure.
Size and colour: It stands between 12 and 13 hh (122–132 cm/48–52 in). Grey and dun are the usual colours, but it may also be dark brown, bay, chestnut or black.
Conformation and character: With its short, powerful neck, a large but pretty head, a rather stocky body and strong sinewy legs the Icelandic Pony has a compact appearance. The heavy mane and bushy tail are especially attractive. The Icelandic Pony is presumed to be the result of crossing the Norwegian Fjord pony with the early Celtic ponies of the British Isles. This incredibly hardy and tenacious pony has keen eyesight and an excellent sense of direction, both of which make it an indispensable means of transport even today on the frequently very rough terrain of the island. Yet it has also captured the hearts of many horse-lovers in distant parts of the world. As well as the three basic paces it also travels at the *amble*, a fast, comfortable cross between a walk and a trot, which has made it a favourite for trekking. Icelandic Ponies are late to mature but are very long-lived. That may be why many of them used to be imported into Britain to be used as pit-ponies.

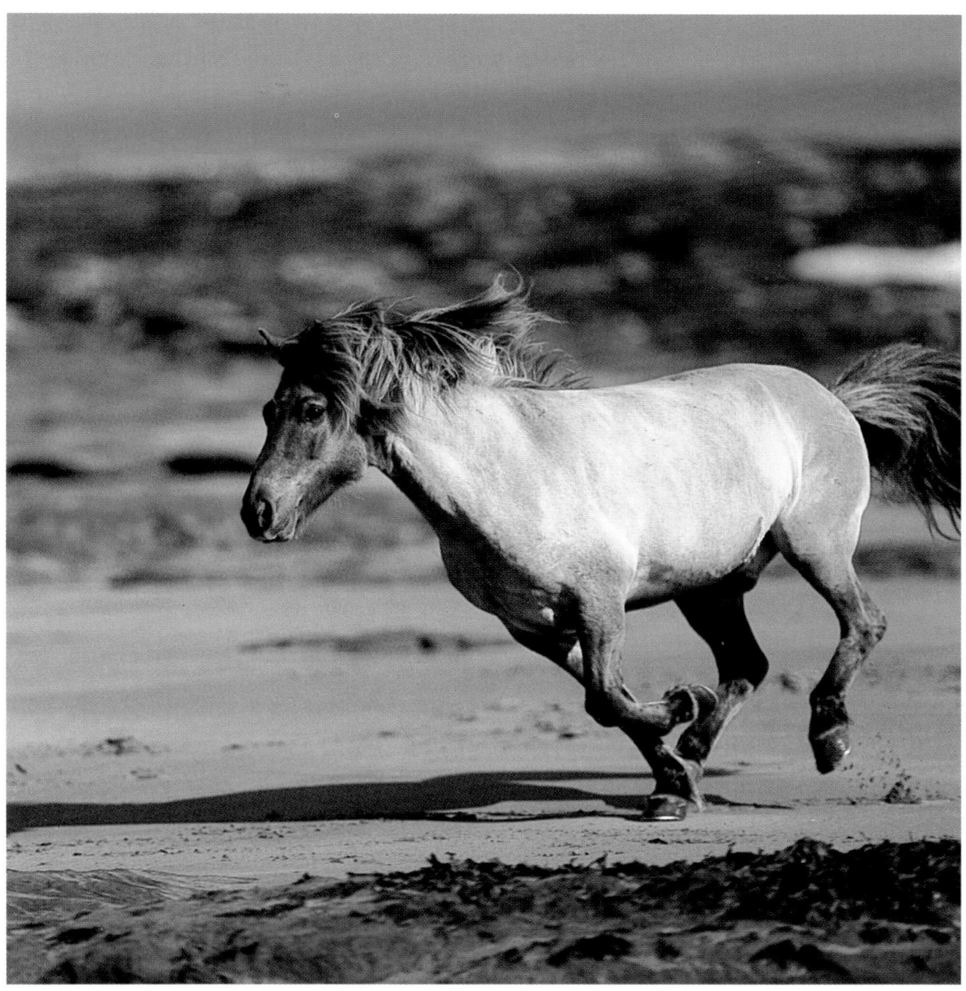

An Iceland pony at full gallop on the Icelandic

Kladruber

Origin: In 1579 the Emperor Maximilian II founded the Kladruber stud, the oldest operating stud in the world, in order to breed Kladruber greys, which are based on Neapolitan and Andalusian horses. Kladruber blacks are bred at the Horse-Breeding Research Institute in Slatinany in the Czech Republic.
Size and colour: Kladrubers stand between 15.3 and 16.3 hh (160–170 cm/63–67 in). Both greys and blacks are bred (see above).
Conformation and character: This large and imposing horse has a short, high neck and a large head with a Roman nose. Also characteristic are the high hocks, round croup and high tail carriage. This spirited, good-natured animal is mostly used as a carriage horse. The Kladruber is slow to mature but can live to a ripe old age.

Knabstrup

Origin: The Knabstrup is the little brother of the Frederiksborg and like the latter comes from Denmark.
Size and colour: It stands between 15.1 and 15.3 hh (155–160 cm/61–63 in). The Knabstrup is always spotted, usually conforming to patterns known as *leopard*, *snowflake* and *blanket*, similar to the Appaloosa.
Conformation and character: This pretty horse is somewhat lighter than the Frederiksborg. It usually has a straight head, flat withers and a straight back with rounded hindquarters. The legs are short and powerful with no feather. Because of its unusual coat markings the active, willing and good-natured Knabstrup is much in demand for circuses, in which its talent for dressage is a distinct advantage and where it is used for bareback riding. The Knabstrup is also frequently used as a general riding horse and carriage horse.

Konik

Origin: The home of the delightful little Konik is Poland, where it is very popular for general use on the land.
Size and colour: The Konik stands around 13.1 (134 cm). They are usually a variety of dun but greys also occur.
Conformation and character: The Konik, a close relative of the Tarpan, has had a great influence on East European breeds of horse and pony. This well-proportioned, powerful and robust pony has clean limbs, sloping hindquarters with a low-set tail, an elongated body and a concave head. It has a slight tendency to have cow hocks. Characteristic of the Konik are its good nature, its stamina and its ability to survive on little food.

Latvian

Origin: As its name suggests, the Latvian comes from Latvia and is hardly distinguishable from the Lithuanian.
Size and colour: It stands between 15.2 and 16 hh (158–162 cm/62–64 in). Chestnut, bay and brown are the commonest colours.

The Danish Knabstrup is a beautiful little cross-breed, always spotted

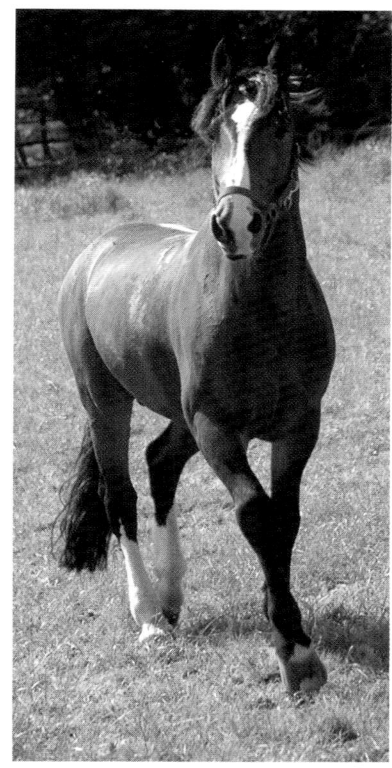

Conformation and character: The Latvian was developed as a result of massive infusions of the blood of Oldenburg stallions into the ancient stock of the Latvian forest horse. The result was a strong, muscular horse with a large head on a strong neck. The shoulders are sloping and the withers prominent. The broad chest and the strong, flat back are an indication of the strength of the original horse. The legs are strong and bony, and the mane and tail have plenty of hair. The Latvian has enough power and stamina to be used mostly as a draught animal and on the land, but is also suitable for riding and even has considerable jumping ability.

Lipizzaner

Origin: The Lipizzaner was first bred in 1580 at the royal stud founded by Archduke Charles of Austria at Lipizza, near Trieste, today in Slovenia. Today they are bred in the Austrian province of Styria, which is also where the horses for the Spanish Riding School in Vienna are bred.

Size and colour: The Lipizzaner stands between 14.3 and 15.1 hh (150–155 cm/59–61 in). Those bred in Austria are almost exclusively grey, whereas dark bays are also bred in Slovenia, Croatia and Hungary.

Conformation and character: The original Lipizzaner was quite a heavy horse, which was already prized by the Romans. In the Middle Ages the Lipizzaner became a favourite jousting horse for knights. However it was also used as a heavily-armoured war-horse, but after the invention of firearms this type of Lipizzaner was no longer so much in demand. So lighter Spanish and Arab stallions were imported to refine the breed. Today the Lipizzaner is a very small, stocky horse with a long, heavy head and often a Roman nose. The neck is strong, often short and always muscular. The back is also strong and quite long. The Lipizzaner has short, hard, clean, strong legs. Its great intelligence and willingness to learn make it ideal for the demands of high school work. Its energy, stamina and docile nature also make it a versatile riding and work horse. Lipizzaners often live to a ripe old age.

Left: The Latvian cross-breed is a good riding horse

Below: The Lipizzaner is a pure-bred horse, well suited to the demands of the 'haute école' riding methods of the Spanish Riding School of Vienna

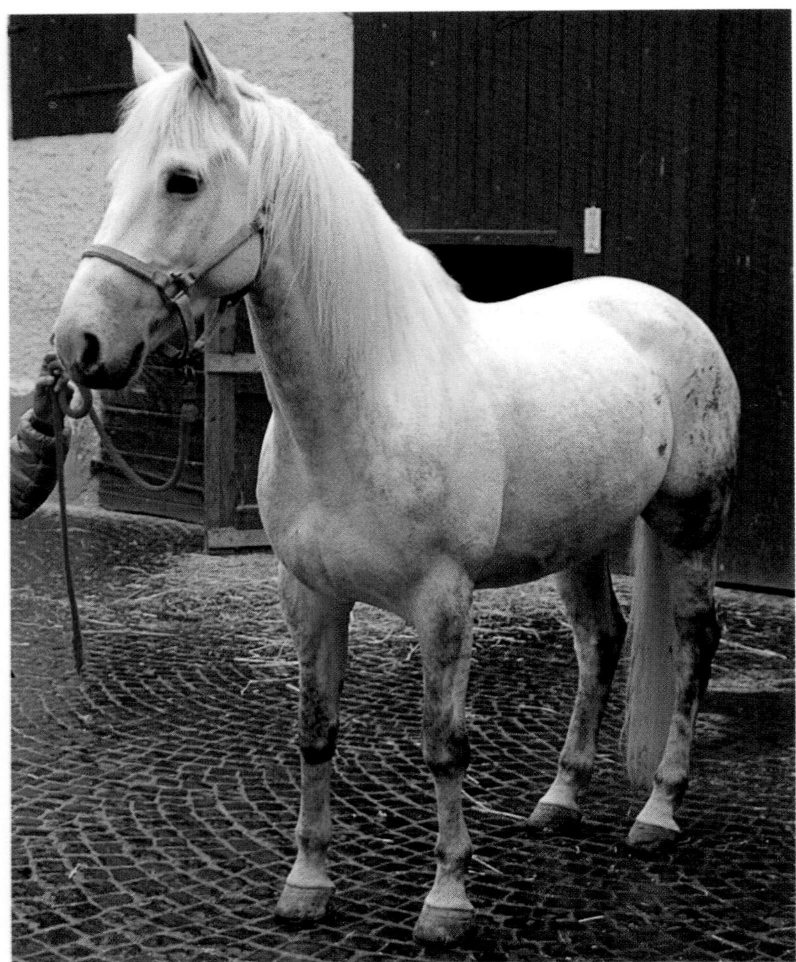

This noble Portuguese Lusitano is a particularly courageous and intelligent horse

crossed with English Thoroughbreds and Arabs but the proportion of Arab blood is always at least 25 per cent. Its speed and stamina make it particularly suitable for showjumping and general riding, and it is less highly-strung than both the Thoroughbred and the Arab. Its good breeding is shown by the head and the beautifully-carried neck in particular. It has rounded hindquarters, sloping shoulders, small hooves and a well-carried tail.

Lusitano

Origin: The Lusitano was originally bred in Portugal and was based on the Andalusian of neighbouring Spain.
Size and colour: It stands a maximum of 15.3 hh (160 cm/63 in). Most are brown or grey but other solid colours are found.
Conformation and character: The Lusitano has a medium-sized head, often with a Roman nose, set on a muscular neck. Its body is also muscular, the hindquarters rounded, and the clean legs are unusually long. The hair of the mane and tail is particular abundant and often wavy. The Lusitano has an even temperament and is hard, frugal, courageous and intelligent. It is mainly used for riding, driving and light draught work but is also often used for bullfighting. The ease with which it can be trained also make it suitable for high school work.

Malopolska

Origin: The Malopolska is a fine breed of warm-blood from Poland.
Size and colour: It stands between 15.1 and 16 hh (156–162 cm/61½–64 in) and occurs in all the basic colours.
Conformation and character: To produce the Malopolska the native primitive horse was

Missouri Foxtrotter

Origin: The settlers of North America needed a hardy horse with plenty of stamina that was capable of hard work day after day. So in the 19th century the Missouri Foxtrotter was bred from English Thoroughbreds, Arabs and Morgans.
Size and colour: This warm-blood occurs in all the basic colours and stands between 13.3 and 15.3 hh (140–160 cm/55–63 in).
Conformation and character: The Missouri Foxtrotter is kind and docile and is today a popular leisure horse. A clean head with small, pretty ears, a short back with slightly-sloping hindquarters, a deep and broad chest, a low-set tail and strong, muscular limbs characterize its attractive appearance. The Missouri Foxtrotter has a special gait, known as the Foxtrot. It walks with the

fore-legs and trots with the hind-legs, giving a very comfortable ride. This sure-footed and nimble horse can travel at between 6 and 9 mph in this way.

Morgan

Origin: The Morgan is the oldest breed of horse in North America and is named after its breeder, Justin Morgan, an innkeeper who acquired the foundation stallion in 1795 in settlement of a debt. All other breeds of horse bred on the Continent of North America can trace their ancestry back to the Morgan.
Size and colour: The size of the animals is between 15.1 and 15.3 hh (155–160 cm/61–63 in). The most usual colour is chestnut, but black and brown are also quite common and other solid colours also occur.
Conformation and character: The Morgan is a very active, muscular warm-blood. Its gaits are not particularly long, making it all the more energetic. It has a very small head, a powerful neck and long, sloping shoulders. The hindquarters are round, the legs are clean and the hooves small and hard. The Morgan horse is tough and healthy and has plenty of stamina. Its intelligence, temperament and devotion make it an outstanding horse for riding, driving and draught work.

Mustang

Origin: The Mustang is the feral descendant of the Arabs and Barbs brought to America by the Spanish in the 16th century. They were the original cow pony, but were also ridden by the Indians, who captured and tamed them. The Mustang is the ancestor of all the horses of Western North America.
Size and colour: The original Mustang was merely a pony, standing only about 14.1 hh (145 cm/57 in). Mustangs occur in all colours.
Conformation and character: Toughness, a notoriously boisterous temperament, sturdiness and stamina typify the Mustang. They also have a reputation for being difficult to handle.
The Mustang has particularly hard legs, a powerful body and a rather common head.

All North-American breeds are descended from the Morgan Horse. It is particularly popular with cowboys

New Forest Pony

Origin: The second-largest of the British breeds of mountain and moorland pony after the Highland, its ancestry goes back to the original Celtic pony.

In England New Forest ponies are often used for hunting

Size and colour: ANew Forest Ponies are classified as Type A, up to 13.2 hh (137 cm/54 in), and Type B, 13.2 to 14.2 hh (137–147 cm/54–58 in). They may be any colour except piebald and skewbald.
Conformation and character: Although no new blood has been introduced for over 100 years, the New Forest Pony is not particularly uniform in appearance. It usually has a very large head on a short, powerful neck, good shoulders, a broad chest and short, clean legs with small, hard hooves. The breed contains a large proportion of English Thoroughbred and Arab blood, some of which comes from Zorah, an Arab stallion belonging to Queen Victoria which was allowed to roam free in the New Forest in Hampshire from 1852 to 1860. Even those running wild see so many tourists that they have no fear of people. Type A ponies make ideal children's mounts and Type B are strong enough to carry adults, making them popular for the whole family and for hunting.

Dutch Warm-Blood

Origin: The ancestors of this breed are the Groningen and the Gelderland, which were crossed with Thoroughbreds, Arabs and French and German warm-bloods.
Size and colour: The Dutch Warm-Blood stands around 16 hh (163 cm/64 in) and occurs in all whole colours, though brown and chestnut are particularly common.
Conformation and character: This exceptionally athletic and good-natured horse is suitable for both riding and driving and excels as a competition horse, both in dressage and driving. It is also particularly attractive to look at. It has powerful limbs, sloping shoulders and prominent withers.

Noriker (South German Cold-Blood)

Origin: The name Noriker refers to the Roman province of Noricum, roughly corresponding to today's Austria, where they were first bred. They are also known as South German Cold-Bloods.
Size and colour: The Noriker stands between 15.1 and 16.1 hh (155–165 cm/61–65 in). Chestnut and bay are the main colours, but all of the other basic colours are possible and some have attractive spots.
Conformation and character: The appearance of the Norikers has scarcely altered since the time of the Romans. It is a heavy horse very suited to heavy agricultural work. The Noriker has a heavy but not ungainly head on a huge, mus-

Right: The Noriker is a powerful heavy draught-horse, native to southern Germany, which is often bred with a spotted coat

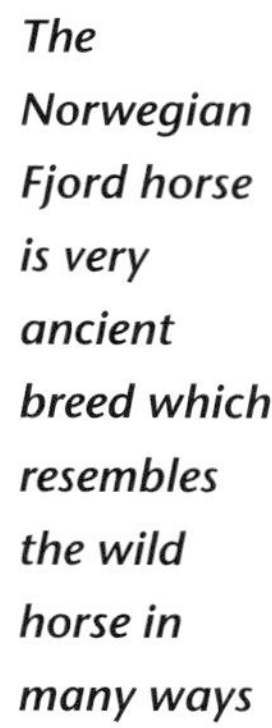

The Norwegian Fjord horse is very ancient breed which resembles the wild horse in many ways

cular neck. The shoulders are upright, the withers not very prominent. The chest is broad, the back is short and sturdy and ends in long, strong hindquarters. The Noriker has clean, strong legs with only a little feather. Being sure-footed it is ideal for use in the mountains. It is tough and undemanding with a pleasant character but is rather sluggish.

Norwegian Fjord

Origin: The Norwegian Fjord is a very ancient breed thought to be descended from the Tarpan. It originates from Norway and was used by the Vikings.
Size and colour: It stands 13 to 14.1 hh (133–145 cm/ 52–57 in). The ancestral colour of the Fjord is dun, but cream is common and bay and brown also occur. The coarse mane is dark in the centre and light on the outside and is usually clipped to show this.
Conformation and character: The Fjord is still very reminiscent of the East European and Asiatic wild horse. It has a broad forehead with bright, gentle, intelligent eyes. The nostrils are large. The head sits on a short, muscular neck. The back is short, the shoulders upright, and the legs are sturdy and powerful. The Norwegian Fjord has a surprisingly powerful pull so makes a good working horse but its very good nature and lively temperament make it also suitable as a children's riding pony.

Oldenburg

Origin: It originated in the former earldom of Oldenburg in northern Germany.
Size and colour: Oldenburgs stand between 15.3 and 16.3 hh (160–170 cm/63–67 in). Most are brown, bay or black.
Conformation and character: Oldenburgs existed inthe 15th century and were the result of crossing local mares with Spanish and Neapolitan stallions. The resulting magnificent coach horses were refined in the 19th century by crossing with Cleveland Bay stallions, and later in the same century a further step to make them lighter and more elegant was taken by introducing a considerable proportion of Thoroughbred blood. The Oldenburg is an extremely attractive horse with a medium-sized head, long neck and prominent withers. The back is strong and ends in muscular hindquarters. The clean, powerful legs are straight. The Oldenburg is characterized by its toughness and stamina which, together with its courage and great jumping ability, make it an outstanding competition horse.

The Oldenburger is much loved because it is an excellent competition horse

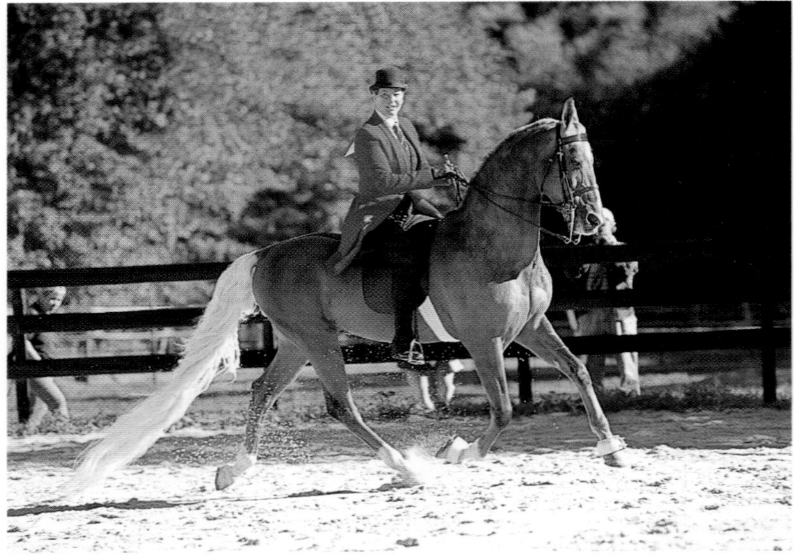

Palominos are identified exclusively by their colour. These golden horses are handsome and elegant

Below: The Paso Fino is a breed native to South America and is now bred all over the world

Palomino

Origin: The Palomino is descended from the Spanish horses brought to America in the early 16th century. Its home is North America.

Size and colour: The golden Palomino is not strictly a breed in the usual sense but a colour, therefore the appearance and size of this pretty horse are rather variable. Attempts are still being made to get the Palomino recognized as a genuine breed, though it already is in the USA. Five shades are officially recognized, ranging from cream to almost chestnut. Mane and tail must be silvery-white and white markings on the face and legs are allowed.

Conformation and character: Once this particular colour occurred it was maintained and reinforced by selective breeding. Palominos come in all sizes. Most of them have a build similar to that of an Arab, a Quarter Horse or the Morgan. Their hardiness, toughness and stamina make them good working horses and they are especially highly prized by cowboys. Their kind nature and even temperament also make Palominos good family riding horses, and because of their splendid colouring they are very popular in the show-ring and for parades.

Paso Fino

Origin: Like all American breeds of horse the Paso Fino is

descended from Spanish horses introduced into America by the Conquistadores in the early 16th century. Its original home is Puerto Rico, but nowadays it is also bred in Europe.
Size and colour: The Paso Fino stands at least 14 hh (143 cm/56 in). All the basic colours occur and many are beautifully spotted.
Conformation and character: The long-legged Paso Fino is extremely attractive to look at. It has a medium-sized, straight head and a strong, well-arched neck on upright, muscular shoulders. The back is strong and ends in round, broad hindquarters. The legs are long with high knees, the hooves are small and hard. Apart from the three basic paces the Paso Fino has an innate ability to move at another pace, known as the *paso*, making it a comfortable and easy ride. This kind, good-natured horse is sure-footed and has plenty of stamina, so it a safe horse for riding, in particular over rough terrain and even in the mountains.

Pinto (Painted horse)

Origin: The Pinto is yet another horse descended from feral Spanish horses and is widespread in both North and South America.
Size and colour: As a colour and not strictly-speaking a breed the Pinto varies very much in size, standing between 14 and 16.1 hh (143–165 cm/56–65 in). Two types of pattern are recognized, *Overos* with white marks on a dark background and *Tobianos* with dark marks on a white background.
Conformation and character: The Pinto is the archetypal „Western horse' of North America. There is a Pinto registry in the US but it is not recognized as a breed. Its appearance is very variable. As a rule it is an attractive horse with a pretty, medium-sized head, large, expressive eyes and small, mobile ears. The neck is carried well, the back is short and strong and the hindquarters are round and muscular. The clean legs are medium-length and powerful with prominent hocks and small, hard hooves. Pintos are excellent general-purpose riding horses with considerable jumping ability. They are also characterized by their great speed, tenacity and stamina. These tough horses were also very popular with the North American Indians.

The lovely Pinto was popular with American Indians

Pony of the Americas

Origin: This Western pony was bred from Shetland Ponies and Appaloosas and bears a close resemblance to the latter.
Size and colour: The height of Ponies of the Americas varies between 11.1 and 13.1

hh (115–135 cm/45–53 in). In colour and markings it is like the Appaloosa, hence it is considered to be a type of miniature Appaloosa.
Conformation and character: This loveable pony has lots of stamina and athletic ability. It is particular popular as a children's riding pony. Its appearance is reminiscent of the Arab.

All current horse breeds are descended from Przewalski's Horse

Przewalski's Horse (Mongolian Wild Horse)

Origin: Przewalski's Horse comes originally from Mongolia, where it still lives wild today. After almost becoming extinct, it is now bred pure in zoos as the last breed of truly wild horse.
Size and colour: It stands between 12.1 and 14.1 hh (124–145 cm/49–57 in). Most are various shades of dun but black and bay also occur. Mane and tail are usually dark and the legs often have horizontal stripes.
Conformation and character: Przewalski's Horse is a very ancient steppe pony possessing great strength and stamina. It can survive even under extremely harsh conditions. It is characterized by a long head, often with a Roman nose, and large ears. The chest is deep and the withers are very prominent. The strong back ends in muscular hindquarters. The strong legs have hard, well-formed hooves. Przewalski's horse often has a rather unpleasant character and is difficult to tame, so it is rarely domesticated.

Quarter Horse

Origin: The Quarter Horse was bred in America by crossing the descendants of the feral horses left behind by the Spanish with Arabs and English Thoroughbreds.
Size and colour: The Quarter Horse stands about 15.1 hh (155 cm/61 in). They are usually chestnut but may be any solid colour.
Conformation and character: The name of the breed refers to its remarkable turn of speed, for there is no horse faster than the Quarter Horse over a distance of a quarter of a mile (400 metres). It is a compact, muscular warm-blood with a short head with medium-sized eyes and ears and a broad forehead. The neck is powerful and is carried well. The withers are not very pronounced. The chest is broad and deep, the back short and strong. The shoulders are long and sloping, the hindquarters are round and very broad. Slim legs with powerful hocks and small, hard hooves complete the picture of this horse.

This reliable, tough and tireless animal has a calm temperament and loyal character. Its speed and agility make the Quarter Horse one of the most versatile of all horses. At the same time it is a

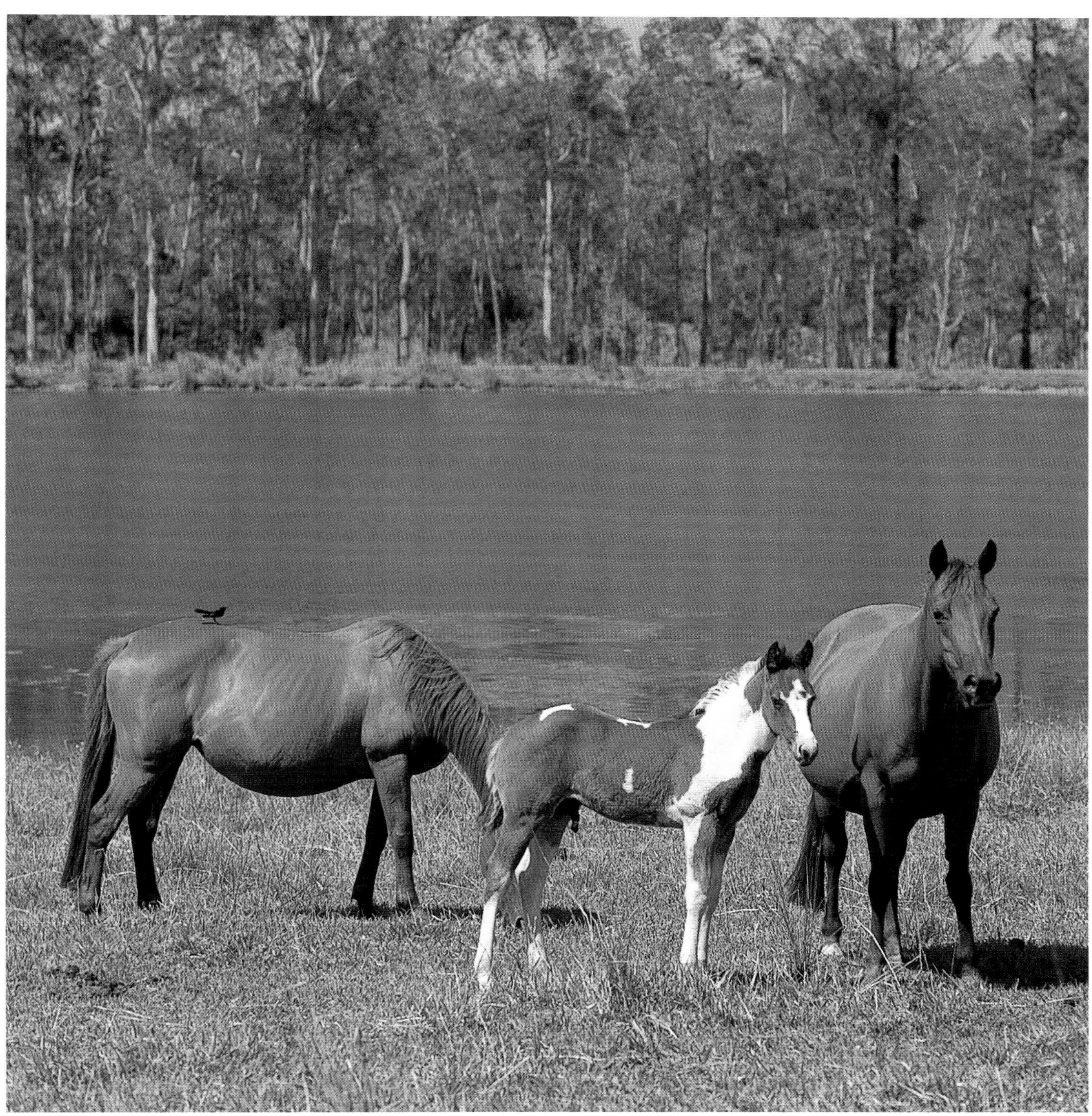

reliable riding horse for all the family, an almost unbeatable racehorse over short distances, an ideal cow pony and a tough competition horse.

Rhenish-German Heavy Draught

Origin: The Rhenish-German Heavy Draught is bred in the German Rhineland region and is largely based on Belgian heavy horses. Its studbook dates back to 1892 but the breed is in all probability much older.

Morgan horses with foals

An impressively powerful horse. The Rhenisch German Heavy Draught horse is ideal for agricultural and forestry work

Size and colour: Its size varies between 15.3 and 17 hh (160–172 cm/63–68 in). Chestnuts, bays, strawberry roans and red roans are bred.
Conformation and character: The Rhenish-German Heavy Draught is a huge, heavy, enormously-strong horse. It has very strong bones yet nevertheless astonishingly free paces. The head is big and heavy but clean and sits on a huge neck. The shoulders are compact and sloping. A short, strong back and the very muscular, round croup, often with a cleft, are typical of the Rhenish-German Heavy Draught. The legs are short and powerful and usually feathered. Its enormous pulling ability makes the Rhenish-German Heavy Draught ideal for heavy agricultural and forestry work.

Russian Heavy Draught

Origin: This sturdy horse comes originally from the Ukraine, where it was bred by crossing local mares with Ardennes, Percherons and Orlov Trotters.
Size and colour: The Russian Heavy Draught stands around 14.2 hh (148 cm/58 in). The most usual colours are chestnut, bay and strawberry roan.
Conformation and character: With its ability to pull very heavy loads the Russian Heavy Draught has proved itself an excellent horse for use in agriculture. It is good-natured and docile. This very compact, stocky animal has a medium-sized head with pointed ears, an extremely strong neck, flat withers, a heavy body, a broad hollow back and powerful, sloping hindquarters. Its legs are short and slightly feathered and have hard hooves.

Salerno

Origin: The Salerno is an old Italian breed which with the dissolution of the Persano national stud in 1972 is gradually becoming extinct.
Size and colour: It reaches a height of 15.3 hh (160 cm/63 in). All the solid colours occur.
Conformation and character: The Salerno gets its particularly good looks from its Spanish forefathers. It used to be used mainly by the Italian army as a cavalry horse. It is of medium size, powerful, with a finely-chiselled head, a long, well-carried neck, prominent withers and a large chest cavity. The shoulders are muscular, the back is short and flat and the hindquarters are sloping and well muscled. The legs are long and clean and end in small, hard hooves.

Schleswig

Origin: The development of the Schleswig heavy horse was influenced by French heavy horses and is today bred only in small numbers in northern Germany.

Size and colour: Its size varies between 15.1 and 16.1 hh (155–165 cm/61–65 in). It occurs in all the basic colours but most animals are various shades of chestnut with flaxen mane and tail.
Conformation and character: The Schleswig is a strong, medium-sized heavy horse. It is thick-set but has very free paces. The head is big and heavy but clean and sits on a thick neck. The shoulders are compact and sloping. The short, strong back and the muscular, sloping hindquarters are typical of the Schleswig. The legs are short and strong and have only a little feather. Its enormous strength makes the Schleswig ideal for medium to heavy work in agriculture and forestry.

Schwarzwälder

Origin: The home of the Schwarzwälder is the range of low mountains in south-west Germany.
Size and colour: The Schwarzwälder stands between 14.1 and 15.1 hh (145–155 cm/57–61 in). Most are chestnut with a beautiful flaxen mane and tail. Other colours of coat are rare.
Conformation and character: The Schwarzwälder is a particularly fine Cold-Blood. It has similar origins to the Noriker but is considerably daintier. It has a small, pretty head, a short, well-carried neck and upright shoulders. The back of the Schwarzwälder is short and strong with broad, muscular hindquarters. The legs are short, strong, tough and attractively feathered. This very small heavy horse is particularly good-natured. Its willingness to work, its toughness, stamina and sure-footedness make it an ideal light draught horse for use in agriculture and forestry, even on rough ground.

The Schwarzwälder is a noble heavy draught horse with its balanced build

Swedish Warm-Blood

Origin: This breed was originally bred in the 17th century at the Royal Stud at Flyinge in southern Sweden specifically to meet the requirements of the cavalry. Over time it was crossed with numerous breeds, at first mainly Spanish and oriental horses, later Arabs, Trakehners, Hanoverians, Thoroughbreds and others. Flyinge is still the main breeding centre, where the selection of sires and dams is governed by strict regulations.
Size and colour: Size varies between 15.3 and 16.2 hh (160–167 cm/63–66 in). All colours, but mostly chestnut.
Conformation and character: The Swedish Warm-Blood is a fine horse for general riding and is also suitable for dressage. It is intelligent, alert, well-balanced and has a particularly pleasant temperament. Being well-proportioned and having long, harmonious paces it has an extremely attractive appearance. It has a straight head, a well-carried neck, lovely, sloping shoulders, clean legs and very small, hard hooves. Typical are the rather flat withers and powerful, round hindquarters. The back is medium-length, flat and muscular. The tail is set high and is carried well.

Speckled grey is a typical colour for the Shagya, which originated in Hungary

Shagya

Origin: The Shagya's original home is Hungary where it was bred from native stock and an Arab stallion, named Shagya, bought from Bedouins in Syria in 1830.
Size and colour: It stands between 15.1 and 15.3 hh (155–160 cm/61–63 in). Whilst most are grey the Shagya does occur in other colours.
Conformation and character: The conformation of this fine horse is somewhere between the English Thoroughbred and the Arab. Its ability to withstand great heat and thirst is almost legendary. Its hardiness, stamina and athleticism make it very suitable for both riding and driving. The Shagya is characterized by its slim build and its very small but long head with big, expressive eyes. The neck is long and muscular, the back slim but nevertheless strong. Also typical are its long legs with small, hard hooves.

Shetland Pony

Origin: The Shetland Pony's original home is the Shetland Isles in the north British Isles. Today it is bred the world over.
Size and colour: Registered ponies must not exceed 40 inches (102 cm) at the age of three and 42 inches (107 cm) at the age of four and over and are thus the smallest breed of pony native to Britain. They are always measured in inches

and not in hands. The foundation colour is black, but they may be bay, brown, chestnut, grey, piebald or skewbald.
Conformation and character: There is evidence that Shetland Ponies existed as far back as 500 BC but there was no attempt at selective breeding until the middle of the 19th century when they were used as pit-ponies. Therefore even today Shetlands still look very much as they did originally. They have a small head with small ears. The nostrils are large, the eyes expressive and kind. Mane, tail and coat are thick and silky and become very shaggy in the winter. The Shetland's short, sturdy legs end in small, hard hooves. Originally they were used for riding and as pack ponies. They often pulled carts carrying seaweed from the shore to the fields for use as fertilizer. Since the beginning of the 20th century the Shetland Pony has become the favourite riding pony for children despite the fact that some individuals have unpredictable characters and despite the fact that it is so strong for its size that it is not easy for small children to control. It is therefore often kept simply as a pet.

Shire Horse

Origin: It originates from the Shire Counties of central England and from East Anglia.
Size and colour: Standing up to 18 hh (183 cm/72 in) the Shire Horse is the giant of the horse world, the largest breed alive today. The predominant colours are bays and browns, but black, grey and chestnut also occur. They almost always have attractive markings.
Conformation and character: The Shire is not only huge but also well proportioned, so despite its size it never looks clumsy. The long, well-formed head with its friendly-looking eyes sits on a long, powerful neck. The powerful chest, the sloping, muscular shoulders and the long, strong legs indicate the enormous strength this animal possesses, for the Shire is not only the biggest but also one of the strongest horses in the world, being able to pull five tonnes. The legs are covered with luxuriant feather. It is a very old breed, known as far back as the Middle Ages. Though no longer extensively used on farms, there has been a recent revival in breeding them for showing, and many breweries still use them for pulling drays.

Suffolk Punch

Origin: The Suffolk Punch is indigenous to the county of Suffolk in eastern England.

The giant Shire Horse is the largest and strongest of all horses

The Suffolk Punch, a heavy muscular draught house, is a very ancient breed

Size and colour: The Suffolk Punch stands around 15.3 hh (160 cm/63 in). It occurs in all shades of chestnut and the only marking accepted is a star or a little white on the face.
Conformation and character: This old breed is recorded as far back as 1506. It is a strong, stocky and muscular heavy breed. It has an attractive, straight head on a thick, powerful neck. The withers are not very prominent and the back is relatively long. The legs are short, sturdy and exceptionally robust. It is easily recognizable because it is the only British heavy horse with no feather on the legs. It was originally bred as a coach horse, but today the tough, biddable and hardworking Suffolk Punch is mainly used in agriculture and for light draught work, and often appears in the show-ring.

Tarpan

Origin: The Tarpan was originally the commonest wild horse in eastern Europe and, together with Przewalski's Horse, is regarded as the ancestor of all our domesticated horses. But in the 19th century it was hunted to extinction and today's Tarpan has been regenerated from the Polish Konik.
Size and colour: Tarpans reach a maximum of 13 hh (132 cm/52 in). Most are various shades of dun with black mane and tail and a black eel stripe.
Conformation and character: Although for the purposes of regenerating the breed individuals that looked very much like the original Tarpans and still had a lot of the blood of the extinct wild form in them were mainly used, it is nevertheless only a domesticated horse in a wild animal's clothing. Profound biological changes, even in the structure of the brain, mean that it is impossible to reverse the process of domestication. The modern Tarpan has a long, large head with long ears and large nostrils. The neck is short and the back is long and solid. The legs of the Tarpan are sturdy and very strong. Most are now allowed to run wild. They are hardy and robust, can survive on a poor diet and reproduce rapidly.

The regenerated Tarpan is a domesticated horse 'disguised' as a wild horse

Tennessee Walking Horse

Origin: The Tennessee Walking Horse originated in the state of Tennessee in the North American Deep South.

Size and colour: It stands between 15 and 16.1 hh (153–165 cm/60–65 in). All the basic colours, with bay, black and chestnut the commonest.
Conformation and character: The Tennessee Walking Horse was not recognized as a separate breed until 1935, although it is much older. It was originally bred by rich plantation-owners, who rode them while inspecting their plantations, hence the alternative name of Plantation Walking Horse. It has a small, pretty head, sometimes with a slight Roman nose, large, expressive eyes and small, pointed, mobile ears. The powerful, muscular neck is long and the shoulders are elegant. The short, strong back ends in rounded hindquarters with a very high-set and beautifully-carried tail. The long, straight legs have large hooves. It is a light, extremely elegant ride-and-drive horse. It is kind-natured, very intelligent, docile and loyal. With its unique fast and comfortable gait, known as a *running walk*, it is also an ideal riding horse for beginners and the elderly. However nowadays it is bred only rarely and mainly ridden in the show-ring.

Trakehner

Origin: The Trakehner is originally from the former German province of East Prussia, where it has been bred for several centuries.
Size and colour: The Trakehner stands between 15.3 and 16.3 hh (160–170 cm/63–67 in). It may be any solid colour but is usually dark.
Conformation and character: The Trakehner is considered to be the noblest breed of horse after the English Thoroughbred and the Arab but as a result of cross-breeding has a high proportion of Thoroughbred blood in its veins. It is a horse of noble proportions with a well-shaped, expressive head and large, bright and kind eyes. The withers are

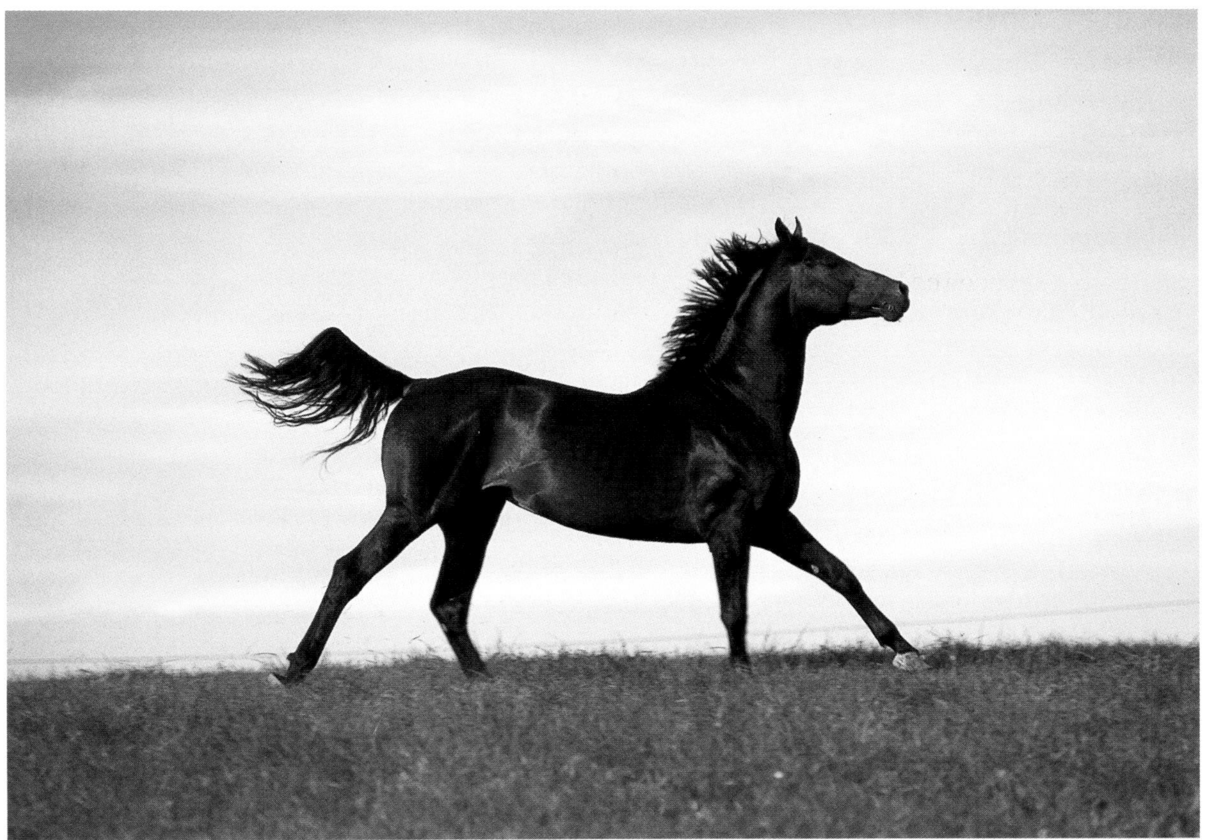

After the Arab and English thoroughbreeds, the Trakehner is considered the noblest of all cross-breed horses

prominent, the shoulders are strong and sloping and the back is flat and muscular. The tail is set high on the powerful hindquarters. The limbs are long and perfectly formed and have small, hard hooves. The Trakehner is outstanding for its stamina, toughness and hardiness. It is a frugal eater and has a lively temperament which occasionally has to be curbed, since its character is not altogether straightforward. As well as being used as a competition and leisure horse, nowadays the Trakehner also plays an important role in refining most of the German breeds of Warm-Blood.

The Welsh Cob is larger than the other three Welsh types and is often used for hunting

Opposite page: Two important German cross-breeds: Westphalian (top) and Württemberg (bottom)

Welsh Mountain Pony, Welsh Pony, Welsh Pony (Cob Type) and Welsh Cob

Origin: These are not separate breeds but four types, all of which originate from Wales.
Size and colour: The Welsh Mountain Pony must not exceed 12 hh (122 cm/48 in). The Welsh Pony and the Welsh Pony (Cob Type) must not exceed 13.2 hh (137 cm/54 in). At 14 to 15.1 hh (142–155 cm/56–61 in) the Welsh Cob is considerably larger. All four types occur in all colours except piebald and skewbald.
Conformation and character: The Welsh Mountain Pony is one of the descendants of the original Celtic Pony and still runs wild or semi-wild in the Welsh mountains. With its huge, kind eyes it is a particular pretty pony. These intelligent and plucky animals make very good children's riding ponies but are also suitable for driving. The Welsh Pony is very similar in character to the Welsh Mountain Pony. Because of an infusion of Arab blood it is somewhat larger and is particularly athletic, so it is especially popular as a children's riding pony and excels at gymkhanas. The Welsh Pony (Cob Type) is the same size as the Welsh Pony but is sturdier and stronger. Because of the Cob influence it is also rather less elegant than the two types just described. Its stamina and hardiness make it suitable for riding, jumping and hunting as well as for driving, and it is still used on Welsh farms. The Welsh Cob is the largest of the four types of Welsh pony. Like the Welsh Ponies (Cob Type) these plucky, powerful and tough animals are mainly used for general riding, jumping and hunting and are driven in traps and light carts.

Westphalian

Origin: The Westphalian is one of the most important breeds of German warm-blood.
Size and colour: It stands between 16.1 and 17.1 hh (165–175 cm/65–69 in). All the solid colours occur, but chestnut predominates.
Conformation and character: The Westphalian has been strongly influenced by the Trakehner, the English Thoroughbred and the Arab and was based on the ideal of the Hanoverian, which it has been

bred to resemble. Often only experts can distinguish from the Hanoverian. At the same time it also very similar to the Trakehner. It is a big horse with a finely-chiselled head on a long well-set-on neck. The back is flat and muscular, the shoulders are long and sloping. The tail is well set on the powerful but nevertheless elegant hindquarters and is carried well. The clean limbs are perfectly formed, and have powerful hocks and hard hooves. With its unimpeachable character and its wonderful, even temperament the Westphalian is an ideal and extremely versatile horse for general riding, showjumping and eventing.

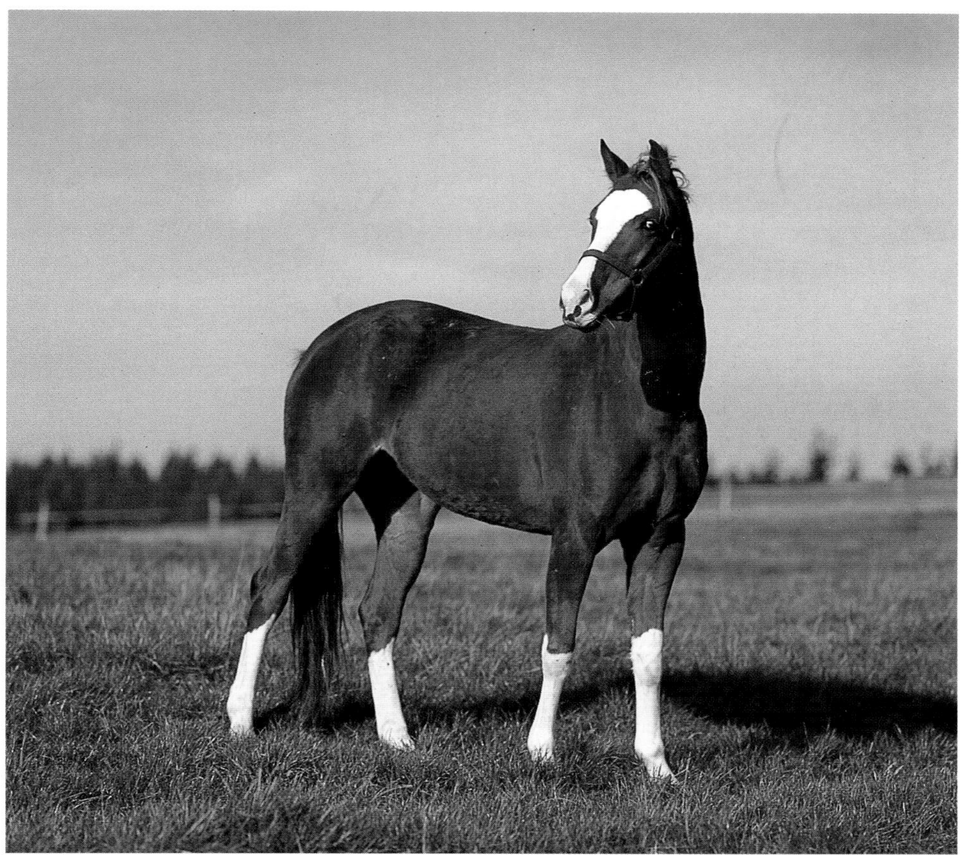

Wurttemberg

Origin: The Wurttemberg is from south-west Germany.
Size and colour: It stands from 15.2 to 16.1 hh (157–165 cm/62–65 in). The commonest colours are brown, bay, chestnut and black.
Conformation and character: The Wurttemberg was bred by crossing various breeds. It contains Neapolitan, Spanish and Arab blood. This gave a powerful, compact, horse with a straight, expressive head, kind, attractive eyes and small, mobile ears. The neck indicates the animal's strength, and the beautiful sloping shoulders are also packed with muscles. The back is short and flat and ends in powerful, very flat hindquarters with a high-set tail. The medium-length limbs have small, hard hooves. Today the Wurttemberg is prized as a loyal and reliable horse for general riding. It is also occasionally used for light agricultural work.

Buying

a horse

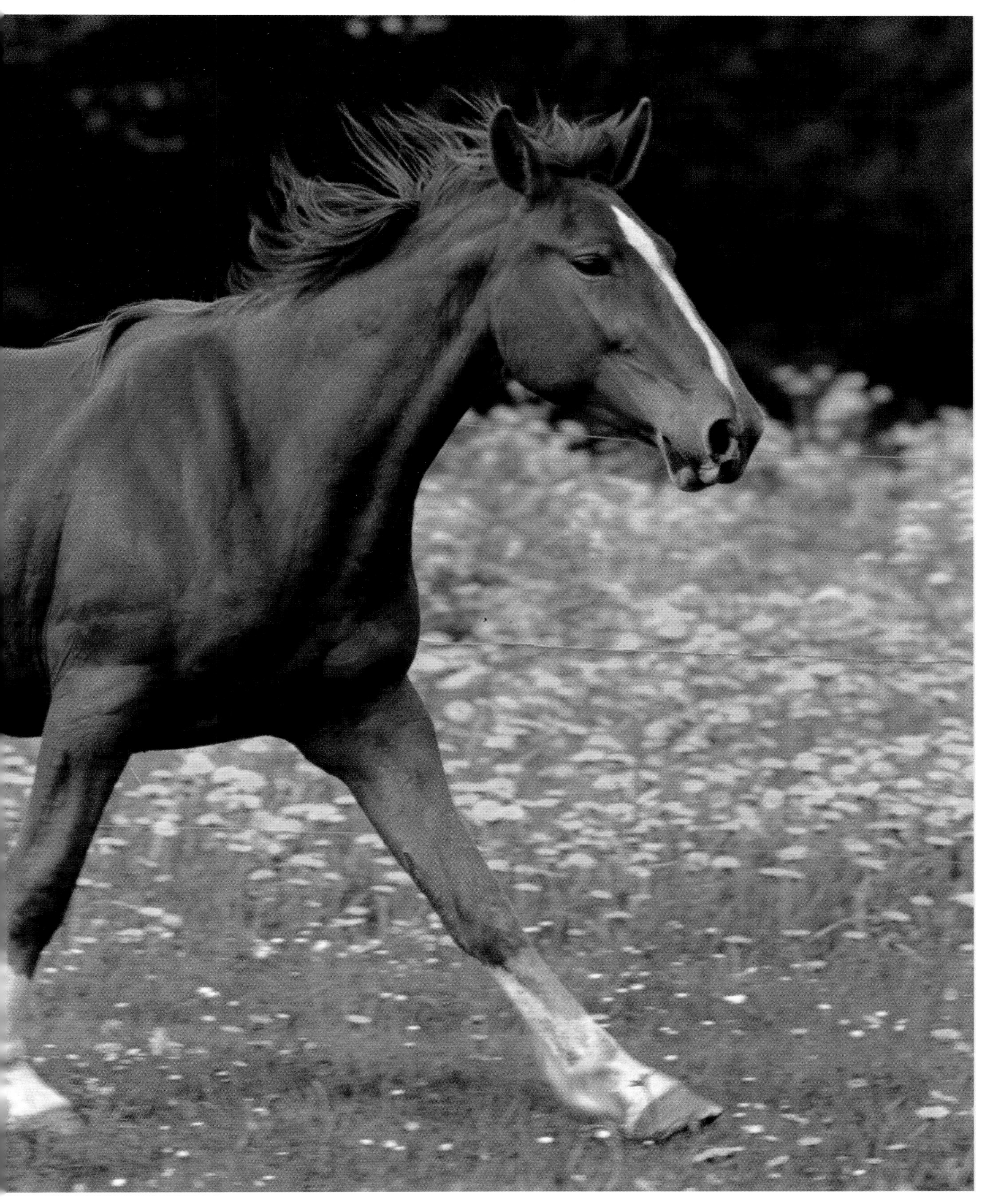

Privately or from a dealer?

The horse-lover who, after reflecting long and hard, decides to buy a horse then has to decide how and where to get the best one. There are professional horse-dealers but also lots of private advertisements in newspapers and specialist magazines. However the purchaser should be aware that private owners often describe their horses as superb animals. Yet on closer inspection it sometimes turns out that the horse does not live up to its owner's claims. Most often the reason is that private owners have

Nearly all horse-riding enthusiasts would somehow love to have their own horse

no real idea of their horses' market value. So before setting off on what may turn out to be a totally wasted journey the buyer should at least ask for a photograph. A video would be even better, showing the horse moving and thus enabling a preliminary impression of the horse to be obtained. Buying a horse is usually very straightforward when the purchaser has known it for a fairly long time and has been able to watch it on several occasions.

The facial expression is also very important when judging a horse

Nevertheless, whether buying privately or from a dealer, what should the purchaser bear in mind when looking at a horse, and how is it possible to tell whether the horse has anything wrong with it? First of all the buyer must ensure that the horse is suitable for the rider. Whilst an experienced rider may be able to cope with a young, unschooled or newly-broken horse, inexperienced riders should choose an older, well-schooled and docile animal. The horse might even have something to teach the rider! Older people too should choose a quiet horse rather than a lively youngster, since there is always the risk of a fall and the resilience of the human body decreases steadily with age. However nobody should consider buying a horse at all unless they have some riding experience.

Deciding on a horse

If you already have a particular horse in mind the animal's condition should be assessed. This requires the faculty of observation, attentiveness and also a great deal of scepticism. Very important when deciding on a horse are its general appearance, its nutritional state, its character and its agility. When assessing the appearance the first thing to look at is whether the whole horse looks harmonious and agile. Are the legs and hooves sound, so that the horse's action is not adversely affected? It is important to check whether it has any scars, which could point to previous injuries, accidents or illnesses. Do not hesitate to ask the owner about this sort of thing. An attractive head may be nice to look at, but attention should be paid to whether the ears look sensitive and mobile and the nostrils clean and healthy. The eyes must be bright and alert, since a horse with poor eyesight may be nervous when approached. It is essential to have a look at the teeth, since they indicate the horse's age. During its lifetime the horse wears its

An expert on horses will be able to tell what kind of horse the foal will develop into, what kind of nature it will have, and whether it will become a good riding horse

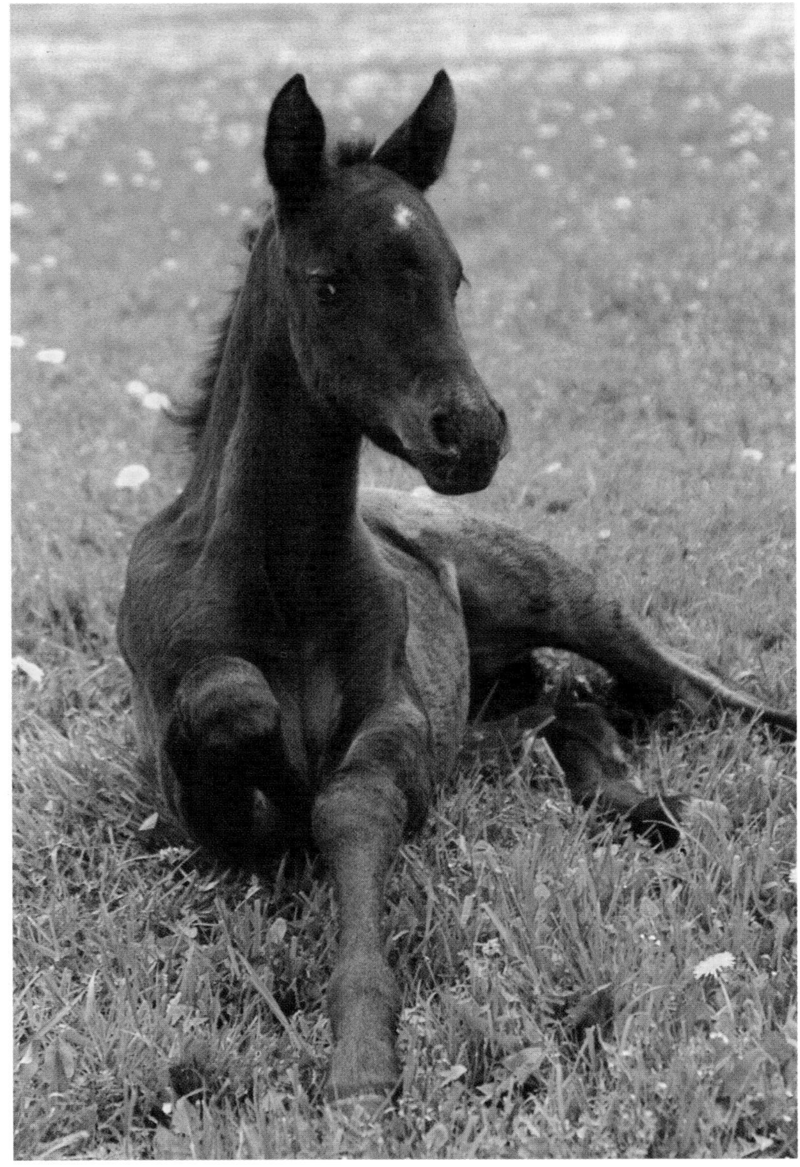

incisors down. With increasing age these front teeth also become more sloping. The nutritional state can also give an indication of potential disease. The horse should be neither too thin nor too fat. If you can see its ribs it's too thin; if you can't feel them it's too fat.

The horse's character is important if you are going to enjoy riding it. You should check whether the animal will allow its feet to be picked up and how it behaves when approached and when the saddle and bridle are put on. You should ask the owner to take it out of the loose-box, and you should watch closely while this is happening. Does it leave willingly and eagerly, or is it hesitant, reluctant or even unwilling to leave? Note whether the vendor leads the horse only by the head collar or by the bit. If the latter, ask the reason, since it is possible that the horse is stubborn. In any case you must approach the horse yourself in order to find out whether it is nervous. If that goes well, stroke the horse. Stroke its head, its withers and right along its back to the hindquarters, and give it a slap on the hindquarters. Notice how the animal reacts! You will soon find out if it is of a nervous disposition.

Then it is time to see the

You can find out a lot about a horse's character simply by observing it from a distance

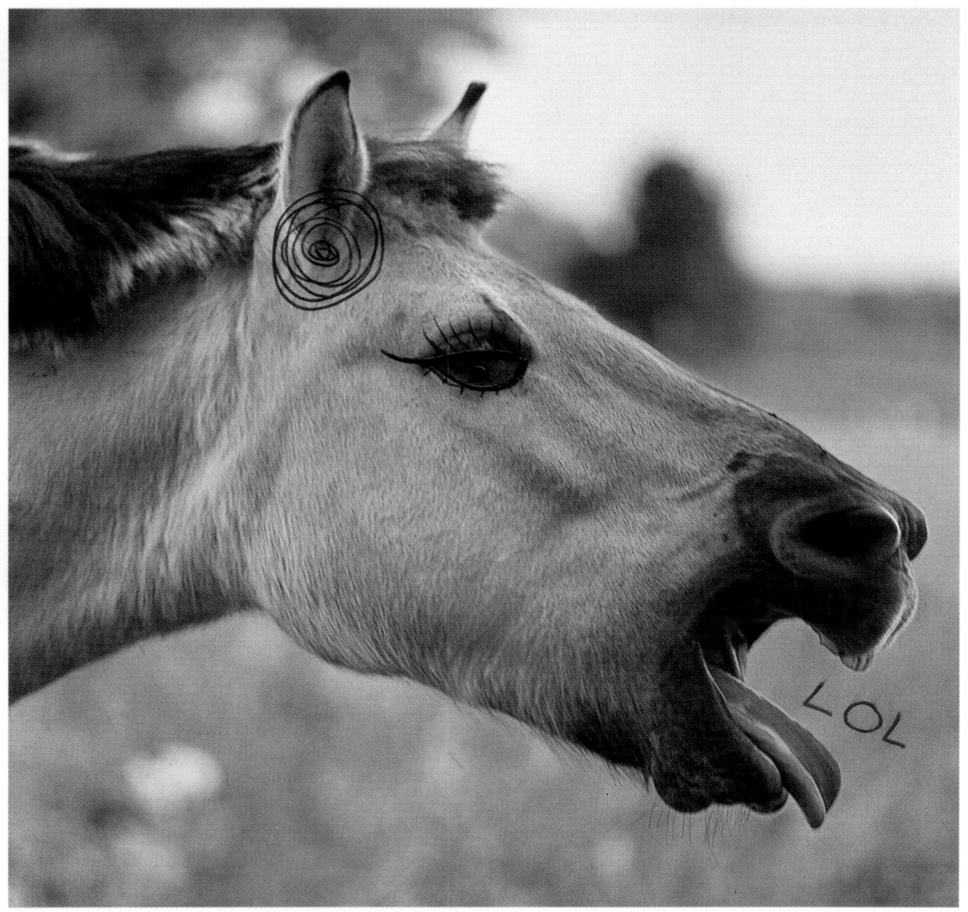

It is the teeth that reveal a horse's age

horse moving, since you still have to find out whether it can move properly, that is to say is not lame. This should be done on as hard a surface as possible, preferably on asphalt. Lameness is immediately obvious on hard ground, whereas on soft ground it could remain unnoticed. Watch the horse going through all three paces one after the other, and pay close attention to how its legs move. Even small jumps can show up slight defects. Watch the rider carefully too, since a good rider can, to a certain extent, use experience to compensate for some defects in the horse. Finally have a ride on the horse yourself too in order to feel for yourself whether it suits you.

The safest thing is to get an experienced vet to go with you. He will not be able to guarantee the state of health of the horse, but as an expert he will certainly have an opinion, which you should take into account when making your decision whether to buy the horse. If it is impossible to have the horse vetted before buying it, ensure you arrange for a trial period before the sale is finalized. During this period have the horse vetted, but by your own and never the owner's vet. The vet should of course be one who specializes in horses. A thorough inspection lasts more than two hours, since the horse's pulse and breathing after exertion must be checked.

If the vet is satisfied he will then issue a certificate of the horse's soundness, but not otherwise. You are strongly recommended to arrange third-party liability insurance immediately, because a horse that takes fright or bolts can quickly cause a lot of damage to property or even injury to people.

Anyone interested in purchasing a horse must insist on being introduced properly to the animal by the seller. This will make things much easier later on

Then comes the pleasure of getting to know the beautiful new horse

The legal aspect

Like all animals, under British law a horse counts as an object. Therefore there is no difference in law between buying a horse and buying a television set, for instance.

Keeping your horse,

tack and equipment

A home for your horse – the right accommodation

In these stables, horses are kept in individual boxes

Horses are kept in many different ways. According to available space, available buildings and time of year horses can be kept in loose-boxes, in stables or in paddocks. Owners and riders of competition horses can best feed their animals regularly and with the right quantity of food if they are kept in. With animals that live out this is not quite so easy, because it is impossible to ascertain exactly how much grass they eat. Horses out at grass are living as naturally as possible, but such conditions are not suitable for race-horses and competition horses.

If a horse spends most of its time inside, its loose-box should measure at least 3.5 x 3 m (11½ x 10 ft). In large riding schools and other establishments where very many horses are housed they may be kept in stables in which the individuals are tethered in their own stalls separated from one another by a wall reaching to approximately shoulder height. If the stalls are arranged along two sides there will be a passageway about 13 feet (four metres) wide down the middle. This sort of accommodation is very easy to keep clean but is suitable only for horses that are taken out every day, that is to say turned out into a paddock or taken out for schooling or on a hack.

However far better than the stall system is for horses to be kept in large loose-boxes. In the last few years, because of increased concern for the welfare and protection of horses, this type of accommodation has become the norm and very few are still tethered in individual stalls. Even better are loose-boxes that open directly onto a paddock. This type of accommodation is not only beneficial for the welfare of the horse but is also very practical from the point of view of the groom and the rider.

As well as sufficient space, temperature is an important criterion for the horse's welfare. A good stable should have plenty of light and be maintained at a temperature of around 15 degrees centigrade. The necessary warmth is best provided by straw placed in the loose-boxes or stalls as bedding. This is also comfortable for the horse to lie down on. The horse should on no account come into direct contact with the cement or wooden floor of the stable but should always be able to lie down on a thick layer of straw or sawdust providing good insulation. Accommodation should also be well ventilated but with no draughts, and should always be kept dry.

It is obvious that a horse is

In this case, the horses have direct access to the paddock

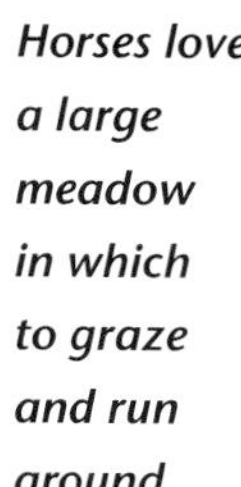
Horses love a large meadow in which to graze and run around

not happy living in its own dung. So for the sake of its welfare particular attention must be paid to cleanliness. Apart from the tried and tested method of mucking the stable out every day, which is expensive because of the huge amounts of bedding needed, it is possible simply to clear out the dirty corners frequently and regularly using a pitchfork or manure fork to remove the dung and wet straw several times a day. It may then be possible, depending of course on the condition of the stable, to change the bedding completely only once a week.

The best method of providing the horse with water is with an automatic drinker, which obviates the need to keep filling buckets up. Also useful is a feed container, which should be fitted in an accessible part of the stable so that it can be easily removed from outside either for replenishing or for cleaning. However this is not essential since hard feed is usually eaten so quickly that there is little risk of a bucket being knocked over. A hayrack is useful though. If there isn't one hay can be fed in a net hung at the correct height. Neither hayrack nor net should be higher than the horse's head otherwise there is the risk of wisps of hay and seeds falling into its eyes as it stretches its head up to feed. On the other hand the net should not be hung so low that the horse can catch its feet in it. Hay should never just be dumped on the floor, since no horse will eat anything that has come into contact with soiled bedding.

You will need a wheelbarrow for carrying soiled bedding away, a manure fork and a shovel for mucking out the loose-boxes and stalls. Obviously a yard broom is also needed for sweeping out dust and the remains of the straw. Another piece of useful equipment is a hosepipe for giving the stable a thorough clean. For moving straw and hay a pitchfork and a rake are also recommended. When cleaning the stable and looking after horses Wellington boots and strong working clothes (jeans and shirt) are recommended as protection against dirt and damp.

Horses like to see what is going on

What horse and rider need

Whether you are just starting to ride or even buying your own horse you must of course acquire a few more things that are essential not only for your own riding pleasure but, more importantly, for the horse's welfare.

Basic items of equipment for a horse that is to be kept in include a stable rug to protect it from the cold, a summer sheet to provide protection from insects, and a sweat rug. If the horse is to be transported its legs should be protected from injury by kneecaps and travelling boots and its tail by a tailguard. If it is to be outside in wet weather it will need a New Zealand rug even if it is not clipped. You will of course also need a head collar, a bridle with reins and a saddle with stirrups and stirrup-leathers.

The horses are wearing New Zealand rugs to protect them from the spring cold

The bridle was invented by the Celts around 2500 years ago. They used a curb bit in order to be able to restrain and lead their horses, hence the expression 'to curb someone', meaning to limit someone's freedom, to 'bridle'.

Nowadays both curb bits and snaffle bits are used. They are attached to the bridle and pass between the horse's teeth. The reins are attached to the bit. Riders or drivers of traps and carriages are said to have the horse 'on the bit'. Dropped nose bands are sometimes used with a snaffle for extra control without the need to use a harsher bit. On the other hand the simple head collar does not need a bit since it is used merely for leading the horse into and out of the stable or paddock.

There are many types of bit on the market. Depending on the nature and temperament of the horse the rider uses jointed or double-jointed bits or those with a small copper key at the joint that encourages the horse to chew. This constant chewing on the bit prevents the horse from biting on the bit and clamping it between its teeth or jaws, which would mean the bit would be useless. The horse should feel the pressure of the

Gaiters protect the horse's legs when jumping

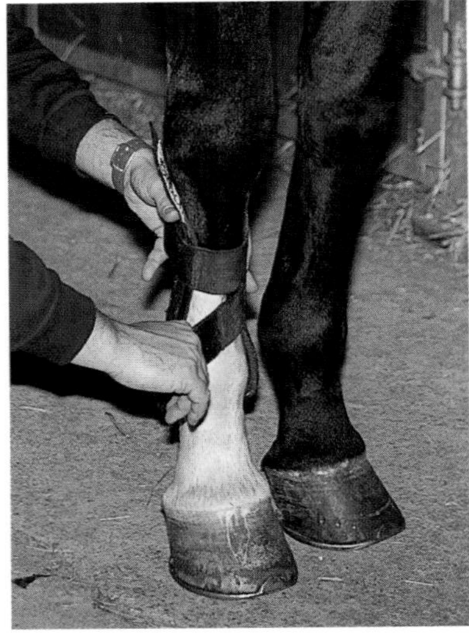

Opposite page: Naturally the horse is happiest without halter and saddle

These two draught horses are wearing very decorative harnesses

Bits and snaffles come in all kinds of shapes and designs, some of them very decorative

reins in its mouth, though as gently as possible. However if it manages to get the bit between its teeth it can resist the pressure of the reins and will ignore the rider's commands. For a sensitive and 'well-brought-up' horse a snaffle with a very soft bar made of rubber or vulcanite is used. However other horses, for instance young stallions with a lot of Thoroughbred in them, may be more difficult to control. It may be best to use a solid bit on them, for instance one made of titanium or stainless steel. Even this type of bit comes in various shapes for use with animals of different temperaments, e.g. with a pair of spoon-shaped plates in the middle to prevent the animal putting its tongue over the bit and thus evading the pressure of the reins. Some bits have cheekpieces that in addition to the pressure on the inside of the mouth also press against the lips from the outside. Even young and very fiery stallions cannot resist the pull of the reins when these are used. It may sound rather cruel to put a metal rod in a horse's mouth in order to make it obedient. However in order to ensure that the animal complies with the wishes of the rider and not vice versa it is essential for the horse to be properly tacked up. In addition, the horse's teeth are not damaged by metal bits if they are fitted properly, that is at the point where there is a gap in the teeth. The bit lies between the incisors - the front teeth which are visible from outside - and the molars at the back. In addition, a responsible rider will not force a harsh bit on an experienced and obedient horse, since a sensitive animal does not react to such treatment with enthusiasm and obedience. It would not have the effect of achieving a rapport between horse and rider - just the opposite.

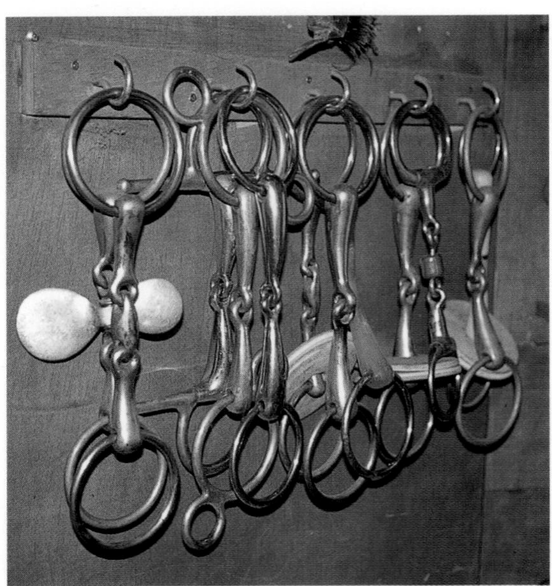

A smart outfit or jeans? The right clothes for riding

The basic clothing for any rider consists of comfortable stretch jodhpurs, riding boots and a well-fitting hard hat. A hard hat is not only an elegant accessory for the fashion-conscious rider, it is essential for safety. Whether riding hat, bowler hat, helmet or top-hat for dressage - none of them shatter and in the event of an accident absorb some of the shock if the rider's head hits the ground or the overhanging branch of a tree. A good riding hat is essential and can be bought for around £40. However you must ensure that it conforms to at least EN 1384, never be tempted to buy a second-hand hat, and if it does get a knock in an accident it must be replaced immediately even if no damage can be seen externally.

Specialist saddlers offer a multitude of jackets, pullovers and shirts for sale. You could fit yourself out completely at one of these establishments, but for hacking or lessons simple and comfortable items of clothing, most of which you will already have in your wardrobe are sufficient to start with provided they do not get in the way. It is best to wear several layers. First a T-shirt to soak up the sweat, then a pullover and over that a comfortable jacket. It is only in films that anyone rides bare-chested and wearing sandals and it is definitely not recommended. In addition, the advice sometimes given to beginners and those who ride only occasionally that jeans are suitable wear for riding is simply not true. Unless you want to end up with extremely sore legs you should, even if you ride on only the odd occasion, buy a pair of proper jodhpurs.

The hard hat protects the rider's head in a fall while the riding jacket will keep the rider warm

Leisurewear is fine when riding for pleasure but it is essential to wear a hard hat always

It is the inside of the rider's knee and thigh that takes the most punishment, so the protection provided by the reinforced sections of proper jodhpurs costing as little as £25 is essential.

Riding boots are also essential, trainers and Wellingtons being totally unsuitable on safety grounds. However there is no need to spend a fortnight's wages on leather boots. Long rubber boots, costing around £35, are just as good at protecting the legs and are much easier to clean. An alternative would be jodhpur boots, costing slightly less, which protect the feet and ankles but not the legs so are nowhere near as comfortable as full-length boots, though they are cooler in hot weather.

If you want to look like a cowboy you can wear jeans with chaps on top. Chaps are a type of leather cover which protects the rider's calves (mini-chaps) or reach right up to the thigh (long chaps). Long chaps cost from £30 upwards. Western-style boots look particularly good with these. Proper riding gloves are another essential item of clothing, not only as protection against the cold but also in order to have a good grip on the reins, especially in wet weather and to prevent blisters. They ensure that the horse is under proper control in all circumstances.

A horse should always be approached slowly and quietly

Horse etiquette – how to understand horses and handle them properly

Every rider should understand some of the horse's language in order to make friends with it but also for self-protection. For a horse in a bad mood can, contrary to the popular belief that horses are so good-natured that they are incapable of harming anyone, deliver a painful bite or kick. A kick from a fully-grown stallion or a powerful mare can cause serious injury or at least be so painful as to put you off riding for life. So here are a few hints on what your horse is trying to tell you. For instance care is needed if the horse pushes its lips out and tenses them, lays its ears back, raises its head and swishes its tail. That means 'I've had enough of you and am showing you how strong I am.' If this happens the rider must be patient. Talking quietly to the horse from a safe distance usually helps to calm it down. If this doesn't work, a sharp word may be needed to let the horse know which of you is the boss.

When you approach a horse it will first sniff you. But

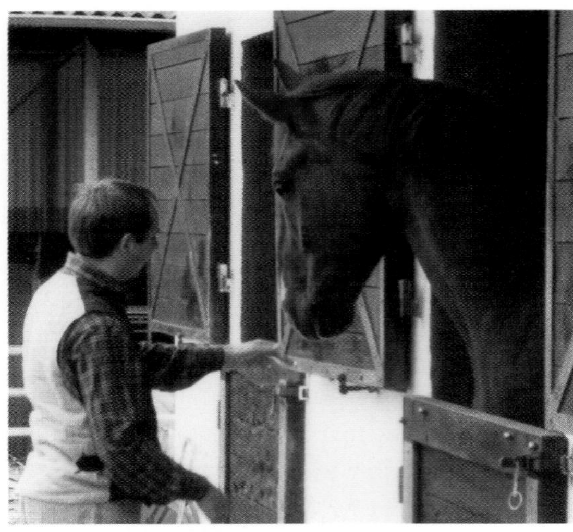

never extend the flat of the hand or you may lose your fingers

If as you continue to talk softly the ears prick up again, the expression in the eyes becomes gentler and the mouth relaxes, this means that everything is all right again as far as the horse is concerned. It has calmed down and is once more in a good mood. Now it is once again disposed to approach you in a manner that is both friendly and inquisitive.

If the horse's ears are only slightly turned round and if it is looking intently in one direction, this means it is feeling neither particularly aggressive towards you nor particularly interested in you. It has simply discovered something that has captured its attention and that it is now observing intently.

In this situation the animal is possibly not inclined to take any notice of the rider, but neither is it showing any feelings of aggression. It is therefore possible to try to approach it quietly.

If the horse lets its head and tail hang down, it may not be in a particularly good mood but neither is it cross with anyone; it is merely bored or having a rest. Horses often rest one of the hind legs at the same time. Do not ask to much of the horse at such times. This is not the time to surprise it, and if you disturb it it may kick you. So approach the animal slowly and do not just plonk the saddle down on its back!

Another thing horses do is known as Flehmen, where the animal lifts its top lip and raises its nose. This enables the horse to get a good smell of an interesting aroma. Stallions do this frequently if there is a mare on heat within smelling distance.

In order to becomes friends with a horse it is of course not sufficient merely to understand its language. It is also important to learn how to handle the animal. A horse is a very sensitive creature and sets great store by certain types of behaviour. First of all, it likes to get to know the rider before it lets you get on its back. You must build up a relationship with the animal so that it will obey your commands. Someone who is a total stranger to the horse cannot simply walk into the stable, saddle the horse and ride off on it. Good-natured as these huge creatures are, anyone wishing to approach them must first win their confidence. At some riding schools the horses meet total strangers every day and carry several dozen different riders around the school or around the lanes, so they do not particularly mind who climbs on their backs. They are interested only in the people who look after them. Really keen riders do not hold such animals in much esteem because of their character, ranging from stoical calm to

complete indifference. However a horse that has to spend the whole day plodding in circles for the entertainment of inexperienced occasional riders or children in the pets' corner of

Above: Yawning when tired. Below: A stallion sniffs the air

Horses spend most of the day in stables, which is why they enjoy ourdoor exercise so much

a zoo has no choice other than to show a lot of patience. Even if these horses do not fulfil the demands of experienced riders, the correct seat, the use of the stirrups and how to control a horse using the reins and other aids can be learned from them. However it is obvious that a pony that has spent its whole life going round in circles as if on a fairground roundabout should not be expected to gallop nor to jump properly. It is, though, possible to learn the basics on such animals.

If you want to learn to ride properly you should go to a good riding school and ensure that you are allocated a good horse. All schools have to be licensed by the Local Authority but this gives no indication of the standard of tuition. To be sure of that, you should choose one that is approved by the British Horse Society or the Association of British Riding Schools.

The first stage in getting to know a previously-unknown horse is to look after it. A horse soon looses its shyness towards someone who feeds and grooms it every day and begins to pay attention to him or her. So when beginning to learn to ride, ensure that you are also instructed in how to look after the horse. If, later one, you decide to buy one of your own and keep it at livery, do not leave the care and feeding of it completely to the staff. The rider who just looks in now and again always remains a stranger to the horse and never knows what reaction to expect. What is the horse supposed to make of someone who uses it only to go for the occasional short ride? It becomes more attached to the person who looks after it and feels disturbed by these occasional visits.

In a paddock or a large box with access to the outside it is rather harder to approach the horse than in a loose-box, where it is relatively stationary and has less freedom of movement. In any case you should always approach a horse slowly, from in front but at an angle, in which position it gets the best view of you. Once the horse has got to know you it will come up to you in order to greet you. If the horse is not interested in your arrival it will simply remain standing in the stable, possibly with its back turned to you. In this case you should speak to the animal in a quiet voice. If it does not immediately react to your voice, walk round the animal with even but determined

steps to its head. While doing this you should ensure that you remain out of reach of its hind legs, since it could kick out at any time.

This applies in particular in the case of horses that you do not yet know, for each horse has its own character and they all react differently from one another. In a loose-box it is easy for an animal that may weigh more than half a ton to use its powerful leg and neck muscles to push you into a corner. Some horses actually like doing this in order to show you who is the stronger.

Now you've got to the horse's head you're over the hardest part. Now you can greet it and let it sniff you. Speak softly to it and slowly put your hand out so that it can smell it and recognize you. Horses greet each other by putting their noses together. In this way they exchange smells and breath.

Now you and the horse are acquainted, and you can begin to put the head collar on.

As horses are herd animals and their behaviour is based strictly on their ranking within the herd, you should always act in a very determined manner when dealing with them. If you dither or hesitate the horse will soon begin to feel dominant. However it is the rider who should dominate the animal, and not the other way round. Otherwise the horse will be riding with you, and not you with the horse!

That is why it is often not as easy to deal with a high-ranking animal, for instance a strong stallion used to leading the herd, as with an animal lower down the ranking.

Always act in a decisive and determined manner, since only in this way will you gain your horse's respect.

If everything has gone well up to now, put the head collar on the horse. As with mounting and saddling up, this should be done from the near (left) side of the horse.

After putting the halter on attach the lead rope. When leading the horse always walk on the near side. A well-trained animal will walk along beside you neither more quickly nor more slowly than you. However if it doesn't, you should give a sharp tug on the rope. But if the horse refuses to move at all, it is no use pulling strongly on the rope. If you do the horse will only turn stubborn like a donkey and refuse to budge at all. It is important that you always place yourself beside the horse facing the way you wish to go and never in front of it.

It is best to get an experienced person or riding instructor to show you how to tie the horse up in the place you are going to groom it, whether outside or in the loose-box. The special safety knot required, also used by sailors and mountaineers, is quite complicated but can be undone later with a single pull.

Horses exchange their breath as a sign of greeting

Putting the saddle and bridle on

For the inexperienced rider putting the bit in the horse's mouth is not particularly easy. It must be in exactly the right position. In order to do this the rider should always stand close to the horse's head on the near side. First the reins should be placed over the horse's head and then the headpiece and the noseband slipped on, with the right hand passing under the horse's head and up to the fore-

In rodeo, the art is to remain on the horse without a saddle

head. At the same time the left hand reaches inside the horse's mouth and places the bit into the open mouth. Once the bit is in position the headpiece can be pulled over the horse's ears and the throat-lash and nose-band fastened. Now the bridle is on but of course in order to ride you will also need a saddle.

Riding without a saddle is suitable only for the very experienced or those who want to get back to nature, since riding bareback or with only a blanket there is nothing to grip onto and it can be very uncomfortable. Certain very specialized types of riding require special saddles. There are many different models made of leather or synthetic materials. The four most important types of saddle are the general-purpose saddle, the dressage saddle, the jumping saddle and the Western saddle. The main difference is the shape.

When a saddle is made the soft but tough material, that is the leather or the synthetic material, is fitted over a saddle-tree. This is made of synthetic material, layers of wood glued together and leather, to make a firm seat for the rider. A saddle-cloth made of sheepskin or some soft artificial fibre must be placed under the saddle to protect the horse's skin from saddle sores. To prevent it slipping sideways the saddle is fastened round the horse's belly with a girth. It is important that the girth should not rub nor pinch either, so it is made of soft leather, cotton or nylon and may be padded at the points where the horse's forelegs require freedom of movement, that is between the belly, thigh and elbow.

The correct way to saddle a horse is first to talk to it in a reassuring way. One again you should stand on the near side and place the saddle-cloth then the saddle carefully on the horse's back. Then the saddle must be positioned in such a way that it sits evenly on the

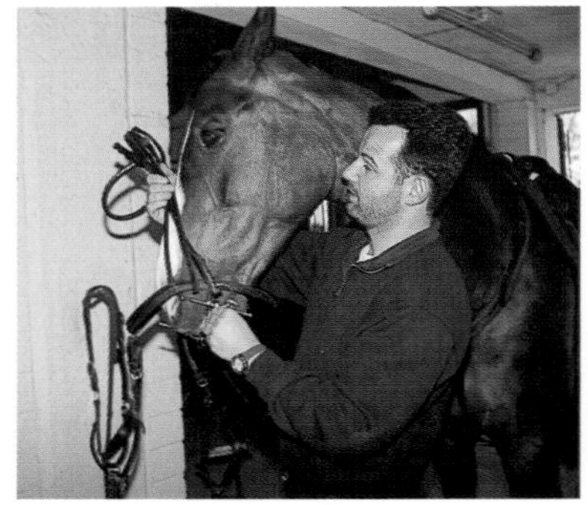

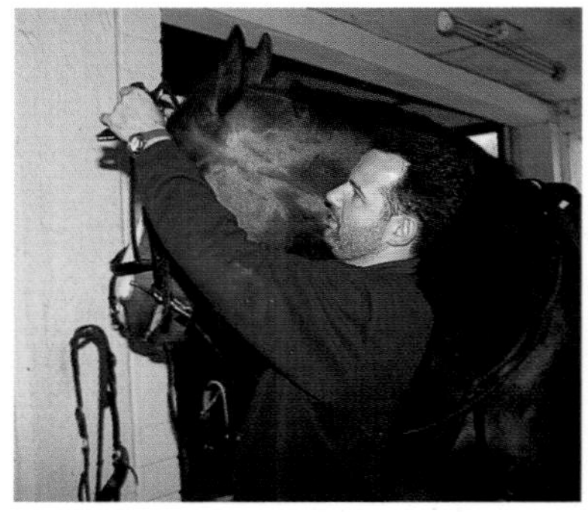

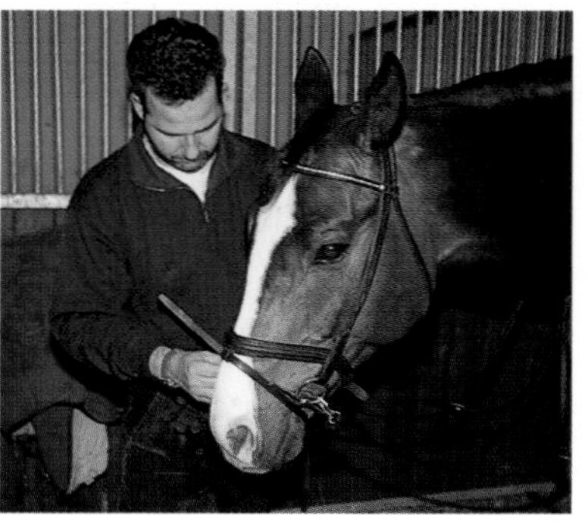

Putting on the bridle on the horse

ribs and on the shoulder-blades. Neither the saddle-cloth nor the saddle should press on any part of the horse's spine. Once they are in the correct position, the saddle can be held in place by the girth, which ensures that it does not rub. As soon as the rider has mounted the girth should be tightened. It may even need checking during the ride, since the movement of horse and rider can make the saddle slip forward and therefore the girth become loose. The girth should be carefully tightened, but it should still be possible to insert a flat hand between it and the horse's belly.

However before mounting the rider should ensure that the stirrup-leathers are properly attached to the saddle (with the safety bars left open) and are at least approximately the right length, although it is a simple matter to adjust them while mounted, and it is easier to mount if they are too long than if they are too short. Stirrups not only give the rider the necessary support for the feet, but they are also useful in helping to guide the horse. Safety stirrups were developed several years ago to avoid, as far as is possible, serious accidents. These do not surround the foot completely, but have a gap on the outside closed with a thick, strong rubber band. In the event of a fall the rider does not remain hanging from the stirrup, which in the most serious cases could mean being dragged several hundred yards by a panic-stricken animal. As is the case with modern ski bindings, if the rider falls the rubber fastening comes undone because of the pressure and the foot is immediately free.

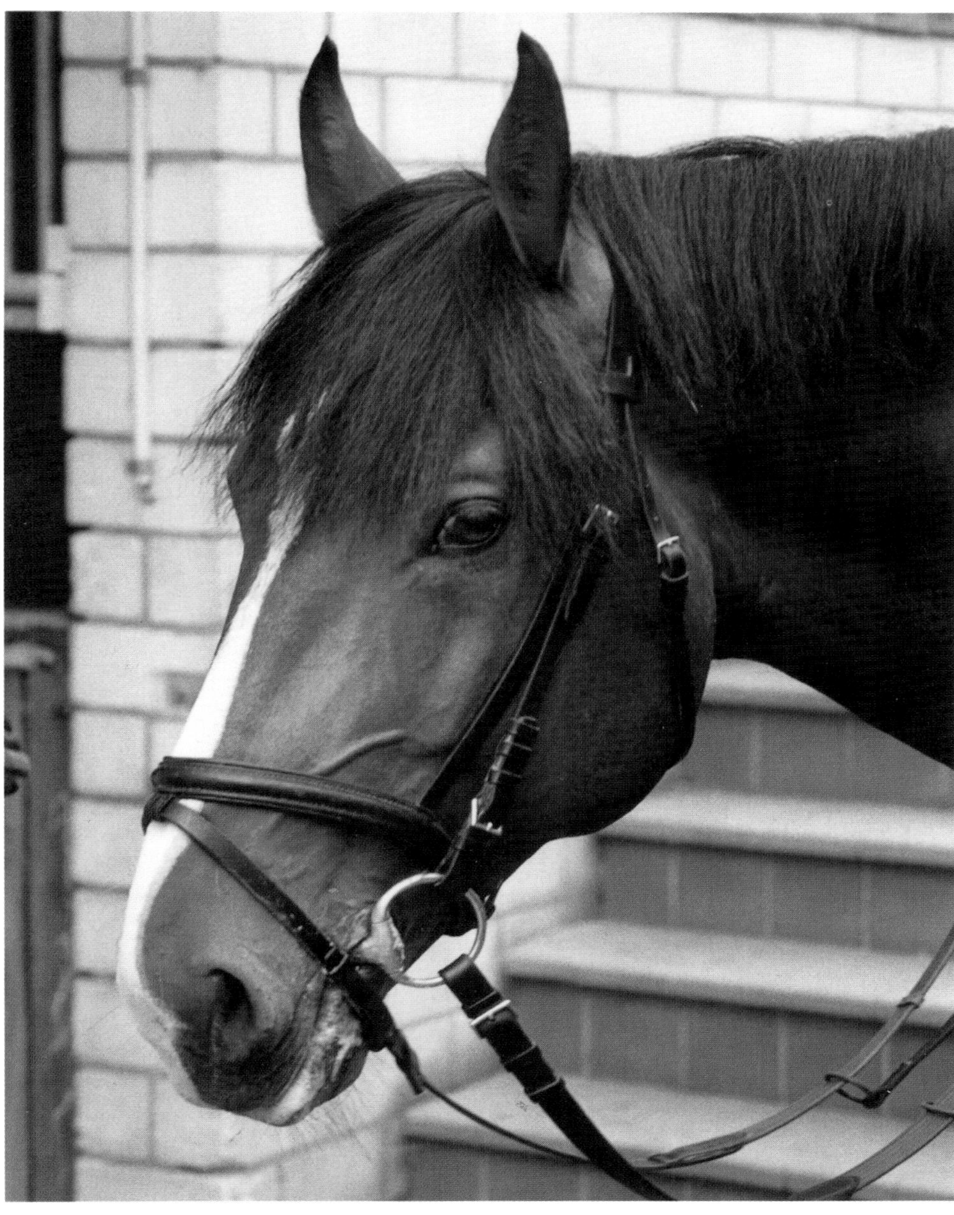

Correctly harnessed with a combined English halter

The saddle and bridle should be cleaned using lukewarm water and a sponge. The bridle should first be taken to pieces and the stirrup leathers removed from the saddle. If saddle and bridle are made of leather they should then be treated with saddle-soap, applied using clean lukewarm water and a clean sponge. Every now and again the leather should be treated with oil to prolong its life, keep it supple and prevent it from cracking. The easiest way of applying it is with a small paintbrush kept for the purpose. Nobody wants to sit on a hard saddle with cracks in the leather! However apply only a small amount and leave plenty of time between applying the oil and next using the saddle to avoid getting it on your clothes.

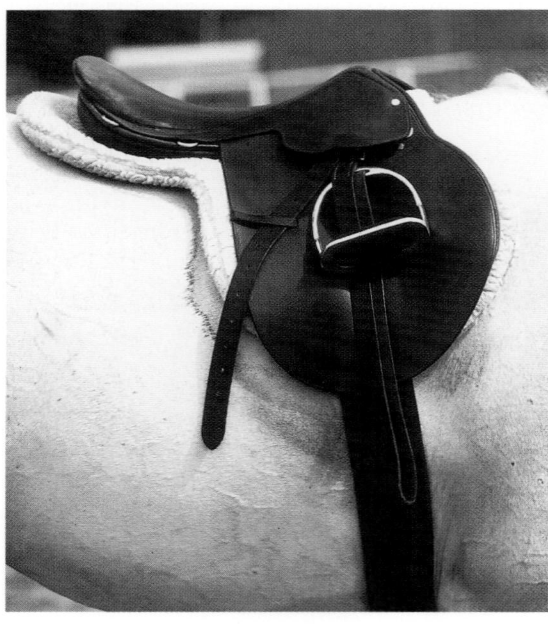

The saddle must fit properly and be in the right place on the horse's back

Even if you have no wish to buy your own horse you must, as a rider, know something about tack. For normal use a simple general-purpose saddle is recommended, and this will also be quite adequate both for cross-country riding and for simple dressage and jumping. It is essential that the saddle be the right size and fit for the horse.

The saddle is fitted from the left side of the horse

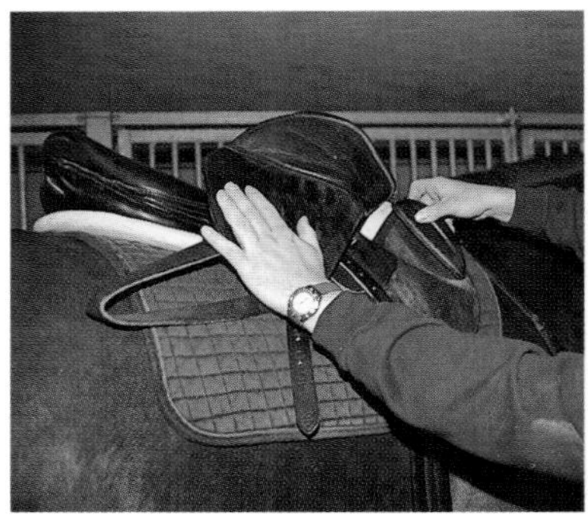

You need to know the names of the most important parts of the saddle, since you will have to know what to do when the riding instructor tells you to grip the knee-rolls and so on. The top of the saddle, the part on which the rider sits, is called the seat. Below it is the skirt, and under the skirt are the stirrup bars on which the stirrup leathers hang. The main parts of the saddle are the flaps on top and the panels underneath, and the knee rolls are the front edges against which the knees rest. The rear of the saddle is known as the cantle and the front is the pommel.. The stirrups, in which the riders feet rest, hang on the stirrup leathers, which must be adjusted to suit the length of the rider's legs. The girth with its buckles is passed under the horse's belly and fastened to the saddle by the girth straps in such as way that it neither rubs nor pinches.

The stirrup bars have a safety bar, which must be kept open so that in the event of a fall the stirrup-leathers come off with the force of the pull. This is a further safety precaution in addition to safety stirrups to prevent a rider that has fallen from being dragged.

There is a special type of saddle for showjumping. This offers the rider considerably more stability on the back of the horse than a general-purpose or dressage saddle. The jumping saddle has special rolls in front of and behind the rider's thigh, which give the rider's legs the required support in the saddle. When the horse takes off the rider remains seated and leans forwards. The higher cantle and the slight bulges behind the thigh prevent the rider from sliding backwards. When the horse lands on the far side of the jump, there is a risk of the rider sliding forwards over the horse's neck. The protruding knee rolls against which the inner thighs rest help the rider to counteract this force and to maintain balance. They are also helpful if the horse suddenly stops before the jump, though they cannot always prevent the rider from sliding forwards out of the saddle, over the horse's neck and to the ground, though a soft landing is always desirable. This sort of fall is commonest during cross-country riding, since horses sometimes refuse before the water or very difficult jumps and stop so suddenly that the rider is catapulted forwards.

Grooming your horse

Not all horses have horseshoes

Among the daily duties of anyone looking after a horse are brushing its coat and cleaning its hooves out. For this you will need the proper tools. To clean the coat you need a dandy brush and a body brush, a curry-comb to remove the hair from the brushes, a mane and tail comb and various sponges. If the animal is actually washed the water is removed from the coat with a sickle-shaped sweat-scraper. A hoof-pick is used to remove hard earth from the hooves, and afterwards hoof-oil or grease should be applied to the hooves with a brush kept for the purpose.

The first stage in grooming a horse thoroughly is relatively simple. Horses enjoy having their coat brushed, their head, back and legs wiped down and their mane and tail combed. However you must take care when picking the hooves out not to be kicked and land in the muck yourself. The secret is to stand very close to the horse so that it cannot use the power of its legs to kick out. Most horses will lift up their hooves when the leg is touched. Hold it up with one hand and with the other use the hoof-pick to removed hardened lumps of earth and stones, taking care not to damage the delicate frog (the triangular-shaped bit in the middle) After a ride they should be picked out again. If the horse is to be ridden in a sand or sawdust school, the hooves should be oiled or greased after the ride and not before, to prevent the sand or sawdust sticking to them.

Once the hooves have been cleaned out the horse should be brushed with the dandy brush, starting at the front and working backwards. Vigorous brushing with this will remove lumps of dried- and hardened-on dirt. The body brush can then be used, always in the direction the coat grows and with small hand-movements. If brushing the horse doesn't make you warm then you're not doing it properly! The main use of the curry-comb is to remove hair from the brushes. Rubber or plastic curry-combs may be used on the horse, but this must be carried out very gently, and only in the event of stubborn caked-on mud. Metal curry-combs must never be used on a horse.

The hooves must be scraped out after riding to remove any stones

The legs are treated in the same way, then the mane and tail are brushed with the dandy brush and the mane comb. Again, a rubber or plastic curry-comb may be used with care on the mane and tail.

Wipe the head over with a clean, damp sponge, not forgetting the eyes, mouth and nostrils, then dry it off with a cloth, known as a stable rubber.

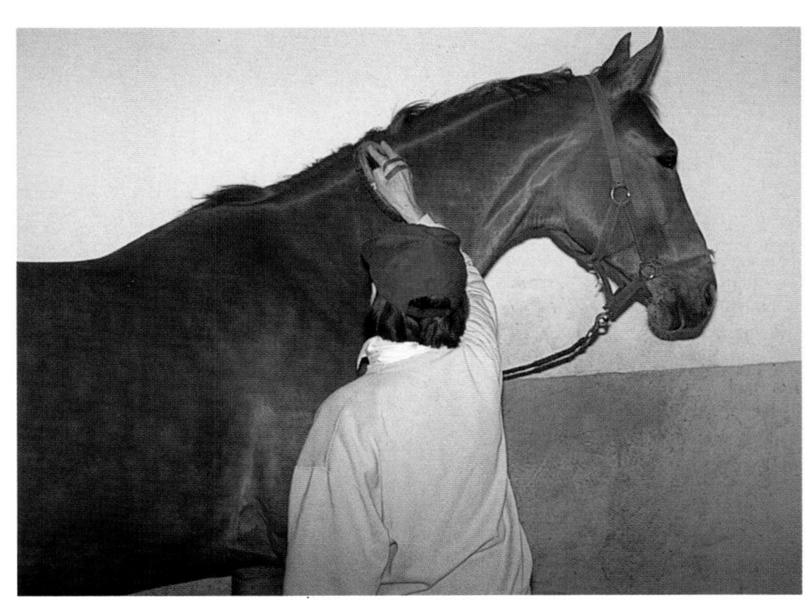

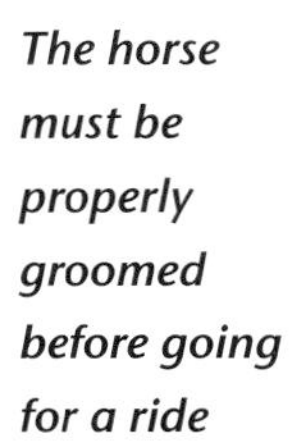

The horse must be properly groomed before going for a ride

The horse goes to the horse's pool for a little splash

Right: Horses gathering their fodder, hay

The dock area should be wiped with a separate sponge.

If the weather is dry and sunny the horse can be washed all over, with especial attention being paid to the parts where it sweats most, that is the neck, the saddle-patch and where the girth goes, in particular behind the elbows where dried-on sweat can cause serious girth-galls on a horse with sensitive skin. A sponge and a bucket or watering-can of clean water, preferably with the chill taken off, are all that is needed. A hose may be used on warm summer days to cool the legs and to remove dried-on dirt. Once the horse has become used to the hose it will enjoy a refreshing shower. Some establishments have a horse-wash into which the horses can be led.

Competition horses are treated differently. Trotters, who are drenched in sweat after a short training session and a couple of laps of the race-course, generally enjoy a full shower. Horses used for trotting racing are often not clipped so they are not as sensitive as animals that are. Moreover, competition horses sweat much more profusely than their cousins who live quieter lives and 'merely' go round a field a couple of times for schooling or are taken on a light hack.

Feeding your horse

There is no doubt that an animal that may weigh more than half a ton needs plenty of food. In the wild, horses have plenty of food available provided they can find enough grazing where they eat grass and other plants that grow wild. Horses that live in stables and are ridden, however, use up much more energy than their wild cousins who wander slowly from one grazing ground to

another in search of fodder. Working or riding horses spend much of their life at work, at sporting events or in paddocks where there may not be much grass. Therefore they need several meals a day. The daily requirements of an adult horse - up to eleven lb of hard feed and up to 10 kg (22 lb) of coarse fodder – should never be fed all in one go but in small meals of 2–2.5 kg (4 - 5 lb). Horses have very small stomachs and can digest only small amounts at a time.

Of course the composition of the feed is important, not only

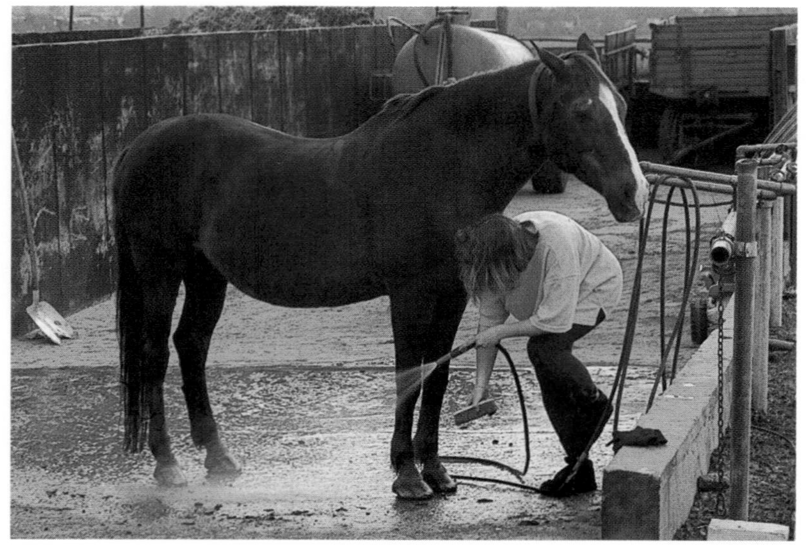

Gentle but thorough. This young rider is cleaning her horse after a ride, spraying it with water from a hose

the quantity. Coarse fodder, that is hay or a mixture of chopped straw and hay, contains a fair proportion of protein and a lot of minerals, which are essential for the horse's health and well-being. It supplies the bulk the horse needs, and should be provided throughout most of the year, since it is only in late spring and summer that grass is sufficiently nutritious even if there is enough of it. Because of the fats, proteins and carbohydrates they contain, oats are a rich source of energy. However many horses react to a good feed of oats by becoming boisterous and restless and trying to get rid of their excess energy by bucking and generally playing up. Linseed contains a lot of protein (25%) but must never be fed raw, only boiled. Barley is also boiled before feeding, and sliced sugar-beet must be soaked so that pieces that have dried out do not swell up in the horse's stomach. Wheat bran may be mixed with hard feed. Too much bran, fed dry, may cause the horse to become constipated, and fed soaked it may have the opposite effect. As in humans, bran can inhibit the absorption of nutrients from other feed. For both these reasons it should be used with caution. By far the easiest, but not the cheapest, way to give hard feed is to buy proprietary horse nuts, which come in different varieties having varying amounts of protein, fats, oils, carbohydrates, vitamins and minerals for the varying needs of individual horses. Horses also enjoy fruit and root vegetables, which also contain vitamins. Salt licks are popular but may mean that the horse takes in too much salt, so it is better to mix a small amount of granular salt into each bucket feed. Clean drinking water must be available at all times. This is especially important when hay is fed, since otherwise it cannot be properly digested. A horse needs 30 to 50 litres (7 to 11 gallons) of water per day. The cir-

What the horse loves best is eating fresh grass in a meadow

Hay is stored to provide the horses with food during the winter

cumstances under which the horse is fed are also important. Do not feed too much at once, and do it in a calm and unhurried manner. And ensure the horse is allowed at least an hour to digest before being asked to do any work at all.

Health and diseases

To ensure your horse stays healthy it is not enough merely to give it sufficient quantities of the right sort of food divided into appropriately-sized meals. Whether stallions, mares or geldings, they must be properly housed and looked after.

The cold bothers horses less than it does people. But a draughty stable is a real health hazard for them

Most horses, left unclipped, can stand any amount of cold. However what they cannot stand is damp, so if they are turned out in wet weather they should either wear a New Zealand rug or be provided with a field shelter, or both. For horses kept in, stables should be dry and free of cold draughts. Horses can catch nasty colds!

Regular checks by the vet are also essential if you want to ensure that your horse stays healthy. Colds are not the only illnesses that horses may go down with. There are several others that you should recognize and know how to deal with. The main thing is that if you suspect that your horse is ill or if it is not its usual self, you should always ask the vet's advice. Grooms, trainers and riders can usually judge the general state of health of an animal. There are some obvious signs of illness that should give rise to immediate concern. A healthy horse looks strong and muscular, whereas a sick horse, unless it is inclined to be overweight, often looks distinctly weak. It gives the impression of being slightly undernourished, its back often looks hollow, and its bones are clearly visible. The flanks also look hollow and the animal lacks muscle tone. This lack of strength is especially noticeable between the hind legs and on the neck. The spine of a sick horse soon becomes prominent and clearly visible under the skin whereas the spine of a healthy horse is surrounded by strong muscles and is hardly visible. A horse's body temperature should be between 99o F and 101o F (37.8 and 38.5o C) but there may be variations of up to 2o depending on time of day, stage of digestion of a meal, the age of the horse and the sex of the horse. Thoroughbreds have a higher temperature than other horses. Temperature is measured by inserting a thermometer into the rectum for about three minutes. A horse at rest breathes only eight to sixteen times per minute, and a normal pulse beats 35-40 times per minute, though the rate for stallions is 28 to 36 per minute and for young horses up to the age of three it is much higher. Excited and sick animals have a faster pulse and a higher rate of respiration, which can clearly be seen from the rising and

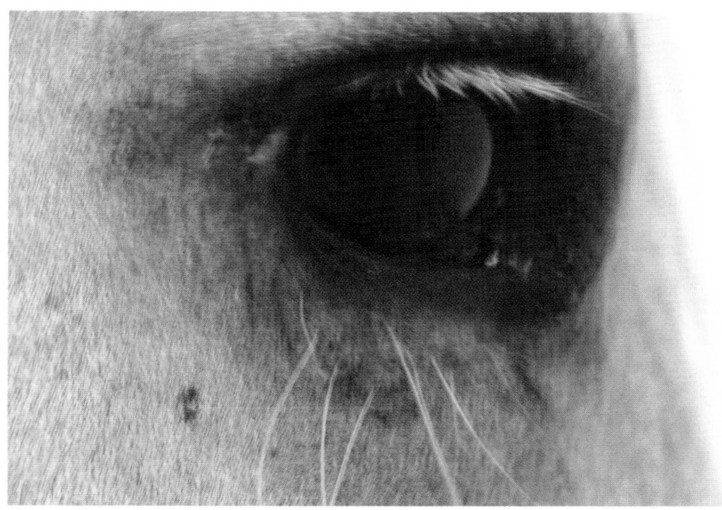

You can tell the state of health of a horse from looking at his eyes

falling of the flanks. Red or pale eyes may indicate inflammation of the mucous membrane or a weak animal. Yellowish eyes point to liver problems. A horse's eyes should therefore always be wide open, bright and slightly pink. If an inflammation of the mucous membrane or a diseased liver is suspected the vet should of course be called immediately since either of these problems will seriously affect the health and well-being of your horse.

The coat of a healthy animal looks shiny and smooth and lies flat against the body. In addition the mane hair of a healthy horse cannot be easily pulled out but remains firmly anchored at the roots. On the other hand if your horse's coat looks dry, bristly and unkempt this is usually a clear indication of incorrect feeding, infestation with worms or even a much more serious illness.

If the horse's general condition is not very good, it may be that it has lice. The animal may constantly scratch itself and the skin may become puffy. However lice may be present even if the horse shows no sign of irritation. They are usually found at the withers, along the base of the mane and at the root of the tail and are easy to treat with louse powder.

The droppings of a healthy horse have not got a strong smell and are only slightly soft but not slimy. A slight touch of diarrhoea is no cause for concern since a change in feed or a move to fresh grazing can often lead to slight alterations in the digestion. However if the faeces smell particularly unpleasant and have a yellowish tinge this may indicate a liver problem or infestation with worms, in which case the vet must be called. Similarly the urine should be almost colourless and should not smell too strong. Blood in the urine may be a sign of kidney disease or diabetes. Horses can also suffer from bladder infections, which manifest themselves by the continuous dripping of urine.

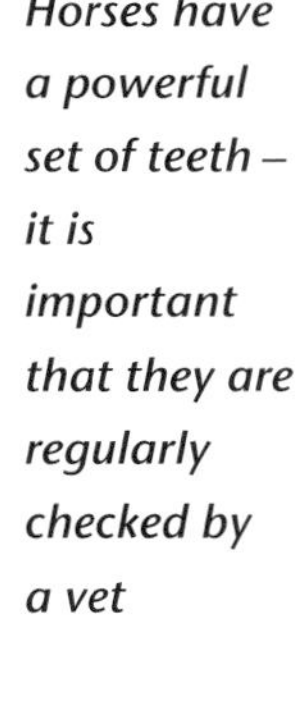

Horses have a powerful set of teeth – it is important that they are regularly checked by a vet

The horse's teeth should also be examined regularly, though obviously only by an expert. The teeth are constantly changing and sharp edges form which may injure the tongue and gums. The vet may need to file the teeth. All horses need to be vaccinated against tetanus, and vaccination against influenza may also be desirable. However the most essential treatment for horses is regular worming, which should be done at least every three months but not necessarily by a vet. Internal parasites soon lead to the horse losing condition and severe infestation can be fatal. If colic is suspected the vet must be called immediately, since this can also be fatal and is very painful for the horse.

Left: A healthy horse has a glossy coat, a handsome pair of ears and clear eyes. It is alert and looks happy, like this Latvian cross-breed mare

Horses do not have to be ill for a vet to be consulted. Their assistance is often requested when valuable competition horses are to be mated. Owners of showjumpers and dressage horses like to have their mares covered by stallions that have already sired good foals. However it is not always possible to drive the mare miles to the chosen stallion, or the act of fertilization may not be successfully completed on the agreed day. Moreover many owners of stallions fear that their horse may be injured in an encounter with a temperamental mare. A mare that is not particularly ready for mating will often kick out with her hind legs and injure the stallion.

Many mares have never seen the face of their foal's father

This is why artificial insemination has now become the norm for valuable competition horses. In this way semen can be sent to the mare safely, and distance is no object. A stallion that has become valuable by competing successfully can thus sire numerous foals throughout the country without ever meeting the mothers of his children.

Training the

horse and the rider

Pony-riding at the fair has nothing to do with real horse-riding

The art of mounting the horse

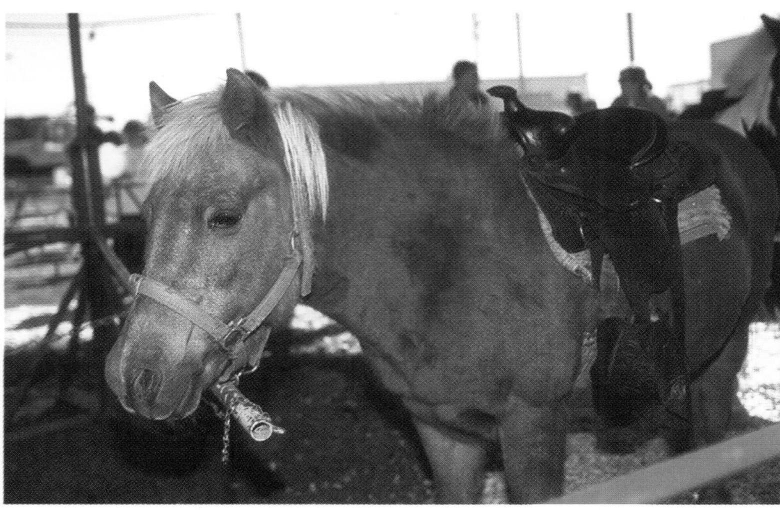

The first task is to learn to mount the horse correctly. correctly. The second stage in learning riding skills is mastering the simple walk, then you can spend time learning how to canter. The canter is easier for the untrained rider than the more complex trot. Trotting requires smooth, experienced movements in order to avoid falling off, since our four-legged friend does sway considerably.

Adjusting the length of the stirrup leathers

However, let us devote ourselves to the first stage of your riding lesson! Before mounting the horse you must check that the saddle and bridle are properly fitted and tightened. Then it is important to adjust the length of your stirrups correctly to the length of your legs. Once you are on the horse it is extremely difficult to adjust the stirrup straps. It is best to have a second experienced person present who will help out, if necessary. To avoid too much adjustment of the stirrups when mounted, it is best to adjust them before mounting. Roughly the correct length is achieved by touching the stirrup bar on the saddle with one hand and adjusting the stirrup leathers so that the stirrup iron touches your armpit. It is necessary to check the saddle girth for tightness once you are in the saddle as they can become loose due to the movement of horse and rider.

Once saddle, bridle and stirrups are adjusted correctly and tightened you can start to mount. If your horse is resteles and will not stand still during your attempts to get into the saddle it you mayleave the saddle faster than getting into it in the first place. A second person should therefore hold on to the reins so that the horse cannot run off once it has recognised you as an inexperienced rider.

Approach the horse from the left as it is used to this. Take the reins into your left hand and feel the pressure of

the horse. The contact to the horse via the reins should already be established before getting into the saddle, as the horse will stand quieter, unless the riding instructor holds on to the reins. Standing sideways and facing the rear of the horse, hold the front of the saddle with the left hand while still holding the reins in the same hand. You are holding on to the saddle and not to the reins! Then twist the stirrup slightly clockwise with your right hand and put your left foot into the stirrup.

You are now holding on tightly to the mane and the reins with your left hand and your left foot is in the stirrup. In order to mount the saddle you need a good swing with a lot of momentum. Grasp the back of the saddle with the right hand and the press the knee of the left leg against the saddle. Then pull yourself up, lightly supporting yourself with your hand and swing your right leg over the horse. At the same time the upper body should be slightly bent forward as this increases the momentum. Make sure that your right leg swings over the saddle and does not kick the horse in the flank – if this happens it means you do not have enough momentum. Such a kick makes the animal nervous and it might understand it as a signal to trot off which would have serious consequences for you since you already have one foot in the stirrup. Too much momentum in your right leg can also could be a disadvantage: in this case you may 'fly' too far and could land on the ground on the other side of the horse, a misadventure

Take the reins in your left hand, turn the stirrup and put your left feet in it, grasp the saddle and swing lightly into the saddle. Then – off you go!

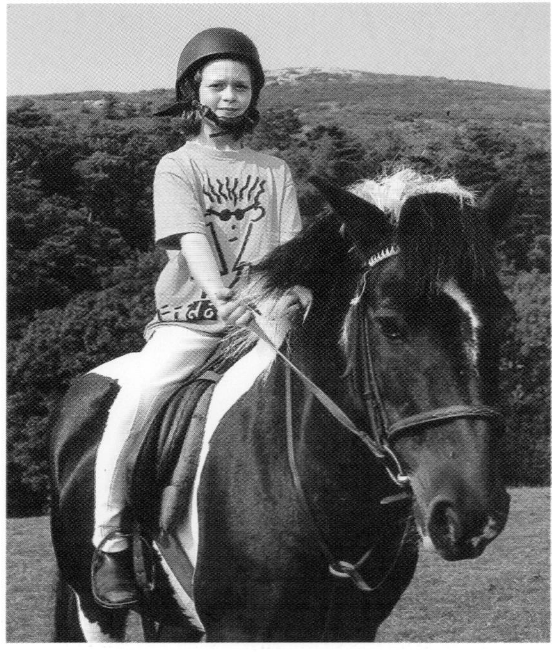

You must start young to be a champion

often seen in slapstick comedies. This is neither good for the back of the horse nor for your posterior! Getting into the saddle correctly must therefore be carried out smoothly with just the right amount of.

The correct posture is pleasanter for the rider and also for the horse

How to ride well: the correct seat

Now that you are on the back of the horse, you must find the correct sitting position. A good seat will hold you and at the same time you must be comfortable. Avoid holding onto the mane, the reins or the saddle too tightly and too tensely, or pushing your feet into the stirrups too hard or pressing your legs too firmly against the flanks of the horse. You might think these actions would give you a tighter hold this way, but this is not the case. Rather, you would soon have had enough of horse-riding after only a few minutes because of the aching muscles and bones such effort will cause. Do the following: sit down relaxed and hold the reins lightly in your left hand whilst maintaining contact with the mouth of the horse. The contact means pulling them slightly so that the horse can feel a very gentle pressure through the bit. Then, when you are sitting straight in the saddle, your right foot will search for and slide into the right stirrup. Now both feet should safely be in the stirrups. It is important to put the ball of your foot into the stirrup and not just your toes as this gives you enough hold so you will not constantly be losing it . Also, you will not achieve a secure seat on the moving horse if your legs are not in the correct position. A rider supports himself mainly with the legs by stretching them downwards as long as possible and by pressing the legs slightly against the flank of the horse. Even the lower leg of the rider does not 'sway in the wind'; they also have slight contact with the horse's body. The slight pressing together of the lower legs and the contact between the knees, flank and the saddle guarantees a relaxed and secure seat. Whether the reins are held with one or both hands depends on which type of riding you prefer or what exercise you are performing. In the 'European' paces – the walk, the trot and the canter – the reins are held in both hands. This makes the 'control' of the horse is

easier and more precise but also simpler.

In contrast, when riding Western style only one hand holds the reins, since the horse is held much more relaxed than with the English horse-riding style. In the Western style the reins are controlled by slightly moving the 'controlling hand'. The rider is much less responsible for the movement of the horse. He lets it go where it wants to without exerting too much pressure or influence.

Holding the reins properly and lightly

Back to the English riding style. You should have a firm but relaxed grip on the reins, otherwise you will not be able to perform the steps and movements that characterise a good rider. This means holding the reins loosely in both hands but always in contact with the horse's mouth. The animal does not like to be pulled at the mouth but be guided sensitively. The arms of the rider are slightly bent and, using the reins, exert slight pressure against the horse's mouth. The head of the animal should be slightly vertical from to the pressure of the reins. Contrary to the Western style rider, the sports and competition rider always uses the contact to keep the horse slightly tensed by using his hands. If the animal has had 'enough' – meaning that the reins are held too tightly it will let you know soon enough. It will then be restless and shake its head. However, if you hold the reins too loosely you will not receive good marks for posture and the horse does what it wants. If the reins are held correctly the front legs of the horse are aligned next to each other (closed) and the head is slightly bowed down (almost vertical). The reins do not droop (frowned upon as 'driving reins') but are relatively tight.

Holding the reins properly and steadily requires a lot of practice and concentration

The reins are not held in the fist. They are taken up between the fourth finger and the small finger and loop out again over the index finger. Thumb and small finger are free and are the 'brakes' if the reins threaten to slip out of the hand. Both arms are

Bareback riding is also possible

The equipment needed for lunging: a lunging rein, a long switch – and a patient horse

bent so that the hands are level with the base of the neck of the horse. This guarantees the highest possible freedom for movement of the rein hand. You are in a position to pull up the reins, control and let them go without too much effort.

If you now know how to mount the horse, how to sit correctly and how to hold the reins as well as gripping the hore firmly with your legs and feet, you are ready to make the first steps.

When lunging you can concentrate on yourself

On the lunging rein: Individual teaching for the beginner

Riding on the lunging rein is a highly intensive form of practical individual instruction and the most successful method of learning how to ride. It is especially recommended to the ambitious beginners who later want to master the art of 'classical' horse riding. With this basic knowledge you could become a show jumper or master of dressage.

Riding on the lunging rein means that rhe riding instructor leads your horse on a lunging rein about 5 m (16 ft) long. The horse proceeds in a circle inside a riding school or outdoors. This method of teaching beginners is so effective because you have continuous contact with the riding instructor who can explain the correct grips, point out your posture and correct your movements. Also, you will feel much more secure on the lunging rein. The horse cannot 'run off' with you and take steps that you are not ready for.

Riding on the lunging rein takes place in a riding school, especially when the weather is bad. The only disadvantage that the beginner should be aware of is that this will generate more costs. It is not only the riding instructor who has to be paid. Most riding schools charge a fee for using the hall on top of the normal costs for stabling and feeding the horses.

Going out in a group, you must already have some riding experience

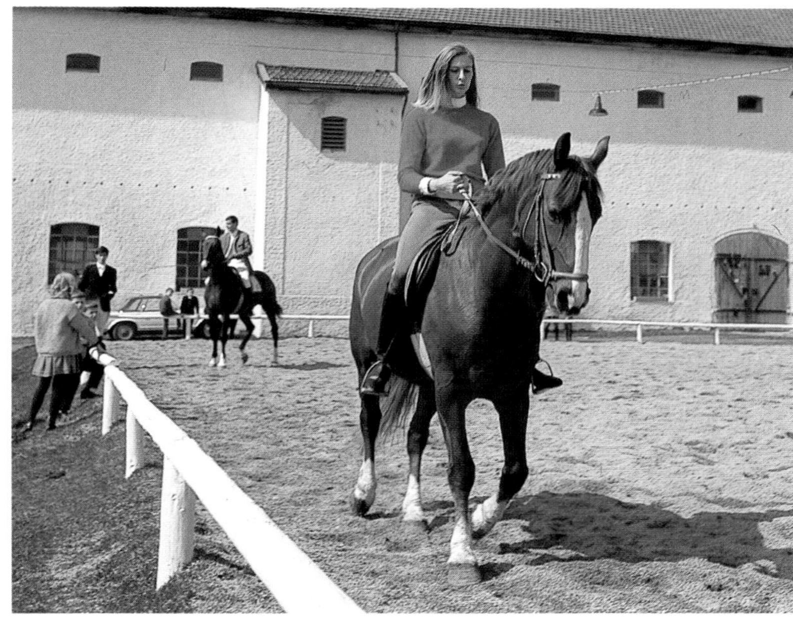

Learning in a group

If your purse does not stretch to taking lessons on the lunging rein there is the possibility of learning how to ride in a unit. Here you ride in a group. At the front is an experienced rider or the riding instructor and the other horses and their riders trot in a single line behind the 'leader'. This means that the riders at the 'back' can also reach their destination without having to be able to control their horse perfectly. Here you can also trust your instructor completely as he has all the horses under control. No individual animal will break away from the group and run off with its rider. The best advantage of riding in a group is that you can concentrate on your own behaviour and not have to cope with possible 'quirks' of your horse. In time you will realise that this large four-legged creature can be 'dominated', that it soon does not just follow the orders of your instructor but also increasingly yours.

But the most important thing when learning the art of horse riding is not to spoil the fun for beginners. Individual riding lessons on the lunging rein are sometimes too exhausting for a beginner. Within a group, however, an eager pupil sometimes feels that progress is not quick enough. The decision of which type of instruction to choose lies with the individual. Perhaps you will choose a combination of both, sometimes riding in a group and sometimes on the lunging rein. This is a good way to learn quickly while still having a lot of fun.

Slow but elegant: The walk

Concentration is very important

The easiest pace for the rider is the walk. The beginner does not need to be afraid of falling off the horse or of failing to keep up with the rhythm of the horse. In this pace the horse walks very slowly and in a sequence of steps where at least two legs are always touching the ground at the same time that does not create any swinging movements. This step sequence is a four-beat gait and is relatively easy to understand. All four legs march forward in the same rhythm: Rear left, then front right, then rear right and then front left: the four hoof steps sound evenly.

A horse at the walk should be brisk, not 'dragging its feet'

This horse takes very long strides

The correct step sequence is the criteria for the even foot sequence in the four-beat gait). With the so-called medium walk the hind legs move forward past the front legs, the extended walk the horse moves somewhat stronger and faster and the collected walk which is taught to more advanced riders in dressage the rear hooves must touch down after the imprints of the front hooves. These three gaits (tempi) – collected, medium, extended – not only describe the speed with which the animal moves forward but also determines the stride of the animal: the faster it walks the larger is, of course, the stride.

The foot sequence of the horse when walking is not only the normal working walk of a calmly walking horsel it also looks extremely elegant when ridden well and dynamically. Of course, the rider has to do something towards it for the walk to be elegant. By slightly tensioning the lower legs with the rhythm of the foot sequence the horse is constantly driven forward. Otherwise it would just walk which is not very graceful. The rider has to slightly imitate the movements of the horse with his body. By straightening his back he supports the forward movement of the animal.

The walk is the most relaxed fun for the rider and is the first pace to be learned.

A harder exercise: The trot

Compared to the walk the trot is a quite complex exercise for rider and horse. Because if it has to go a little faster the horse often starts cantering which for many sports and riding disciplines is not desirable and leads to mistakes or, in the case of trotting races, disqualification. Trotting is not very popular with beginners because to start with it feels as wobbly as a broken chair. With every second step the rider is lifted out of the saddle. Contact between rider and horse is lost regularly for a brief moment and this feels like sitting in an ejector seat. If you are not experienced enough to catch the momentum of the horse by copying the movement smoothly the rhythm of the foot sequence is lost and you 'slam' back into the saddle every time. This is very uncomfortable and after a few minutes trotting the beginner will have aching bones. Trotting is extremely exhausting and demoralising if you have not mastered it.

The entire momentum of the trot is generated by the

A trotting horse on the race-track can reach incredible speeds

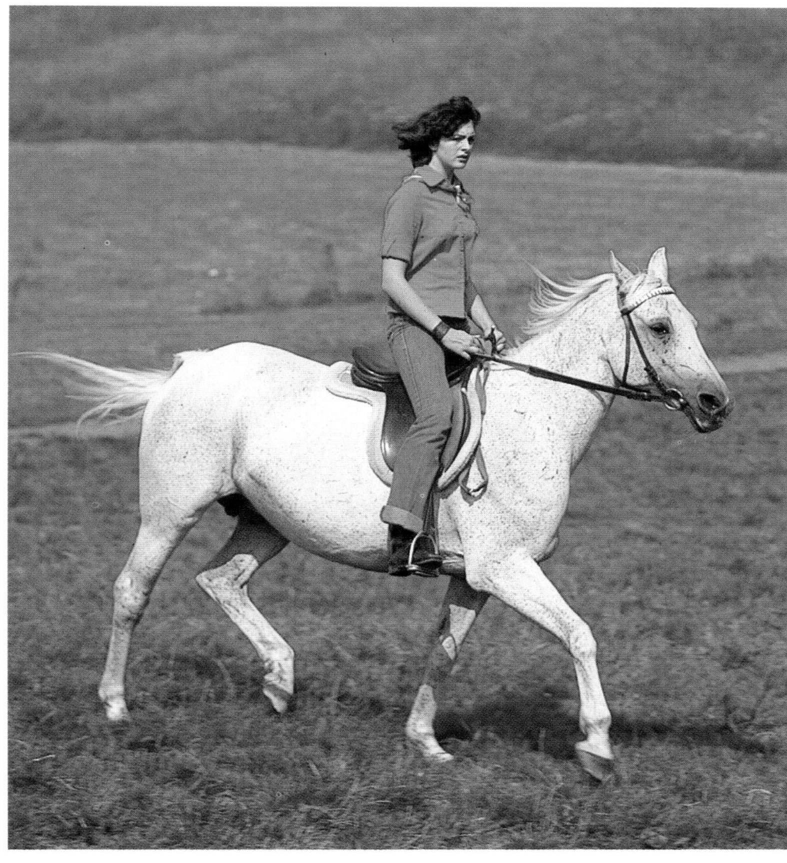

When you have become used to the rising trot it is time to get used to trotting in a sitting position. The simplest way of being able to 'sit' during trotting is to follow the movement of the horse. This could initially be a problem because you must recognise the rhythm of the movement of the horse first before you can start copying it. But learning to trot is not half as bad as the initial pains in your posterior may lead you to believe.

Trotting is really just sitting...

The momentum of the horse transfers itself automatically onto the hips of the rider when sitting whilst trotting. However, due to the diagonal foot sequence, the rider swings slightly to and fro and absorbs the actual up and down of the horse by lightly swaying his hips.

This does not mean, however, that you have learnt trotting. Now you have to get to know the four trotting paces.

Start the horse moving by driving strongly with your legs near the saddle girths (start). Then practise the working trot with slight up and down. With medium trot the horse has more freedom from the reins, it takes bigger strides and swings its head more. In collected trotting the horse moves evenly and calmly the head is just about vertical – that means slightly

foot sequence of the diagonal two-time beat. The horse rests on the left hind leg and the right front leg in order to 'jump over' to the opposite diagonal. When trotting you can hear two even hoof sounds. The horse 'jumps' from the legs front right and rear left onto the opposite legs: rear right and front left.

When the legs of the horse are put down diagonally at the same time, the entire momentum of this little leap transfers onto the rider. Now there is the question of how to get the horse to stick to this sequence. By holding the reins tight and by pressing with your legs you can give the command 'trot' from a standstill position or from walking. You have probably seen riders who lift themselves out of the saddle and stand up in the stirrups for a brief moment with every second step. This simplifies the trot and does not strain the back and posterior of the rider. This way of moving is called teh 'rising trot' because of its relative tranquillity. It is significantly slower than a full trot. The up and down of the rider, however, must not be exaggerated; it is only a soft rising out of the saddle. Standing up in the stirrups must also not be carried out with too much force, as you have to sit down in the saddle again with the next step. And this must be quick because even when performing the rising trot the foot sequence is not exactly slow.

This horse is showing off its high spirits

raised. The fourth speed of trotting is the extended trot: With this the hind legs make giant strides and the back of the horse swings strongly but evenly.

When riding dressage, changing from collected to extended trot will not make you win but the spectator is impressed by its elegance.

Horses at their fastest, in full gallop

The canter: A three-beat sequence

The canter is a fast, more 'natural' three-beat movement of the horse. As the horse jumps more than it walks when cantering it is also called the three-beat jump sequence. And as the foot sequence in cantering always starts with the 'outer hand' – outside is the foot that faces the outside even when on a circular riding ring – there is a difference between the right and the left hand canter. The horse can start cantering with either the right or left hind leg. Counting starts when the outer hind leg moves. When starting a right hand canter the foot sequence starts with the rear left then the legs jump simultaneously on rear right and front left (is also called inner diagonal) and finishes with the front right leg that in this case is called the leading leg. You can clearly hear three hoof sounds; the second is – because the diagonal leg pair 'hits the ground' –significantly louder than the other two. In this sense the legs of the horse carry out a counter-clockwise 'circle'. If you want to change directions the horse changes into left-hand canter for which the left front leg provides the momentum.

It is expected from a dressage rider that he can tell the horse to change canter. On command from the rider the animal jumps from right into left hand canter and vice versa. However, this is not only a required exercise in dressage. Changing hand when cantering is also necessary to avoid straining one side of the horse too much. The rider has to know which aids must be used, how to apply the reins and pressure with the legs in order to carry out the command.

For the beginner it will be easier to start cantering by letting the horse change into canter from trotting. Young horses which do not know the aids of the rider too well will also start cantering from

Even an indoor riding school is large enough to let off steam

trotting. By slackening the reins and slight bending forward of the body – push yourself more strongly onto the stirrups and bend the knees slightly – the rider tells the horse to change from a fast trot into a canter.

Well-trained horses accept the command to canter as follows. The rider straightens his back, takes the horse tighter between his legs and sits down in the saddle as necessary for cantering. When cantering the rider shifts his weight to the inside level with his hip and there is more weight on the inner stirrup than the outer one. Of course, the inner rein also pulls inwards and indicates the direction. After applying a half-halt using the right rein (more in the section 'Applying aids': half-halt and halt) it is time for the canter. The reins slacken and the inner leg drives harder against the side of the horse just behind the saddle girth than the outer leg which is positioned slightly further back. These aids must be repeated continuously during cantering so that the horse maintains a fluid cantering sequence. The rider sits loosely in the saddle (half-seat) and supports himself in the stirrups the same as when trotting.

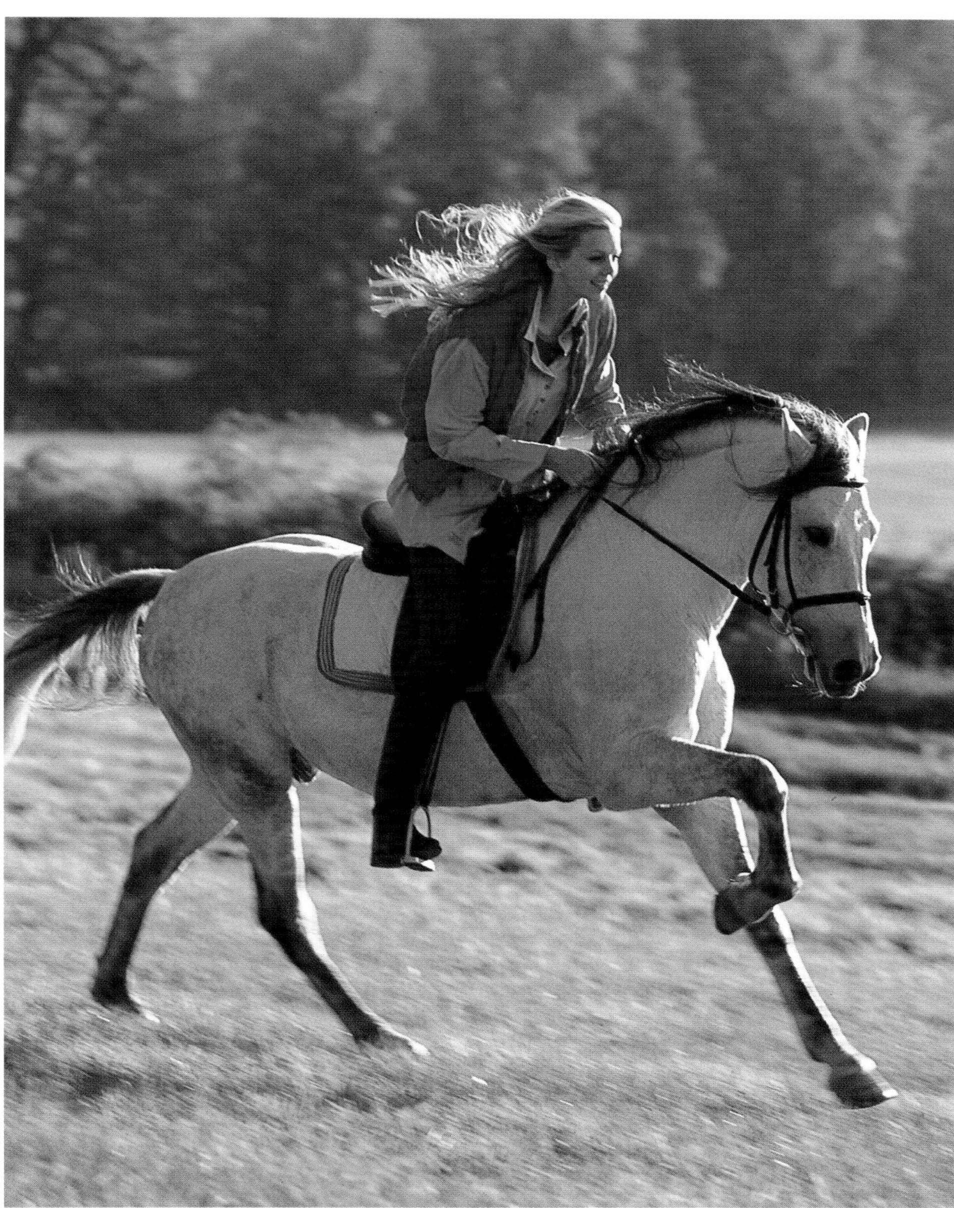

A lively canter in the country is always great fun

Of course, the correct aids, just like the clutch in a car, cannot be taught by theory alone. Here the phrase 'learning by doing' can also be applied. Trotting and cantering can only be learnt correctly during lessons. Even if you are the most talented rider in the world, in your first lesson you will never mount your horse, give it a little kick and canter elegantly into the sunset. Handling animals must be done patiently and with high concentration. Mastering the various paces and their tempi does not only depend on the horse alone. Even an experienced rider is not always able to give the aids to a horse

that has just been broken: it may not recognise whether the rider want to canter on the right or left hand. Even the horse needs time – possibly years – before it will understand the aids its rider is giving him. Only after a long period of training a horse will know what the rider wants when he straightens his back, shifts his hip, gives the aid with the legs and 'holds on' to the reins.

The change of leg in dressage is not for beginners

Changing the canter: A task for experts

The simple change of lead is from a standing position; the flying change of lead must be managed whilst cantering. When performing the single change the rider 'moves over', i.e. he gives the command for canter from the other side of his hip and his legs, there is more pressure on the inner side than the outer side. In order to master the flying change of lead you need a lot of riding experience. It is expected in the highest dressage classes. Here the horse has to shift the load from the right to the left hind leg without taking an intermediate step. The rider indicates the impending change to the horse by shifting his weight to the other side whilst in the flying phase between the jumps. The horse jumps from one diagonal pair onto the other in one stride. This is aesthetically a very demanding 'step' for the horse as it seems to perform a small 'leap'.

This horse is waiting to be given aids as it waits for the next lesson

Applying aids

The aids are used to communicate with the horse. You use them to let the horse know what you expect from it. There are various different aids including action of the seat and use of legs or of reins.

Actions of the seat are achieved by straightening your back and the possible shift of the weight via the posterior by slightly moving the position of your hip. This signals to the horse that now a different stride is required. Leg aids drive the horse forward but also to the side and action of the hands are the tightening, the loosening or the slackening of the reins and pushing the horse sideways. Only a combination of all three will give the desired effect. Thus the horse clearly understands what is expected from him.

Very well trained horses who also know their riders very well could react on just voice commands – one word of his rider and the horse will

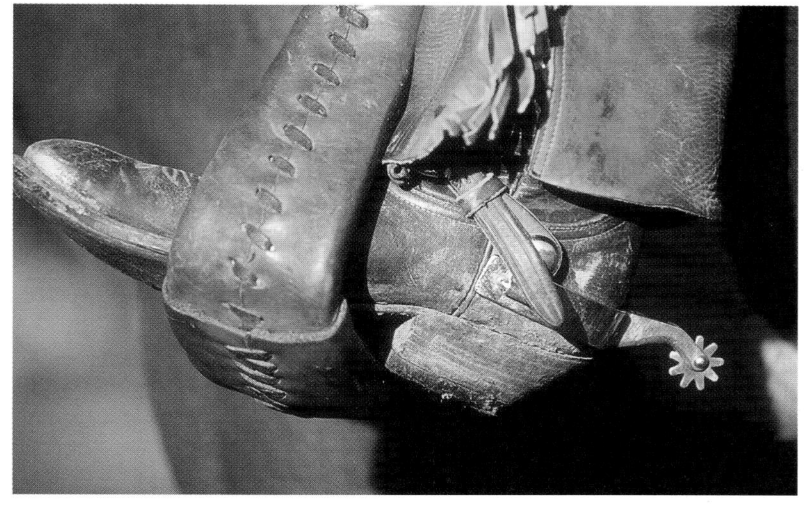

This type of spurs are only for cowboys. You could seriously injure a horse with them

sequence or pace. For the half-halt – executed with straightened back and driving legs – the reins are slackened and then retightened slightly. The horse recognises that a command is soon to be executed due to the straightened back and the simultaneous slight driving: a turn or a further aid for changing from walk to trot. The half-halt is also used to tell the horse to know whether to stop, canter or to jump.

Artificiial aids are the riding crop (whip) and the spurs. Riding crops are really only used in sports where high performance is required. Riding crops are no longer used in international dressage competitions. However, in training or show jumping these riding crops are a regular occurrence. Riders also use their riding crops in three-day events. The show jumping or event crops are not very stiff and have a flat, mostly brush-shaped 'swatter' which is the part making contact with the horse. They generate more noise than pain and do not hurt the horse. The dressage crop that is also used for the general training of the horse is also quite soft and very long so that the rider can use it with a flick of his wrist without having to take the hands off the reins.

Different spurs are used in the English types of riding. The rider straps them onto his boots in order to emphasise his leg aids. The small metal knobs at the heel of the boots that are used today do not cause pain or injury to the horse when used correctly. However, they are only recommended for use by experienced riders as the 'novice' can quickly but unintentionally cause bleeding injuries to his horse when using them.

Where is the brake? The half-halt and the halt

When using the halt the horse prepares itself for a new command from the rider. There are half-halts and halts. The half-halt is used to signal the horse to slow down or to change into a slower foot

The half-halt prepares the horse for a change of leg or a change of tempo, while the halt makes the horse stand still

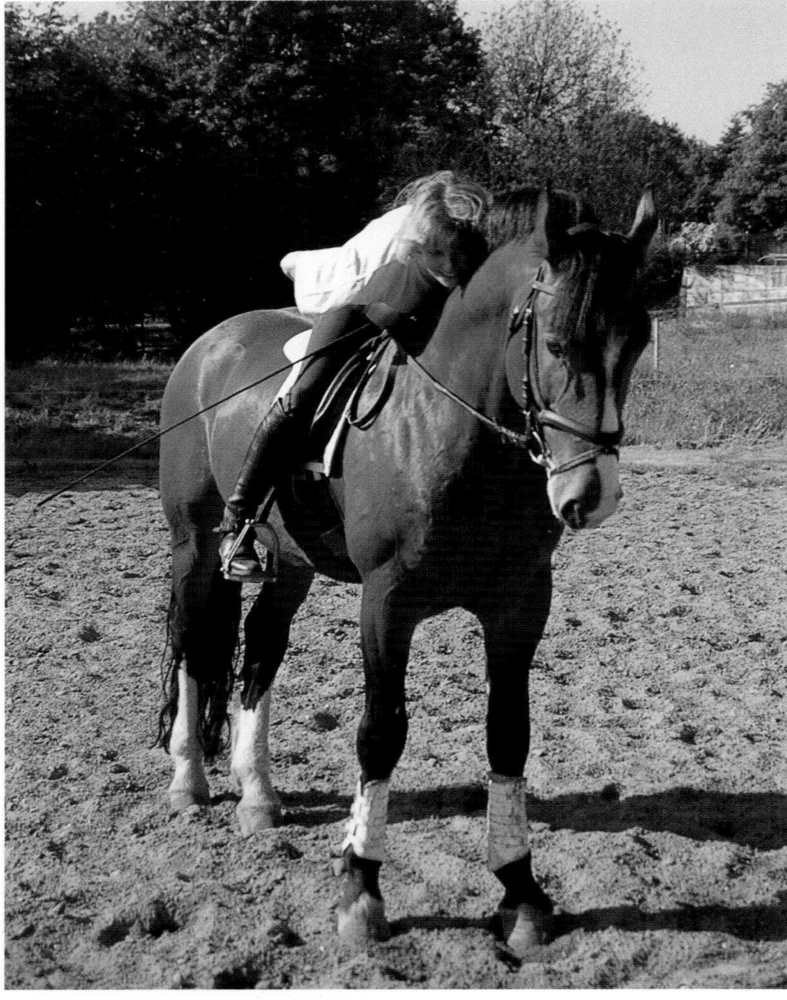

Even a horse should be praised when it has done well

perform a more 'ordered' movement. Halts are used to stop the horse and to make it stand correctly.

Stopping the horse is just as important as learning to brake in a car or stopping on skis. If you do not know how to stop a horse you will not only helplessly slide around in the saddle but you will be subjected to the horse's will until the horse stops by itself when it has tired itself out. Fortunately, stopping is one of the easiest lessons in horse riding: The halt is carried out by straightening your back (this also needs to be practised) and a slight tensioning of the reins (leave your hands 'standing', or pull them back slightly). And, if you apply slight pressure to the belly of the horse with your legs as if you are driving it forward a well-trained horse will stop immediately. If these aids are applied together the hind legs of the horse will stop under the centre of gravity of the horse and thus soften the momentum. If you pull the reins too tightly, however, it will not have the desired effect. If a horse does not react to the aids with which you are introducing the halt a sequence of half-halts will surely convince it to stop.

You cannot control a horse with long reins

Indicating direction

You will, of course, have to indicate the direction to the horse. 'Controlling' when riding means to use your legs. The one-sided pressure with the legs will always cause a shift in the rider's weight. Additionally, the reins are used to give a well-proportioned impulse. And now you have combined the three basic aids and the horse changes its running direction – it performs a 'curve'.

However, make sure that you do not lean into the 'curve' too much. If a rider tries to shift his weight by bending his hip it could all go wrong. If the hip bends the centre of gravity moves towards the opposite side and the horse walks into the opposite direction.

Also, do not lean your

upper body towards the direction in which the horse is supposed to 'bend'. The back of the rider must always be straight. Also, the outer rein and the outer leg should not loose contact with the horse when changing direction.

Otherwise the animal loses its guidance and will not move – as requested – collected. The aim is to have rider and horse move forward in harmony. Neither one must 'run off', or you will certainly lose 'style marks'.

In order to do well in a show, you need a well-trained horse, but of course it all depends on the rider's skill

Dressage: Training of horses

Apart from the equestrian sport of dressage, the term dressage also describes the complete training of riding and draft horses, that is, the disciplining of horses with the aim of it reacting to the aids of the rider.

The word derives from the French verb dresser, which means ' to train' or 'to drill'. Dressage as a sport is to prove that the horse will perform certain learned tasks on command from the rider. A working or hunting horse will also perform a turn, a curve, a parade or change of pace on a signal from the rider or driver. But alongside the already introduced exercises like halt, starting, paces in walk, trot and canter there are riding figures that are only performed in this sport. Outside dressage competions, you are unlikely to see a trotting horse that walks backwards, a show jumper that performs right hand and left hand cantering sequences or a Western horse that performs the perfect sideways step.

Two hard exercises: Riding backwards and riding sideways

Riding backwards is an exercise that is only performed in dressage. Here riding backwards represents one of the basic exercises. No dressage rider will gain recognition if he is not able to make his horse walk backwards in orderly steps. Walking backwards is a difficult exercise for the horse as it is extremely unnatural. A horse will only voluntarily walk backwards if it is moving away from danger. 'Backwards' therefore is an exercise that any horse will only perform reluctantly. Here you can see very clearly how much the horse listens to its rider or how well it is trained. This means that beginners are rarely successful when they want to give the horse the command for 'Backwards'. Therefore a few words about the aids. First get the horse's attention using a half-halt followed by a halt. The horse now stands with its legs closed. Now the rider drives the horse – with his back straightened – using his legs as if he wants to make it go forward. The horse now walks backwards instead of forward as the reins have stood still or the fists holding the reins are slightly turned inwards. This seems to be a miracle for the novice. The rider can also support the horse by slightly tilting his upper body forward. Try it if you have a very well trained horse! After four steps, however, you should stop again. How does that work? Do not drive forward anymore and let the reins go. If this worked the horse deserves to be praised. You will be praised by anyone watching you.

Walking backwards is one of the most difficult techniques in dressage

Riding sideways is even more difficult than going 'in reverse'. No beginner will try to do this exercise – and will not be allowed to do so – because it is the domain of the most experienced riders. These 'specialists' take up the reins tighter on the side towards the horse must go. At the same time they shift their weight onto this side and drive with the relevant leg just behind the saddle girth.

This is the start of the complex sideways movement, the so-called leg yielding. Furthermore, to make it even more difficult the rider is asked to ride sideway steps like Shoulder In, traverses and half-passes. These exercises, however, belong to the higher category of dressage and are performances almost fit for the Olympic Games.

Turning on horseback

With reference to turning the horse into the direction in which its head is pointing there is a difference between forehand and hind hand turns. This does not mean that the horse uses its forehand or hind hand to start the turn. When turning on its forehand the horse turns by 180° whereby the front legs are practically standing still and are the centre of the circle. When turning on the hind hand the hind legs of the horse remain still and it walks in a circle just on its front legs.

A right forehand turn means that the horse turns around its forehand towards the right (clockwise). The inner rein (in this case the right one) moves the horse into position, the right (inner) leg drives behind the saddle girth. If you now want to attempt a hind hand turn shift your weight to the inside and put more weight onto your right bone in your posterior if you want to do a right turn. The inner leg is level with the saddle girth and the rein indicating the position is slightly slacker. So that the horse does not repeat the forehand turn but understands that it is to turn on its hind hand the outer (in this case the left) leg presses against the horse behind the saddle girth.

However, all these exercises are part of higher dressage – the hind hand turn is one of the most difficult dressage exercises. Only start practising when you are already a good rider who is perfectly capable of using his legs, hold the reins correctly and sit correctly in the saddle as well as being able to straighten your back and shift your weight.

Alongside the forehand and hind hand turns by 180 degrees you often hear the command 'right/left turn' or 'short half-turn' right/left turn means that a turn of only 90 degrees is to be made. And the short half-turn only means to change from trotting into walking and turn around whilst moving. A hind hand turn of 180 degrees is carried out when walking and then the horse immediately changes into trotting after only taking one step in the walk.

The turn is an attractive exercise. A beginner, however, should only observe this exercise rather than trying it too early, as it is quite exhausting for both horse and rider and would not be any fun. And, putting determination aside, riding should be fun!

For changes of any kind the horse must be given precise aids

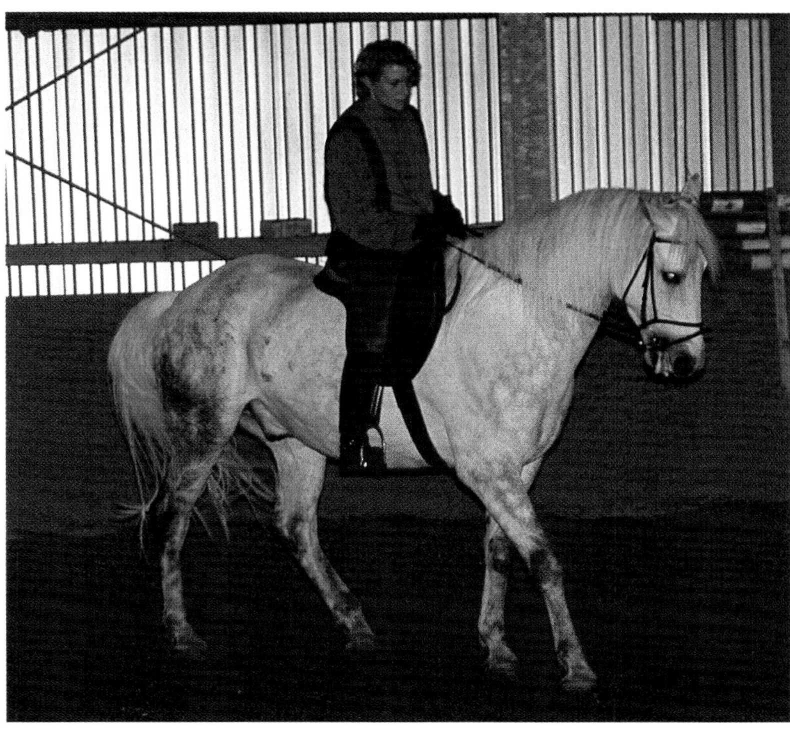

Characteristics of riding in the Western style

English or classical riding like dressage or show jumping require a high measure of rider's know-how, sporting determination and discipline. In order to become a classical rider you not only need a very well trained, high performance and often expensive horse but also numerous riding lessons and training units.

But when you're watching movies and documentaries you see the cowboys apparently effortlessly mount their horses and ride across the prairie. To the excitement of cross-country riders this Western style has returned to the old world. It is becoming more and more popular as the rules and exercises are simpler and not so rigid as in 'classical' riding. Of course, you still need to know certain basic rules if roaming around the countryside on horseback is not to be cut short.

The difference to the classical riding types is already visible in the clothing. There is neither any for riding boots when riding Western style. However, we still recommend the hard hat for safety reasons although it does not 'go' with the outfit of a Western rider. After all, cowboys do not wear lavish clothing in the 'Wild West'. A casual outfit is a 'must' for Western style riders. A simple shirt and jeans plus cowboy boots are the correct clothing. If you want to be an especially elegant rider you need a pair of leather riding chaps.

After the Western style rider has thrown on the correct 'work clothes' he mounts a crossbreed about 15.3 hh (63 in/1.60 m) in height. This is significantly smaller than the racy show jumpers or dressage horses. Originally Mustangs in particular were used as western horses in America. Today, Appaloosas, Quarter Horses and Pintos are suitable for Western style riding but today Haflingers and Norwegian Fjords are used for Western riding in Europe.

A further difference to the classical riding is the significantly bigger and heavier saddle. Compared to a dressage saddle it almost looks like an armchair. At the front of the saddle there is a large knob known as the pommel, which is used for securing the lasso. Even the reins are different from those used in English style: they are split and are

A stylish cowgirl

If you have to sit in the saddle for a long time you must be comfortable

held in one hand only.

Today, the saddle girth is secured with conventional buckles. Traditionally a tie knot was used in Western style riding, using straps without buckles. The saddle girths were knotted, the strap being pulled through an eyelet and then secured to the saddle like a loop.

As far as riding itself is concerned there is a marked difference between Western and classical style that starts when mounting the horse. It does not need to look so elegant and practised – the main thing is to get onto the horse at all. Simply stand next to the horse facing forwards. With the left hand grab one of the reins but without pulling them, since the horse is trained to move with the slightest movement of the reins. The left foot is put into the stirrup facing forward and the right hand grips the front edge of the saddle or the pommel. Thus you can pull yourself into the saddle with the aid of your right hand and your left foot. Once you are sitting straight, the right hand grabs the right rein and the left hand the left rein and the right foot is placed into the right stirrup.

When riding Western style the main thing is – and that is the good thing – to keep

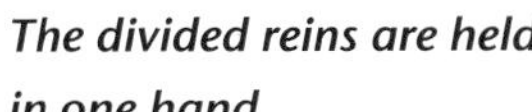

The divided reins are held in one hand

Both horse and rider's outfit and equipment must be comfortable and appropriate

everything, from reins, legs and sitting position, completely relaxed. This means you can sit in the saddle totally relaxed. Horses trained for Western style riding are especially obedient animals that react to the smallest command. This means you do not have to put too much effort in to keeping everything in order. However, even this relaxed riding style has its rules. Sitting straight is also an important rule when riding Western style. Your legs are significantly further away from the horse than in the English style. They are stretched slightly forward and have no contact with the horse. The feet of the rider point slightly upwards and the heels point downwards. They do not give any impulses to the horse but instead swing with the rhythm of the horse.

The reins are held with the right or left hand, as the cowboy has to have one hand free for working, that is, throwing the lasso. The reins run between index and middle finger into the hand so taht either thumb or index finger is used to hold on to the reins. The arms are slightly bent. The reins must be of equal length and must never be tight; they always need to be slack.

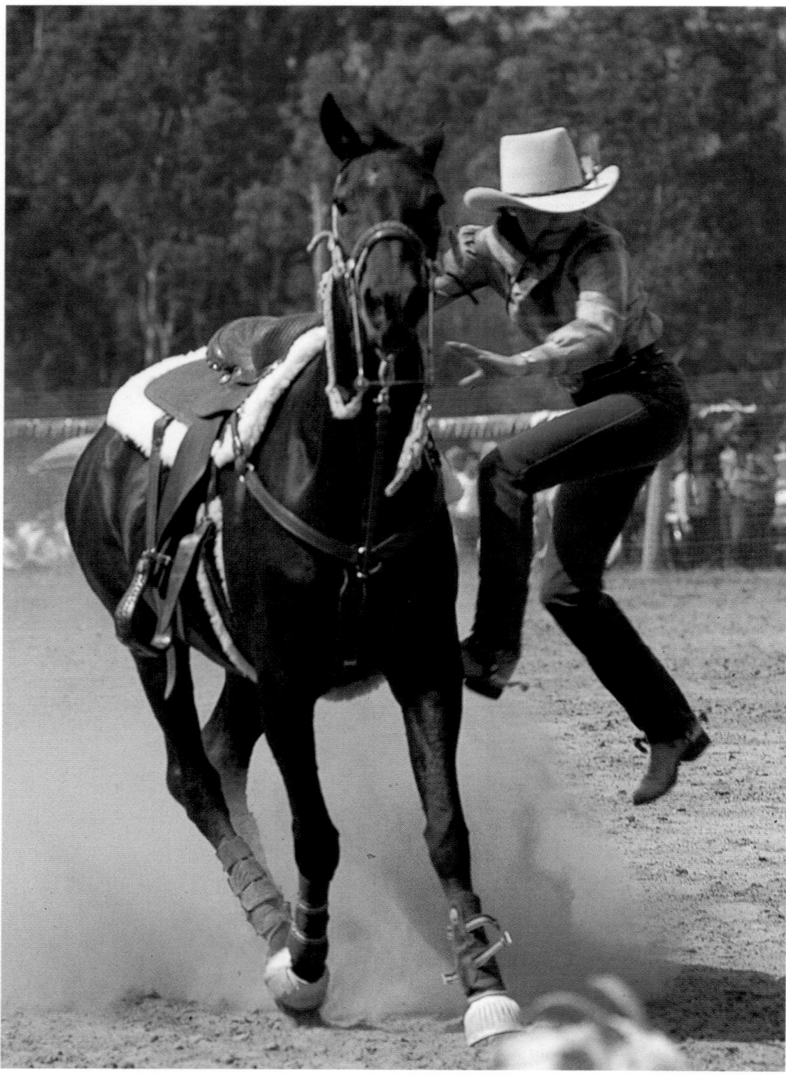

Horse and rider must be very used to each other to perform tricks such as this

If you now want the horse to move the same aids apply as in English style riding. However, in Western style riding the aids are only given if the horse needs to change pace or direction. This means there is no constant contact when moving forward – it is completely unnecessary. When starting off shift your bodyweight forward, the reins get even slacker and the legs giving the command 'start' are level with the saddle girths. This is more than enough for well-trained Western horses to make them move. If the horse 'refuses' because it does not feel like it or has realised that you are not very experienced a slight smack with the end of the rein (replaces the riding crop) could be necessary. The most important aid, however, is the leg pressure that is only repeated when you want the horse to move faster. Otherwise: leave the horse to it.

As you have surely seen in movies, cowboys steer their horses by simply moving the reins to one side. A 'good' Western horse knows instantly that it has to change direction. If you have not yet mastered this to and fro with one hand you are allowed to hold the reins in both hands or to position the so-called rein bridge. Here the reins – they are placed crosswise on the back of the horse before mounting – are held as the closed rein we recognise from the English style.

Using the outer leg you give a brief impulse, the inner rein indicates the direction to the horse. However, it is only tightened briefly and then slackened immediately. In this movement, however, the horse is supported mainly by the other rein, that is the outer one. The rider moves the rein over the neck of the horse to the inside. Thus the horse feels the pressure of the rein at the outer side of its neck and wants to 'pull away' from this pressure. It moves away from the pressure of the outer rein and the outer leg – it reacts the opposite way to the horses that are trained in the English style. The Western horse does not like the touch of leg and rein at all and reacts sensitively. If you want to perform a very tight right turn or start turning use your inner leg. It should exert soft pressure directly at the strap.

A well-deserved pause after a long ride

The paces in Western style

In contrast to classical riding Western style riding does not mention the trot or the canter. The Western style has its own paces and tempi. The slowest trot is called jog; the walk is called Walk. The speed is controlled with impulses given with the leg (faster) or by straightening your back and light holding of the reins (slower). In the jog the horse moves in a rather slow trot, which is significantly easier to sit than the classical trot.

Then next faster speed is the so-called lope – it is a type of slow canter.

In order to adjust the speeds of the horse precisely and to make the horse stop again you require further aids. In order to perform a stop fit for the movies – the so-called sliding stop – you require a lot of practice. This 'full braking' where the horse digs its hind legs into the ground – and you are the envy of the beginners – is

The whole repertory of 'western' riding is performed at a rodeo

The cowboy should always have his lasso at the ready

only achieved from a faster pace called the swaying canter and is seldom used by leisure riders. In order to achieve sporting performance the Western style riders ride the so-called Fast Rack that is comparable to the extended canter of the 'English Riders'.

Western horses are used to the human voice giving them commands. That is why they react very well to calls – just like you have seen in cowboy films. Thus the Western style rider tells the horse to 'walk' when he wants to start off; 'jog' when the horse is required to move faster and 'hoi' means that the horse needs to stop.

This means that if you suddenly want to stop from awalk, trot or canter, you should shout 'Hoi' and hope and pray that the horse slows down gradually and does not perform a sliding stop. Shift your body weight backwards whilst straightening your back. Press with your leg and slightly lift the reins. The less strong these aids are the more gently the horse will stop. The professionals amongst the Western style riders use stronger aids to perform an impressive sliding stop.

Even when riding Western style it is not always straight ahead through the prairie. Experienced riders will know how to make their horses go backwards and sideways. But we do not want to enter deeper into the higher art of horse riding but limit ourselves to how to dismount 'like a cowboy'. When standing still take the reins into your left hand, the right one holds on to the saddle horn. The right leg now swings across the back of the horse (the right hand gives support) onto the ground. Now you are back on your own two legs.

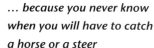

... because you never know when you will have to catch a horse or a steer

Once you have already practised the first steps in riding Western style and are no longer a novice anymore, and provided you have the necessary trust in the horse, it is time to venture into the open countryside. To go outside on your own with your horse is a completely new step after your first riding lessons and also a great challenge. But do not exaggerate the path towards military riding is long. The animal misses following the other horses – and you do not have the protective voice and corrective intervening of your instructor.

When in the countryside it may sometimes happen that you have to jump over small fences – be it voluntarily or involuntarily. For this you need the correct posture so that you do not fall off as soon as the horse makes its first jump.

In order to survive these little jumps you should have practised the half-seat beforehand. First make your stirrups a little shorter so that you can stand up in them. Then bend your upper body forward, press the knees into the saddle and lift yourself slightly out of the saddle. It is especially important that you do not try to hold on to the reins. They always have to be held loosely as the horse needs a lot of freedom for its head and neck when jumping. The only other thing you have to do now is to make the horse start cantering and lead it straight towards the jump. Now the horse is cantering towards the obstacle; you should leave it be because the animal knows best what speed it needs to overcome the obstacle and where it has to jump off. By pressing your knees against the saddle and standing up in the stirrups your body keeps its balance and is stable. The 'show jumper' has to rely on this, as there are no other means of support. Your upper body must copy the movement of the horse during the jump and also balance it. If you are not in equilibrium with the horse you either fall backwards when jumping off or fall forward when landing. And this is not only painful for you but it also puts too much strain on the horse.

You should not only keep these instructions in mind if you want to become a good show jumper but also when you want to ride across the countryside – maybe even as a Western style rider. Many hobby riders that are quite confident in the saddle when riding along smooth bridle paths can be gripped by panic when their horse eagerly runs towards a fallen tree and attempts to jump over this small obstacle. If you know how to balance this lofty momentum these little jumps are not that bad – and you can enjoy horse riding!

Equestrian

sports

Crowd pulling equestrian sports

Although horse riding is no great competition for football and tennis in Europe or for football and baseball in the USA, it nevertheless attracts great interest among television viewers and sports fans.

Spectators enjoy horse racing for the excitement and the gambling, as well as their interest in horses

The reason for its popularity is the fascinating dynamics of the beautiful big animals; the elegance of the riders in the disciplines of dressage and show jumping, the racy head-to-head finishes of trotters and gallopers, as well as the almost artistic performances in eventing competitions. Apart from the sporting and aesthetic aspects of horse riding, horse racing offer the spectators a chance to live dangerously and bet money on the outcome of the race, either through luck or skill. It is possible to win large sums of money with relatively small stakes on a racecourse if you have the right 'nose' for the horse or a gamble respectively. But luck always plays a big part when betting on a horse. Even experts who are extremely familiar with the racing scene, who know each and every horse and who are on 'first name terms' with almost every jockey cannot guarantee success. Experts are also carried away with excitement that cannot be surpassed when the horse race along the home straight after the last bend. 'Who will be first? How much will I win or lose?' – this is the question that thousands of spectators and horse enthusiasts ask themselves in the stands of of a race course, or when following the racing on television. Bets on horses can be placed at the bookmakers almost every day.

Apart from racing, show jumping is also very popular with spectators. This may be because the points system can be easily followed by anybody! All competitors who make a clear round, that is, without refusing any jumps or knocking any

over, mgoes through to the second stage, which is timed. The fastest clear round is the winner.

Dressage, however, means having to look for many different evaluation criteria and the verdict of the judges is not always clear to the layperson. The marks for horse and rider are given on of many different criteria – but more about this later.

Horse riding is also on offer at the Olympic Games and attracts up to 20,000 spectators and av very much larger audience in front of their televisions. Since 1912 equestrian disciplines have been included in the Olympic Games. Even here show jumping is the centre of attraction for the public, although many people take pleasure in watching the almost artistic performances of the dressage competitions.

Unfortunately, the performance sports – especially show jumping – have had bad publicity in the past ten years. A growing concern of the protection of animals and a greater awareness of the methods used to make these horses achieve these wonderful performances caused the press to speculate about doping and overtaxing of the horses.

In 1990 it became known that show jumping horses were 'barred' in order to jump better, higher and further. Whilst in training a 'bar' was hit onto their feet so that they developed more respect for the fences – a radical method that could cause pain and

Top: The three-day event, show jumping and dressage are the Olympic Games equestrian events.

A jockey before a race

injury. Not only animal rights protester but also show jumpers across the world showed their anger. 'Barring' has now been prohibited for many years. Doping, however, is not only a subject in swimming or shot putting. Unfortunately some horses are injected with drugs to make them jump higher, run further and faster which has led to intensified checks during the past few years.

Since 1994 the FEI (the Fédération Equestre Internationale, the International Equestrian Unionwith over 100 members) has prohibited almost all substances that are not given as healing products, even local anaesthetics and painkillers that provide temporary pain relief and thus make the participation in the competition possible.

But the equestrian sport` do not only mean large sums of money, famous horses and record times. Many horse fanciers spend their spare time with horses and show their knowledge and skill of their horse in local competitions. Apart from time they have often invested large sums of money even if they do not own a horse thousands of opounds. Horse riding is not an inexpensive hobby. Even without buying famous stallions and mares, the training, examinations by the vet, riding lessons and the transport of the animals to the competitions is extremely hard on the pocket.

Dressage is particularly elegant discipline: note the perfect posture of the horse and rider

Complex artistry: Dressage

Dressage is a tradition based on sophistication rather than on military precepts. The most famous riding school – The Spanish Riding School of Vienna – was founded in 1572.
The art of horse riding that is taught there was elevated even more due to the writings of the French horseman François Robichon de la Guérinière in the 18th century. In the book *Ecole de la Cavalerie* ('Riding School')Guériniere described the art of horse riding and developed exercises, figures and basics, which are still valid today.

Dressage horses as well as their riders require long and intensive training in order to master to most difficult steps and hoof beats and to keep ahead in the competition. Even dressage horses that do not take part in national or international competitions but only in local or regional dressage competitions are trained for at least half an hour every day. After all, it takes months until the turns and sideways movements are learned even when using a mature and well-trained horse.

And this is not all. The horses must cope with many exercises during the dressage competition – and all this with perfect posture. The dressage exercise requires that a pirouette (a turn during canter in a very tight circle) as well as a 'shoulder in' or *travers* (both are sideways movements on two hoof tracks) is performed and that the horse can cope with the flying change of lead and a *passage* (highly artistic trot) as well as a *piaffé* (trotting movement on the spot).

The first and foremost aim when training dressage horses is to teach the horse to be collected, that is to make it learn to shift its weight more onto its hind hand so that the fore hand is not strained and has more mobility. Only this collectiveness will result in the 'sublime' horse riding that makes dressage so aesthetically pleasing.

When being trained for dressage the young horses are chosen according to the following criteria. A horse for dressage should have a high head and strong hind legs, that is, an overall strong build. This is probably why the bigger horses are preferred because of their majestic look, which emphasises the elegance of the steps. The character of the animal is also important. It should be willing to learn and patient because it needs to learn many exercises during a long development process.

The aesthetically pleasing effect of dressage is achieved especially through the supreme posture of the upright and collected moving horse – whether its walking, trotting, cantering or a hind hand turn. The steps of the horse in dressage should be equally roomy and lively as well as fluid and smooth. To the joy of the spectators and judges the horse obviously 'works' extremely hard. During a half-pass (forward sideways movement), for example, the head points towards the direction of movement – just as if the horse is watching exactly where it is stepping.

In order to achieve all this dressage horses are trained extensively for four or five years for which riders and horses need to have the appropriate riding environment. The complicated dressage steps can only be learnt in a large arena. An international dressage arena measures 20 x 60 m (66 x 200 ft) and has five spots on which the various exercises have to be performed one by one.

The extremely difficult movements in dressage require total concentration on the part of horse and rider

Furthermore, the dressage rider should have the correct equipment A multi-purpose saddle that does not fit the horse 100 percent does not fulfil its purpose here – not even as an emergency solution. If you have the right enthusiasm and if you do not want to put too much strain on your horse a 'made to measure' saddle must be used.

Just like the horse, the

Whether in the free programme or during the compulsory exercises, all the horse's movements must be 'quiet, supple, relaxed and flexible'

rider has to display certain characteristics if he wants to make dressage 'his' sport. The main requirements are willingness to learn, patience, sensitivity and the ability to maintain the direct contact to the horse – not just with legs and reins but also with the voice. Without determination and enthusiasm the development in dressage is extremely limited. A lot of work and energy are always required when you want to achieve international recognition.

The most successsful equestrian nation in the Olympics is Germany. OIn the Sydney Olympics 200, the German team won both the Show Jumping and Dressage gold medals, while Australia was victorious in the Three-day event. German dressage riders have been unbeaten in Olympic Games since 1984.

The discipline of dressage goes back to the military performances given in military academies in the 19th century. Since the Olympic Games in 1912 in Stockholm individual riding competitions have been a fixed part of the programme. When the Olympic Games took place in 1924 in Paris demands were made on rider and horse for the first time that resembled the dressage exercises of today. In the same year the team competition was introduced. Complicated steps such as piaffé and passage were demanded from the participants for the first time in 1932. Since the Olympic Games in Berlin in 1936 horse and rider showed the collected canter and the pirouette for the first time. Women have only been allowed to participate in dressage competitions since 1952.

In order to remove some of the stiffness from dressage and to simplify the regulations for the layperson, Freestyle has become more and more popular. Here aesthetics and harmony between rider and horse are much more in the foreground than during the compulsory competitions. An additional factor for the popularity of freestyle is the music used which gives the whole exercise smoothness, elegance and transparency.

The Grand Prix and Intermédiare competitions in international competitions are ridden in an arena measuring 20 x 60 m (66 x 200 ft). In ordinary competitions the riding arena only measures 20 x 40 m (66 x 131 ft. The judges award marks from 10 to 0, with 10 being the highest (excellent). The mark 1 means a very badly performed exercise and 0 is for the non-performance of a required sequence. The judges adhere to the numerous rules and regulations set by the Fédération Equestre Internationale (FEI) when evaluating the performances which – apart from the numerous steps and exercises – demand that the horses be 'calm, lithe, relaxed and flexible' and that they 'obey willingly and without hesitation' The main thing is that the horses perform their sequences extremely fluidly without being driven too much by the rider. Therefore it is hardly surprising that the education of a good dressage horse is not achieved with force and crop alone. In the best scenario the horse must be able to perform the exercise freely and on its own. Ideally it should be able to perform a half-pass without the rider. Patience and trust are the most proven methods for successfully training a horse for dressage.

Spectacular jumps: Show jumping

In contrast to the artistic but rather artificial looking dressage, show jumping reminds you of the day-to-day aspect of horse riding. For centuries, jumping over fences and fences has been a necessity for rider and horse when hunting and fighting battles. But show jumping has only become a sport since the end of the 19th century. During the Olympic Games in 1900 long jump, high jump and jumping against the clock were separate equestrian disciplines. Only after the Second World War were the rules unified and the factors of time and type and quality of the jumps that are still valid today were established.

The criteria when judging show jumping can easily be understood by the layperson. For example, the rider is awarded penalty points when a fence falls. In national and international competition the misbehaviour of the horse, falling of the horse or rider and, of course, taking too much time are also faults attracting penalties. As the jumping abilities of the horses are almost the same at this high level, time is often the deciding factor for win or defeat.

Show jumping. The competitors must complete a circuit of various jumps in a set time with as few mistakes as possible

Fun for sports fans and gamblers: Flat racing

Even in ancient times horse racing – in those days mostly chariot races – aroused the enthusiasm of the public. This is the con-

The horses in the satrating gate before the race begins

Horse racing has been a very popular sport since Greek and Roman times

clusion inevitably drawn from the fact that it was included in the programme of the ancient Olympic Games in 624 BC. Today there are various types of races – even chariot racing is still practised . The most popular types of horse racing are flat racing and, in some countries, trotting, because they take place nearly every day. The betting shops in every city make it possible for enthusiasts to bet on a horse every day be it in Britain or in France.

The simple sport of cantering is also called flat racing. Alongside the flat racing there is also the steeple chase (see below).

Flat racing is simply a race over a distance, without anyjumps. It is run by thoroughbreds that originated from the English Thoroughbred breed in the 18th century. The classical races are for three-year olds. Three-year old thoroughbred stallions and mares race over varying distances. But horses of other age groups also take part in flat races: there are races for two-year olds and also races for horses more than three years old.

The thoroughbreds are very temperamental so that it can look quite alarming to the spectator when the jockey canters down the racetrack at over 50 km/h (30 mph or more) on horseback. Furthermore, the horses used are of very large; with a height of 15.3–16.3 hh (1.6 to 1.7 m/63–67 in) they are very tall but at the same time extremely slender.

Flat racing has a very old tradition. Its popularity with reigning monarchs in

The horses gallop at speeds of up to 60 km/h (37 mph) to race for first place

Below right: After the race the horse and jockey are greeted with applause – if they have won

Englandgave it the name of 'the sport of kings'. It became established as a popular sport in the 18th centry. The Jockey Club, the sport's governing body, was founded in 1750. The classic British flat races for three-year-olds are the Derby, the Oaks, the St Leger, the 2,000 Guineas and the 1,000 Guineas.

Flat racing takes place over various distances. Shorter distanmces call for younger horses achieving high speeds over a relatively short distance, while 'stayers' are horses that have enough endurance over longer distances. The jockeys themselves also require stamina, which is a very important part. They must not weigh too much because light weight is an advantage in horse racing. Jockeys require great courage and determination. They are not the perfect riders in the sense of classical style, but a good posture on the horse is important since the horses 'fly' across the racetrack at high speeds. The slim, tall, fast animals run 100 m (110 yards) in less than seven seconds and a kilometre in about one minute, representing speeds of 60 km/h (37 mph). Obviously the rider must have a good hold on his or her horse. Falling at these high speeds in the middle of the racetrack can have fatal consequences.

The jockey does not sit in the saddle but stands up in the stirrups and tries to assume as balanced a position as possible. It is important that a jockey should know his mount and be able to judge its endurance. During the race he must concentrate on determining the speed of the thoroughbred so that the horse does not exert itself too early – at the same time, however, he has to keep an eye on the competition.

All Thoroughbreds are listed in the General Stud Book, first published in 1813.

The use of two-year old horses was and still is a sore point in racing. The breeders and owners of the two-year olds have great interest in the young animals taking part because they can not only win prize money but they are also acquiring racing experience which will stand them in good stead when they compete later in races for three-year olds. Animal protectors, however, maintain that these very young horses could be physically damaged when used in competitions. Investigations – which themselves were controversial – showed, however, that the start of training and the resulting demands on the horses do not harm their consitution and is not in conflict with animal welfare. In classical races, run by horses that are three years old, the animals are particularly successful when they have already raced as two-year olds. This is the reasoning by the trainers and the association for the use of young thoroughbreds.

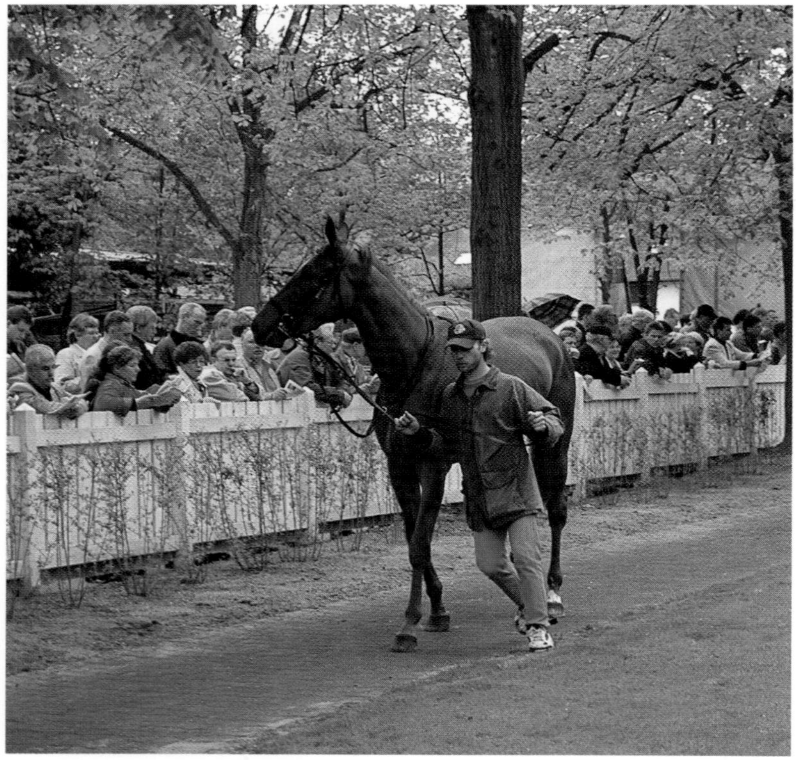

The highly-strung temperament of the thoroughbred becomes apparent before the race when they are introduced to the punters

Between 5 and 15 horses are at the start of a flat race.

For the betting man on the race track there is always a programme, which gives all the details of the individual races, horses, owners, trainers and jockeys. The number of starters, their age and sex and their successes and placings on previous outings of the individual horses are all listed. So every visitor to the racecourse can build his own picture of how strong the participants are and which horse is worth betting on. Ante-post bets, that is, ones that have been placed beforehand at the bookmakers, are made public, and the prices change as the time of the race approaches. Thus the betting man knows how the quotes are before the race starts.

A visit to the race course is always an eventful and exciting event because there will always be several races.In contrast to dressage and show jumping competitions these races attract many spectators even when the weather is inclement; the betting is moderate and the combination possibilities can easily be copied. And, of course, the object of a race is much easier to understand than the points system of dressage competitions.

Here is a simple summary of betting on horses. A stake can be placed on a horse to win. The odds offered will vary among the competing horses. One horse may be the favourite because it has already won several races. The chances of it winning are thought to be high, so the odds offered are low. An outsider is thought unlikely to win, and the odds offered are correspondingly greater. If the favourite wins you might only receive double your stake, but if an outsider wins you could receive 20 or even 100 times your stake.

Apart from betting on a winner the visitor to the race course can also bet on a place. This means betting that the horse selected will finish in one of the first three places – if there are only six or fewer it will be for the first two places. In this case the odds are, of course, lower than when betting on the winner. Furthermore, the horse enthusiast has the chance to enter a two or three way bet. This bet is on horses that cross the finish line in first, second or third place. However, based on 10 horses starting, the two-way bet gives you 180 possible variations for crossing the finishing line. With the three-way bet the chances of receiving winnings from your stake are even lower.

The start and the finish of a flat race marks its two difficult moments: the start and the determination of the winner. First, it is not easy for jockeys and start helpers to get the horses into the starting gates. These moveable starter boxes are necessary because the animals are too eager to prove their speed. Due to their fiery temperament you cannot just line them up at the start. However, as the animals are naturally scared of the boxes it always takes a few minutes until all horses are lined up. As soon as all horses and riders are ready inside the starter boxes the race is started immediately by opening the boxes. This avoids heightening the restlessness of the animals. If a horse 'bolts' before the actual race it has little chance for a good place. The thoroughbreds have to save their strength for the race and not exert themselves beforehand. At the end a race is often decided by photograph.

As well as flat races, race horses compete in steeplechases. Horses that have been successful in flat racing also take part in steeplechases. These have as many as 30 fences and other obstacles for the horses to jump.

The most famous steeplechase in the world is the Grand National at in Aintree, England, which first took place in the year 1837. Unfortunately, this great sporting event which takes place near Liverpool every year has often received bad press due to dangerous and often fatal falls of horses. Despite the fatal accidents, the Grand National in Aintree has always been the

Steeplechasing is particularly popular in Britain

A steeplechase is very fast and spectacular

number one crowd puller. It cannot be denied, however, that some of the spectators only come to see the spectacular falls and the unsurpassed difficulty of this event. The dangers for horse and rider are the extremely high price for the astounding performances that are shown during the steeplechase.

Break-neck speed in the sulky: Trotting races

In trotting races there is no rider on the horse. The animal pulls a small extremely light cart with two wheels, the so-called sulky, on which the driver sits. In this sport the driver does not only have the main responsibility for the placement but also the greater health risk because he occupies a more dangerous position than the horse. Thus it could happen – even if only rarely – that the driver cannot hold himself in the small seat and falls during the race. This fatal 'mistake' can happen when the horse suddenly changes from trotting into a canter. Apart from severe injuries that the driver could sustain due to the other sulkies the team is also disqualified because of the change from trot into canter.

Trotting race events as well as flat races are amongst the horse competitions where the organisers put the emphasis on making money through the bets that are placed. Trotting races are exclusively financed through the bets placed and the 'operating costs' are enormously high. The purchase price of a promising racehorse could well be from £15,000 to £30,000, and for the top horses the purchase price has no upper limit, often reaching £300,000 or more. On top of this, there are the wages for grooms and trainer of the racehorses. A successful trainmay charge £1,000 a month or more for training the animal. This high investment only pays for itself if the animal is winning races with large prize money. However, even the best trainer and the perfectly trained trotter mare cannot give any guarantees!

The horses used in trotting races appear to be smaller and more delicate than show jumpers or flat racers. Furthermore, in the trotting races it is expected from the animals that they run at excessive speed in a normally slow pace, which is not natural for them. Therefore, a lot of training is required to discourage the trotters from starting to canter when reaching higher running speeds.

The El Dorado of trotting races is in the USA. There the racetracks are mostly over 1600 metres (one mile) long, which the best horses run at average speeds of over 60 km/h – and this while pulling a sulky! In the USA many trotting races are run in the more unusual parallel step. This means the horse does not put down the diagonal pair of hooves but the lateral, i.e. the parallel pair of hooves. In order to practise this running style (amblers) the horses are bound at their hind and front legs using a special harness on one side, which prevents them from using the diagonal steps.

In trotting, the participants pull a cart, known as a sulky over a distance of a mile (about 1500 metres)

The peak of horsemanship: Three-day events

The three-day event used to be called 'military' and demands many varied performances from horse and

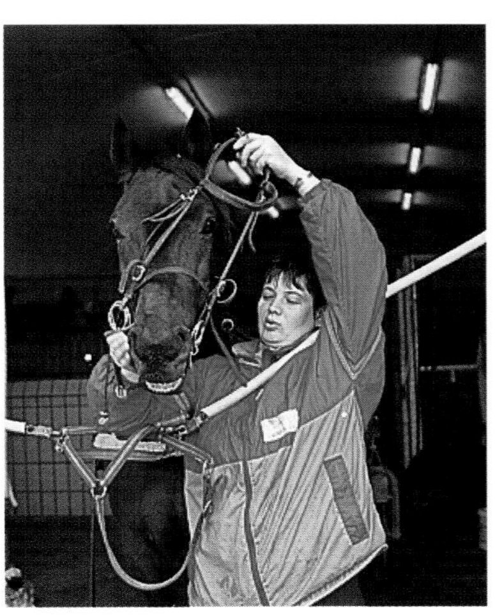

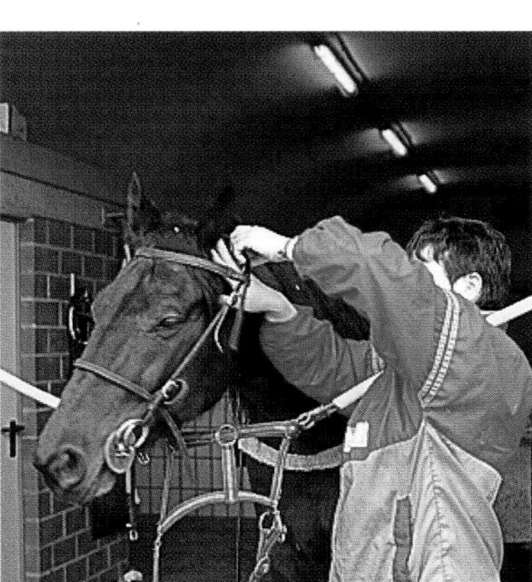

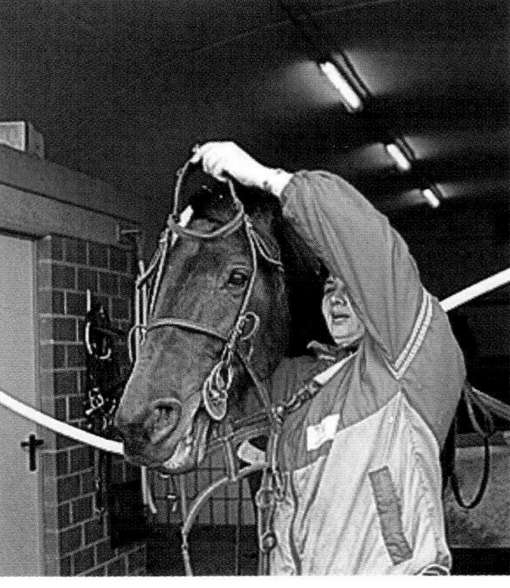

The cross-bred horses bred for trotting must be slowly accustomed to the sulky. This horse is being carefully groomed before training

rider. The competitions range from dressage to a cross-country race of 25 to 30 km (15 to 19 miles) with numerous fences. On the obstacle and cross-country course the horses have to jump over 32 various fences. With a duration of 90 minutes this is a true 'marathon' of the equestrian sport. The water ditches demand every strength and obedience from the horses. The ditches always cause the most spectacular falls that often have serious consequences for horse and rider.

Due to the very different demands the horses selected for the three-day events are very good jumpers, i.e. have great power in their hind legs but on the other hand are lighter than pure show jumpers and have a very good constitution – a mixture between show jumpers and race horse is ideal.

Since 1912 the Three-day event known as the peak of horsemanship because of its demands on horse and rider – has been one of the Olympic disciplines. However, it is highly controversial because it has often caused severe or even fatal injuries and the horses often exerted themselves to the point of exhaustion. In 1996 the International Equestrian Association (FEI) therefore decided on new competition rules for the 1996 Olympic Games in Atlanta. The association took into consideration the very high temperatures in Georgia which the horses had to cope with. It was recommended to the three-day event teams to give the horses three weeks to get used to the climate in Atlanta. Furthermore, the races should take place during the cooler morning hours, which meant relatively moderate temperatures. The distances were shortened and there were fewer fences. Furthermore, the compulsory break was extended from 10 minutes

The most spectacular of equestrian sports: the three-day event

to 15 minutes so that the horses could cool down. Thus the following regulations were introduced in Atlanta 1996. During the first phase the horses ran about 5,000 metres (3 miles) for which they were allowed 23 minutes (220 metres/minute). In phase B of the three-day event seven fences had to be jumped over a distance of 2,760 metres (just under 2 miles); the third phase contained the cross-country part over a distance of 7,700 metres (nearly 5 miles), instead of the previous distance of 11,000 metres (7 miles), which had to be run within 45 minutes. After a brief ten-minute stop to refresh the horses during the third phase and the mentioned compulsory break of 15 minutes was last competition with 35 fences was over a flat race distance of 6,270 metres (nearly 4 miles). In total it was still a race over almost 21 km (13 miles) and with over 35 fences, which had to be completed in one hour 50 minutes.

Acrobatics on horseback: Vaulting

Vaulting became a performance sport after the Second World War and the first Championships for the vaulting teams took place in 1963. An Individual Vaulting Championship began in 1986. Since 1984 there have been regular European events – every two years – and since 1986 there are also World Championships.

Vaulting is a gymnastic, acrobatic exercise on the back of a cantering horse and in synchronisation with the movement of the horse. The animal runs on the lunge rein – be it inside a hall or outside – in a circle with a diameter of at least 13 m (43 ft).

The exercises are performed in walk, trot and canter. During competitions they are performed in canter only. The horse does not have a saddle but is equipped with a vaulting belt. The belt has two grips for the rider. The horse is not driven with the stirrups or the legs but only with the voice and the help of the holder of the long lead.

Vaulting is mainly a sport for young horse lovers. They can start vaulting at the age of seven. In team vaulting the members must not be older than 18, in individual competitions they must be at least 16 years old. For many children this acrobatic gymnastics means the start of a career in horses or as a rider. Especially girls show a high

In the three-day event, the horses jump over high obstacles, run across water-ditches and 'hurl' themselves down steep slopes

Acrobatics on horseback is now not just a circus performance but a competitive sport

interest in acrobatic horse riding. The basic conditions for the vaulting are a very flexible body and the talent to be a good gymnast. Because the main emphasis here is the completion of complex acrobatic exercises. When vaulting, balance and mobility of the athletes is extremely important. Jumping ability, support strength in the arms and strong ability to spread the extremities are also necessary requirements for the high art of 'horse gymnastics'. That is why beginners are in 'dry training' first: they learn the gymnastics ability on a vaulting horse and are only allowed onto a moving horse when they are able to sit up in a fashion typical for vaulters. With the force of their arms and the momentum by jumping off with both legs from the ground whilst running the vaulters swing themselves over the back of the horse into a sitting position behind the belt. And this, of course, has to look very elegant!

During the compulsory section the vaulters always show the judges and the spectators the basic seat, the sitting without a saddle and without holding on. Then they perform the

Standing on the back of the horse is one of the basic exercises in equestrian acrobatics

'flag': a figure where they support themselves on one knee and one hand and the free leg and free arm are stretched out upwards. The 'mill' is a sitting position where one leg is stretched up as vertical as possible and with a half-scissor like movement the vaulters demonstrate a swinging split above the horse's back whilst facing the front or the rear of the horse – similar to the easier exercises on the artificial 'horse' which we know from gymnastics. Even standing up on horseback must be carried out according to special rules. First move both knees softly onto the back of the horse. From this crouching position let go of the grip handles and stand up without holding on. Both arms are stretched sideways. This position must be held over four cantering steps if the vaulter does not want to risk having points deducted. Then the figure 'flank' is shown: swinging both legs backwards into a type of 'bent' handstand with the subsequent bending of the hip. The legs are now closed behind the horse and are moved softly back into the sitting position. In the second part of the 'flank' the vaulters swing away from the horse in the same way. The legs are swung upwards to the rear with much momentum and the arms push the vaulter forcefully towards the outside. He should reach the ground with the legs next to the horse – level with its hind hand – and run off next to the horse.

Strength and suppleness are needed in equestrian acrobatics

In Freestyle acrobatic exercises are added to the compulsory exercises, which are born out of the imagination of the vaulters and create a high variation of figures.

Imported from the Wild West: Riding Western style

Riding Western style as a sport has its origin in the history of the horse on the American continent. The Spanish brought the horses over the ocean and the settlers on the 'new' continent used the horses for working the fields or rounding up the cattle. The dynamics and the toughness of the cowboy working with the lasso were also transferred into competition in modern riding Western style. Of course, the USA is the leading nation in riding Western style. Barrels in the competition often replace the cattle – during Barrel Racing the western riders canter around

the barrels. Whilst doing this they show how to control the horse and how obedient and fast the animal is as well as their own know-how in the saddle. In today's rodeo competitions there are competitions involving real cattle, especially in the USA. The sport cowboys catch the cattle with the lasso (roping); they separate cattle from its herd (cutting) or fight a bull that needs to be pushed over from the horse's back. In an actual rodeo there is also the breaking of 'wild' horses, i.e. horses that were 'made wild'. Most participants in rodeos are professional riders.

In the 'Wild West', cowboys catch the cattle with a lasso

If you cannot afford your own horse or live in a city the only thing left to do is to change to an 'Electric Rodeo', which is a moving robot that imitates a horse or a bull.

Games played at break-neck speed: Polo

Polo is an equestrian sport where the speed and mobility of the horse is just as important as the ability of the players to hit a ball with their mallet. Polo was played 2500 years ago in Persia and China and reached Europe via India in the 19th century. British soldiers serving in the Indian Army were very fond of the sport which was widely

Barrel racing is a discipline in 'western' racing: the cowboys gallop with their horses as fast as possible around a course, marked by barrel. In the United States, wagon racing – with wagons reminiscent of those used in the conquest of the West – is very popular. In chariot-racing, more widespread in Europe, it is more a question of skill and training

played in India and they soon arranged competitions in Britain. The first polo club was founded in Indiain 1859, and the first competition held in England took place in 1870. It was introduced into the United States in about 1876 by James Gordon Bennett. Despite the long association of polo with England, the Argentinians were soon the best polo players in the world. They bred a cross between the Criollo and various thoroughbreds to produce polo ponies which are notable for their speed, endurance and toughness in all countries.

In polo each team consists of four players who try to hit the ball into the opponent's goal, which is 3 m (10 ft) high and 7.3 m (24 ft) wide. Although a player must not cross over the riding line of the opponent nor the flight path of the ball, polo is certainly not

Polo horses must have speed, stamina, perseverance and toughness . Polo is mainly played by the upper echelons of society

Below: Prince Charles playing polo

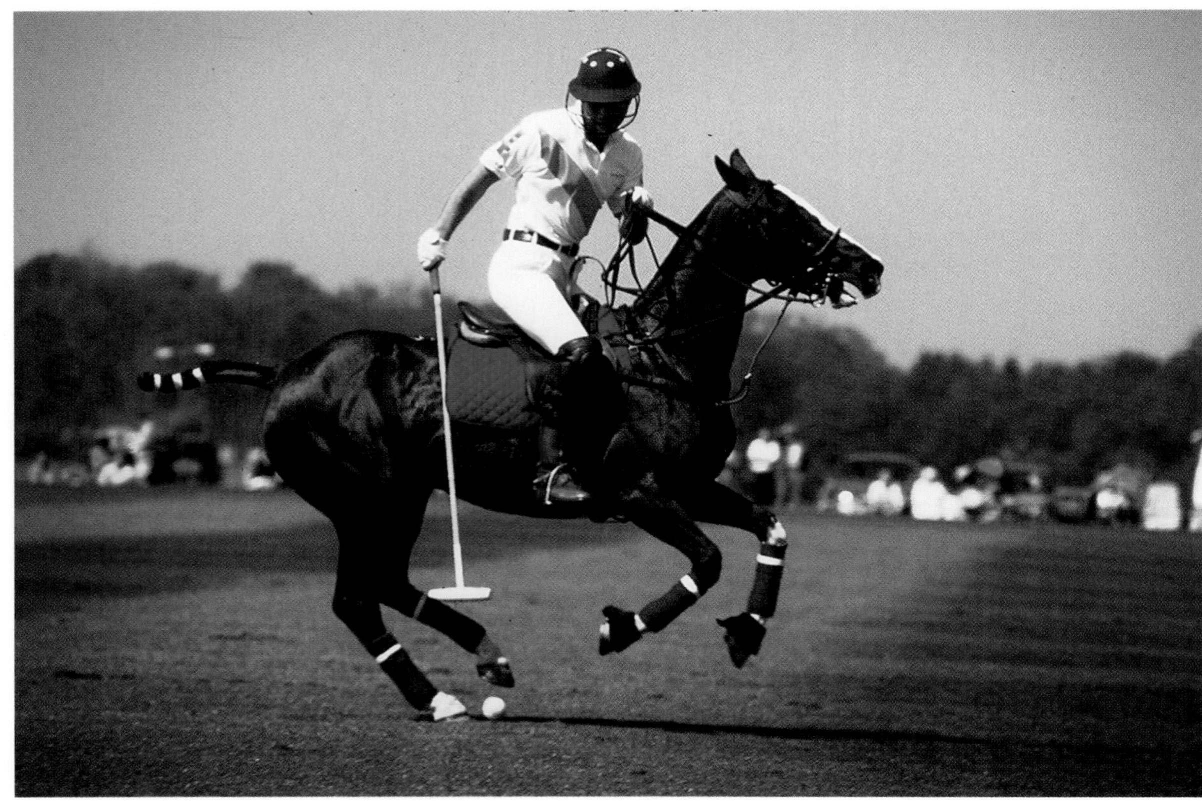

without its dangers. Pushing away and hooking with the mallet as well as hindering the opponent during the stroke is permitted. Therefore the players protect themselves with boots, special helmets, gloves and knee protectors. This not only reduces the dangers when falling but also when hit by other mallets.

The playing field measuring 270 x 180 m (300 x 200 yd). It consists of five or six periods each of 7½ minutes called chukkas, so the whole game is lasts 37½ minutes or 42 minutes. This sport is performed at a fast canter and the extreme speed is extremely draining for the horses and especially bad for their joints. Therefore they are changed at the longest after two chuckers.

In polo the aim is to balance the varying strengths of the players by applying handicaps. A very good player can enter the game with a handicap of up to ten; a novice starts with a bonus handicap of minus two. Each handicap point is valued as one goal to the opponent. So if the handicaps of four team members amount to eight between them and the opponents have six, the score opens at 2–0 to the latter, the weaker team.

A characteristic of the speedy and rather rough looking game are the reins. For the rider to be able to control the horse effectively during the game he has to hold the reins quite tightly. As he only has one hand available – the other one is busy holding the mallet – a special double bridle was developed to which two pairs of reins are attached. A change in direction is performed by pressing the reins against the neck – just like riding Western style.

Polo makes great demands on both the rider and the horse. Pushing, hooking and obstruction of the opposition are all permitted

Chariot racing at lightning speed and Carriage driving

Chariot racing has a long history. Whether the horses were used in farming for pulling a cart or used when the first chariots were invented – the use of horse carriages for working or transport was the predecessor of the sporting competition. The sporting discipline in competitions and fixed rules especially requires the skill, the obedience and the endurance of horse and driver.

Even the Ancient Olympic Games had chariot racing in their programme. Races with single or multiple teams had already established themselves for about 1000 years as a favourite sport of the Greeks.

In modern times carriage driving developed itself especially in England. Towards the end of the 19th century the first carriage driving clubs were founded there. And, although automobiles have pushed out carriages and horses since the end of the Second World War the sporting enthusiasm for driving two- and four-hand teams continues. Since 1969 guidelines set by the International Equestrian Association (FEI) have been in place for three-day events of single, two and four teams and the first International Driving competition was held in 1970.

First drivers and horses on an arena measuring 40 x 100 m (130 x 330 ft) must perform a dressage exercise with team control. The second part of the competition is a marathon drive across country and in the third part an obstacle course must be completed.

The drama of driving is the highest in the second phase. When driving cross-country the 24 to 30 km (15 to 19 miles) long course must be driven within a set time. The spectacular drive leads through water ditches and tight 'alleys' with natural and artificial fences. But the actual obstacle course follows this marathon run. The obstacle course follows a winding route around cones. This means that driving not only demands the mobility and the skill of the animals as well as the endurance, the power and the courage of both driver and horse.

The high point of the driving season in England is during the Royal Windsor Horse Show.

In carriage driving, the driver shows his ability to control the horse and cart wile manoeuvring across difficult terrain

In chariot-racing what matters most are the agility, skill and stamina of the horses and driver. In order to be able to cross such a deep ditch, the horses need a lot of strength

Glossary of

horse terms

Action:
Posture of the horse and movement of its legs in the various paces.

Aids:
Various signals used by the rider to inform the horse of his wishes. Natural aids are the voice, reins, hands, legs and weight. The whip and spurs are artificial aids.

Albino:
Horse whose coat is white from birth in contrast to the grey horse whose coat lightens gradually

Amble:
Smooth quiet pace in dual tact. Because of the almost smooth walk of the horse the amble can be easily sat and is therefore highly suitable for beginners and older riders when riding leisurely across country.

Black:
Basic colouring of the coat: a completely black horse.

Bow hocks:
Incorrect conformation of the hocks which point outwards.
Boxy hoof:
A hoof which is too narrow and upright. This is an inherited fault.

Brand:
In earlier times the mark with which an owner marked his horse.

Breaking in:
The training of the young horse to obey the rider and his aids. Breaking in normally takes about two years.

Breeding:
The systematic selection of the parents for producing offspring to achieve a target. Since the horse became a domestic animal man has performed this breeding selection. The result is today's horse breeds.

Broken wind
Chronic respiratory disease of the horse. It indicates serious lung or heart disease.

Brown horse:
Basic colouring of the coat; a brown horse has a black mane, black tail and often black legs. The colour brown ranges from light to dark.

Build:
Body structure of the horse. If the harmony of the body is not ideal it has 'build faults', e.g. 'overbuilt' (see below)

Calibre:
Ratio between weight to height of withers. The calibre is calculated as a quotient of the body weight in kilograms divided by the height in centimetres.

Cannon's circumference:

Circumference of the front leg measured between the knee and the fetlock. It says a lot about the strength of the horse and should be 20–22 cm (8–9 in) in cross-breeds and 18–20 cm (7–8 in) in ponies.

Change:

(French = changer = change)
Change of hand, especially in flying canter change

Chestnut:

Basic colouring of the coat; a chestnut-coloured horse with mane, tail and legs of ths ame colour. The chestnut colour can range from light to very dark.

Chukka:

Section of a game of polo lasting 7½ minutes.

Colic:

Overall term for various stomach and intestinal diseases of the horse that can be extremely painful. The animals visibly suffer with colic and a vet should be called immediately as an exact diagnosis is necessary.

Collection:

Basic training aim of high school (haute école) riding, chiefly seen at the Spanish Riding School of Vienna. A collected horse pushes its hind legs further underneath the body towards its centre of gravity. The legs are used more for carrying than for driving forward so the front legs are not strained and are more mobile. The horse shifts its weight onto its hind legs. It is nly in this way are many exercises of high School riding possible.

Concentrated feed:

Special grain feed consisting of oats, barley, corn, wheat und rye that can be bought ready-mixed. It increases the performance of the horse but must not be fed too much.

Cross-legged:

X-like crossing of the hind legs. This is present mainly in ponies or old breeds as it has largely been bred away for visual reasons. However, it is not a 'fault' of the horse since x-legged animals are often safer when going cross-country.

Crupper:

'Rear end', near the hip of the horse. The powerful musculature of the crupper is the 'engine' of the animals, dictating the physical performance of the horse.

Curry comb:

Cleaning instrument made of rubber or plastic for cleaning the coat when it is very dirty. The curry comb is essential for the proper cleaning of the horse. A

metal curry comb is use to clean other brushes, never the horse.

Dry:
Term for the appearance of head and extremities. A dry head and dry legs are strong but not fat but bony, wiry or muscular with tight smooth skin.

Eel stripe:
A black horizontal line across the back of the horse running from the mane to the start of the tail. The eel stripe was a typical characteristic of wild horses and can still be seen today, especially in duns (e.g. Norwegian Fjord).

Equines:
(from the Latin *equus*, horse)
Belonging to the horse family, Equidae, which includes horses, asses and zebras.

Fetlock:
The lowest joint of a horse's leg. Hairs on the legs, especially on heavy horses

Foal:
Young horse up to the age of two years.

Foot mange:
Skin disease of the hind legs caused by parasites.

Forehand:
All parts of the horse that are in front of the rider, i.e. withers, neck, head, chest and front legs.

Format:
Ratio of body length to withers in height. It is used to differentiate between the sexes (mares are mostly long rectangular, stallions are square or tall rectangular) and also in describing breeds.

Foundation:
Structure of the limbs and their connection with the skeleton of the horse. The foundation should not be too light, but balanced, broad and deep with legs that are not too long and sry.

Frame:

The proportions of the horse's body. There are big and small framed horses. The frame is the entire size ratio of the individual body parts including the extremities to each other.

Gag bit:

Snaffle bit in which a rounded cord runs from the cheek pieces through bridle rings, connected to the reins. It is used to avoid the horse 'tilting' in its movement.

Gelding:

Castrated stallion. The habit of castrating stallions to make them calmer and more obedient has a long history. The animals are often castrated at the age of one to two years. They cope well with the operation performed by a vet and keep their playfulness and youth for a long time.

Girth:

Distance round the body measured from behind the withers. When the girth is sufficient there is enough room for heart and lungs.

Glanders:

Highly infectious and dangerous disease. The victim must be put down.

Good doer:

A horse is a 'good doer' if thives and looks well on a relatively small amount of food. Some breeds of horses that do not seem to process

their feed – they have the characteristic of always looking thin.

Grey:
Basic colouring of the coat. A grey horse ranges from white to dark gray. Grays are born dark and can take up to ten years before they develop their final colouring. Depending on birth colour they are called light grey, flea-bitten (with dark speckling), iron grey, and dappled (with dark rings). Horses that born white are albinos.

Height measure:
Height of the horse from ground to withers measured with a rod standing parallel to the front leg with a horizontal height-adjustable arm that indicates the exact height. Height is measured in hands, one hand being 4 inches. So a horse of 14.2 hh has a height of 58 inches (147 cm).

High school (haute école) riding :
Dressage training of the horse with the aim of completeness in the Classical Art of Horse riding, as practised at the Spanish Riding School of Vienna.

Hind hand:
All body parts of the horse that are behind the hand of the rider, i.e. withers, hips, tail and hind legs

Hoof scraper:
Hook-shaped instrument for cleaning underneath the hoof

Horn split:
Split in the hoof horn which in the worst cases requires long-term orthopaedic treatment

Horse brush:
Brush with a looped strap for cleaning the coat of the horse.

Horseshoe:
An iron shoe for the horse in the shape of an irregular open ring that is nailed onto the hoof and protects the hoof from wear and damages. Horseshoes can also be used to correct faulty positioning of the hooves. They are also a good luck charm.

Hunter:
Breed of the English or Irish hunting and jumping horse. It is mostly bred from thoroughbred stallions and heavy crossbreed mares.

Jockey:
Rider of horses in horse races. He or she may be professional or amateur.

Kick out:
Horse kicks with its hind legs

Mange:
Rare but severe skin disease caused by mange mites. Mange is highly infectious and must be reported.

Markings:
White marks on head and/or legs of the horse

Molars:
An adult horse has 24 molars, six on each side of the upper and lower jaw

Nail prick:
All injuries of the hoof due to entry of sharp items into the hoof.

Passage:
'Spanish step', a lesson of the Spanish Riding School. It is trotting in the highest completeness where a diagonal leg pair seems to briefly levitate above the ground.

Overbuilt:
Body shape where the highest point of the cruppers is higher than the highest point of the withers. The forehand is thus more used which is unfavourable for some exercises of the horse, for instance dressage.

Pedigree:
Details of date of birth, parentage and ancestry, markings and owner of a horse in the main studbook and other documents of the breeder's association. The word comes from the French 'pied de grue' meaning 'cranes foot', referring to its similarity to the lines of a genealogical pedigree chart. To qualify as pedigree, a horse's ancestry registered in the breed's stud book.

Periodic eye inflammation:
The most dangerous eye inflammation of the horse. It is also called 'moon blindness'. It often occurs in a four-weekly cycle and can lead to permanent blindness. There is almost no chance of a cure so periodic eye inflammation is a quality fault.

Phlegmon:
Painful inflammation of the subcutis and swelling of the lower extremities.

Quality:
Special ability and exquisite appearance of a horse as the result of good breeding and first-class training

Ram's head:
The term describes a horse with a very strongly outwardly bent nose.

Refining:
Breeding of thoroughbreds or fine crossbreed horses to evolve into mainly heavier, more powerful horse breeds. The objective is to achieve a more elegant appearance but also a livelier temperament.

Roughage:
This is necessary ballast to keep the intestines of the horse healthy. The best roughage is good meadow hay from the first cut. When distributed over the entire day the horse is occupied with nibbling the roughage and thus prevents the forming of bad habits.

Rounded horse:
Horse with round and closed looking exterior and short legs.

Running machine:
Device where horses are moving in a circle whilst attached with long leads so that they do not become bored and keep 'in shape'. Also helpful to avoid bad habits.
Selection for breeding purposes:
Accurately determined official breeding permit for stallions.

Spavin:
Rubbing of a bone and inflammation of the hock, which can cause lameness of the relevant leg in the long run.

Stable vices:

Aggressive behaviour and other problems, such as crib-bitin and wind-sucking, caused by boredom when the horse is inside its stable too long and not exercised. Remember that horses are gregarious animals and need a lot of exercise.

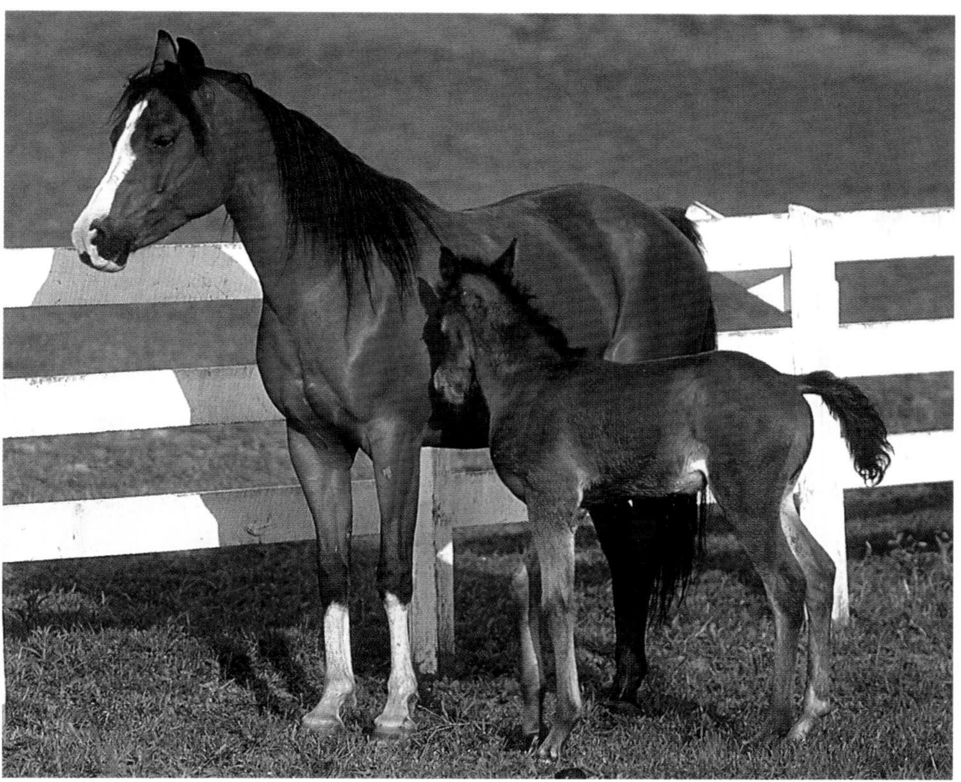

Staggers:

Severe and non-curable brain disease of the horse that is a quality fault.

Strangles:

Infectious catarrh of the airways in which the mucous membranes become inflamed.

Swan's neck:

Long and strong neck with a pleasing bend in the upper area. Horses with a swan's neck are often better for driving than riding.

Swayback:

Sometimes seen in older horses, when the back dips excessively in the middleBending of the spine downwards. Sway back can develops due to being ridden too early and can reverse itself again if the horse is left to 'rest' on the meadows.

Weak back:

(also back lameness)
Weak hind legs or swaying walk, often due to back disease.

Weaving:

Bad habit of the horse. It sways from left to right or vice versa inside its stable. Weaving is due to boredom and lack of exercise and can be 'infectious' to other horses. It can be avoided by moving the horse into a larger box and giving it enough exercise.

Whistling larynx:

Restriction of breathing due to inflammation or disease of the airways.

Windsucking:

Swallowing of air due to boredom. Windsucking can 'infect' other animals and is very undesirable.

Withers:

Central point of the body. Starting point for the shoulder and back muscles of the horse. The withers should be as high and long as possible, reaching well into the back. The horse's height is measured from the withers.

i love lucy
shes da best
lucy's betta dan da rest

she likes horses
don't know why.
she'll give johno
her cherry pie.

lucy and jezzo
what a bunch of bezzo's
is she a lezzo?
everyone thinks so

yeah yeah yeah
gay gay gay
wheres jamie gills?
have a nice punkin day

GET ON EH

ily girlfriend, fae jezzo.
X

KU-208-553

Lawns, Hedges and Fences/Volume Two

Collins Step-by-Step Guides

Lawns, Hedges and Fences

Volume Two

by Adrienne and Peter Oldale

Collins/Glasgow and London

Printed in Great Britain by
C. Tinling & Co. Ltd.
London and Prescot

SBN 00 435441 9

Contents

Introduction

It is not difficult to grow a lawn. Indeed, a presentable domestic lawn can be made in many places without using any seed, plants or turf, simply by keeping the natural wild weed grasses mown short!

Britain, with its relatively moderate temperatures, no great extremes of heat or cold, and with a moist atmosphere nearly all year round, is ideally situated for growing good lawns.

Yet many amateur gardeners expend much time and effort preparing a new lawn. As if grass were an exotic and temperamental plant, the ground is dug, weeded, raked, treated with weedkillers and fertilizers, often for months beforehand.

Then the expensive seed is scattered (meticulously measured to the tenth part of an ounce), and the resulting seedlings are cherished like delicate children.

This is all very well if unlimited time is available for gardening, or if the utmost perfection is aimed at.

But the majority of garden makers are not so keen.

They are ordinary men and women whose main aim is to build a lawn that will look green and pleasant at all times, will not be too difficult to maintain, will withstand the occasional rough children's game and does not cost the earth to make or look after.

This book does not set out to deal with the

perfect lawn, its building or its care. But what is given are full details about the making of domestic lawns which fulfil most people's needs and which will be cheap in time and money both to make and maintain.

In most new gardens, after the essential paths are made, the first gardening operation will be making the lawn, closely followed by either planting a hedge or erecting a fence.

Although open-plan gardens are now acceptable, it will be a long time, if ever, before the independently fenced plot disappears. Most of us prefer to have our own special plot, no matter how small, rather than an anonymous share in the finest of communal open spaces.

Boundary markers of some sort are usually provided by builders of new houses, at least for the rear gardens, but these are often cheap and crude. Replacing or improving these provides business for the makers of fencing and for the nurserymen who sell hedging plants.

In addition to the fence or the conventional hedge, there is now a pleasing trend towards the use of semi-formal screen plantings, often of flowering shrubs, which serve the purpose of a hedge without the hedge's uniformity and its need for regular, energetic maintenance.

The lawn and the boundaries account for much of the cost of any new garden. This book gives details of the main choices in methods and materials. Although no single volume could cover all the possible needs of every garden, we hope that most readers will find enough information to help them make a sensible plan within a budgeted cost, and carry out that plan in as easy and swift a manner as possible.

Tool Kit

Only good tools are worth buying. Cheap tools are a continual source of aggravation. They are also harder to use.

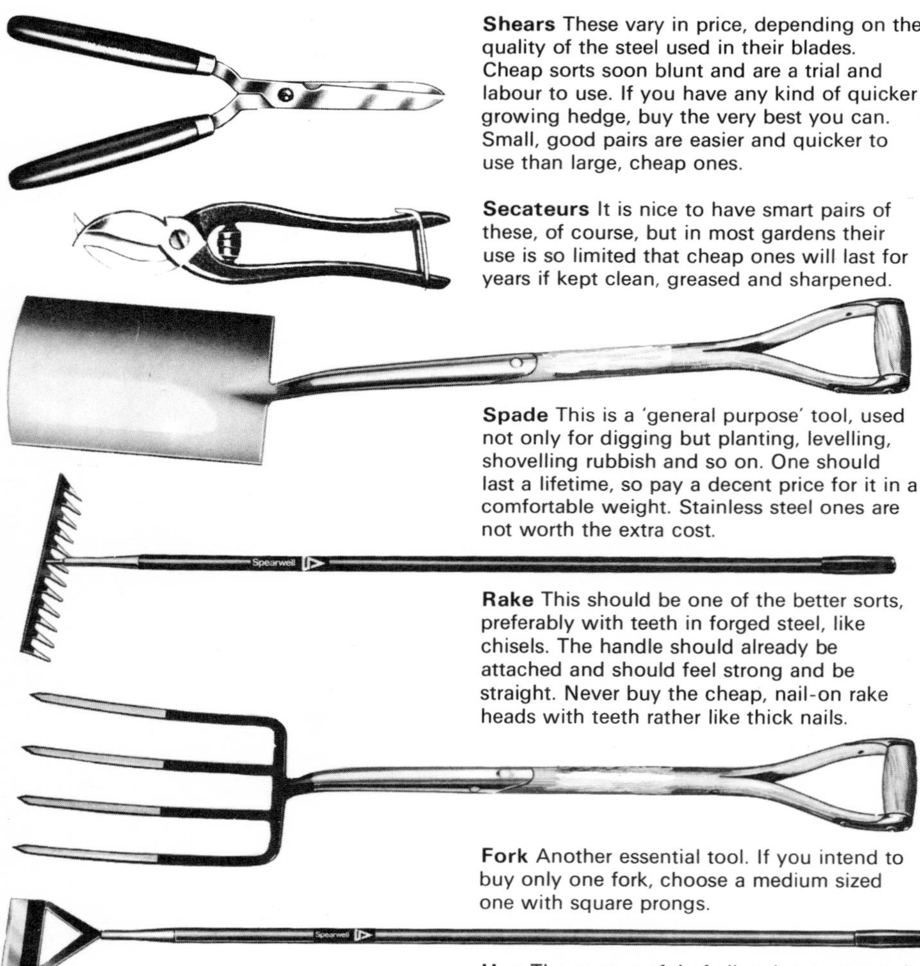

Shears These vary in price, depending on the quality of the steel used in their blades. Cheap sorts soon blunt and are a trial and labour to use. If you have any kind of quicker growing hedge, buy the very best you can. Small, good pairs are easier and quicker to use than large, cheap ones.

Secateurs It is nice to have smart pairs of these, of course, but in most gardens their use is so limited that cheap ones will last for years if kept clean, greased and sharpened.

Spade This is a 'general purpose' tool, used not only for digging but planting, levelling, shovelling rubbish and so on. One should last a lifetime, so pay a decent price for it in a comfortable weight. Stainless steel ones are not worth the extra cost.

Rake This should be one of the better sorts, preferably with teeth in forged steel, like chisels. The handle should already be attached and should feel strong and be straight. Never buy the cheap, nail-on rake heads with teeth rather like thick nails.

Fork Another essential tool. If you intend to buy only one fork, choose a medium sized one with square prongs.

Hoe The most useful of all maintenance tools. Cheap ones bend and are useless. Do not buy those pressed out of sheet metal. Choose one with a solid steel blade and neck.

Wheelbarrow You can get away for a long time with quite a cheap barrow in a small garden. In many cases a couple of buckets serve just as well. But for a largish plot try to buy one with a strong steel body and pneumatic tyres.

Only buy tools or materials when they are necessary to do a particular job. The shops are full of unnecessary oddments and gadgets.

Clearing the land: how to get rid of weeds

Most new garden plots are more or less covered in weeds. The first job to be done is to get rid of at least the worst of these. Sometimes the growth is so heavy that the soil is completely concealed.

There are several ways of tackling this problem. You can dig the weeds under. You can try to burn them off. You can dig them out and burn them in heaps, or rot them down to compost. You can even poison them.

Let us take these methods in order.

1 Digging them under. This is only possible if the labour of doing a proper job is acceptable. It is not simply a matter of up-ending the weeds in the soil. Many sorts will take this in their stride and will be sprouting busily again before the plot is completely dug! Weeds must be buried so deeply that they are deprived of all chance of recovery. This can best be done by trenching or double digging. The weeds are skimmed off with the spade and buried in the bottom of the trench and are then turned *under* the trench with spade or fork. Double-digging is shown on page 12. This method, though laboursome if the area is large, does result in the ground being improved both by the digging itself and by the rotting of the weeds. If you do intend to trench the ground then this is as good a method as any.

2 Burning the weeds off. This is generally useless simply because although the weed tops are burned, the roots, though shocked, will often recover soon. In some cases the burning may actually stimulate stronger growth! It is effective, though, where the weeds are mainly annuals, like Groundsel, that spring up from seed and die in one season. Flame guns are a handy, controlled, but slow way of doing this.

3 Digging them out. This is probably the best of all methods, especially if the weeds are then made up into compost. The whole plant is removed so that there is little left to regrow. Annuals or perennials are equally effectively dealt with. Moreover, compost properly made on a heap with the correct chemicals, makes a better food source and fertilizer than almost anything else. Better than where the weeds are dug in and rot underground. The snag is that this is the longest and most finicky method.

4 Poisoning them. This is quick, easy and effective. Of course you have to buy the poison and this is not cheap. There are several varieties, but generally speaking they are either the chlorate type of plant poison or the more modern systemic or hormone weedkillers.

Sodium chlorate dissolved in water will kill *all* plants over which it is generously poured. The poison remains in the soil for about six months during which no planting can be done. It is cheap (you can buy it in bulk from farm fertilizer dealers etc., much more cheaply than in small packs at shops). Though not poisonous to any degree, it is very inflammable and can explode if it is allowed to combine with some organic materials. Always keep it in tins, not bags or sacks, and use it all at once. It looks like sugar and a saved pound or two may turn up unidentified in later years.

The systemic killers are very effective. Some sorts kill *all* plants and can be used like chlorate. Others only kill grass or other special plants. The best sorts become inactive as soon as they touch the soil, though the *plants* which the spray touches will die. It is possible to plant ground treated with some of these killers straight away. This is a point best checked with the maker's instructions.

One must always realise that although these systemic killers are on public sale, and are generally perfectly safe if handled *according to the directions,* they are all in fact virulent poisons of one sort or another. Moreover, their long term effects are not always clear. Some disappear from the soil but may reappear in the water of rivers and streams. Others remain, apparently inert, in the soil itself.

Never store them other than in their original labelled containers.

If you use them at strengths other than those given in the directions you will probably do more harm than good. A hefty dose may have *less* effect on your weeds than the milder, correct dose.

We can say then that *digging in* is laboursome but effective; *burning* only handles annual weeds well; *removing and composting* the weeds is best for improving fertility and *poisoning* is quick, effective and easy, but unlike all the others, costs money.

Cultivating the land: why digging is necessary and how to do it

All garden plants depend on the soil for food. Some soils are more suitable than others for growing the plants we need. This suitability is a complex business. It is not simply a matter of the soil containing chemical plant foods. It must also be sufficiently porous to allow water to drain away freely and yet not so open as to become totally dry. Most garden plants do best where the spaces between the soil particles are filled two-thirds with water and one third with air.

To make a soil fertile, the first step is often to *cultivate* it by breaking up the natural large pieces into smaller, more easily-worked particles. This is particularly important on heavier lands such as clay, for they will retain so much water that many sorts of plants simply cannot live in them.

At the other extreme are the sands which need no cultivation to make them drain freely, but which must be dug nonetheless to mix in manures.

The two main methods of cultivation in use today in small gardens are digging and rotavating. No machine has been commercially produced that 'digs' in the conventional sense, like a spade, but the Rotary Cultivator has been very highly developed and gives similar results if properly handled. Few gardens are large enough to warrant the *purchase* of a large Rotavator but one can be hired, with or without an operator, to do special jobs.

As the prime object of cultivation here is to break up soil as far down as possible, it is obviously important to compare machine with hand digging. The *apparent* depth to which a machine digs is often greater than the true depth. However, the larger sorts on clay or the smaller ones on lighter land may do as good a job as hand digging.

There is no doubt though, that when a new garden is being made there are parts, such as rose beds or the run of hedges, where the greater depth normally reached by hand digging is essential. Double-digging, which we describe later, will give the best possible preparation for most purposes in small gardens. It is not necessary to do such deep work *everywhere*. As a rule lawns in well drained land need only 6 in.-deep cultivation. But double digging makes a good start in all places where shrubs, trees or perennial flowers are to be grown.

The most economic plan is to cultivate by rotavating or 'single-digging' the large lawn area, but to double-dig carefully all the flower beds and along the hedges.

There are many growers who never dig the ground at all. This is because they apply large quantities of compost—well-rotted leaves, kitchen waste etc.—to the ground surface. The compost gradually accumulates in a rich, soft and fertile bed whose rotting action gradually extends beneath the ground.

Surface dressings of peat may be given and should be heavy enough to improve the soil texture and to smother any germinating weeds.

All this is quite effective and can be adapted to small or large gardens. It takes time, though, and money. Time to prepare and develop the large volumes of compost needed, and money to buy peat in fairly large quantities.

In our opinion it is best to start off by giving a deep cultivation, and then to make as much compost as possible for future surface dressings. By using peat generously each spring, weeds on beds can be kept down and the need for future digging reduced or even removed.

Single digging simply means turning over the ground surface 8 or 10 ins. deep and breaking up the soil as this is done.

In late autumn or winter digging the lumps are not broken up but left in bulky ridges exposed to the frost. The water contained in the large clods is frozen, and expands to shatter the lumps into much smaller particles which are easily raked down in spring.

This depth of digging is too shallow to bury surface weeds, which should be skimmed off beforehand, or poisoned.

Although a spade is commonly used, a fork may be found easier at times. There is also a patented Terrex spade that is designed to reduce the effort of digging. In Britain the short spade or fork handle is commonest, but there are some gardeners who prefer the long-handled Continental tools which can be used without bending. Although these are made in Britain they are not generally obtained locally and must be ordered specially from manufacturers.

Double digging is planned to increase the depth of cultivation to about 16 ins., so that the underlying soil levels are broken up. However, a special technique is necessary because such deep-lying soil is always much less fertile than the top few inches. If the 'subsoil' is brought to the surface and the topsoil buried, the results are disastrous. Double digging keeps the subsoil below, yet mixes it with manures to improve its fertility.

1

1 Starting at one end of the plot, take out a trench about 10 ins. wide and deep. In narrow beds this trench will extend for its full width, but in wider plots for only half. Scoop the soil removed into a barrow for replacement later.
2 Next fork over the bottom of the trench, mixing in any available manures, especially natural rotted manures such as farmyard clearings or composts. Break the soil up thoroughly.
3 Now dig back from the first trench for 10 ins., using the spade to dig out the soil
4 and to drop it on top of the dug subsoil of the first trench.
5 This action will form another trench, the bottom of which is forked over. The plot is dug from end to end in this way, the soil removed from the first trench and put in the barrow being used to fill up the last trench.

2

4

3

5

Using a Rotavator is not simply a matter of wheeling it over the ground. Use a definite pattern of work, as sketched out here, to give even digging without underground ridges developing. Do not attempt to reach the full depth of digging in the first pass across the ground. Two or three inches deep may be all that is possible on heavy land. Second and subsequent passes will deepen the digging as desired. Continuous working in one direction only will tend to result in subsoil ridges. These can be avoided by changing direction several times. Rotavators commonly *appear* to dig deeper than in fact they do. This is because they 'fluff up' the soil behind them above the original ground surface. The true depth can be checked by leaving a strip of soil undug, and using this as a guide.

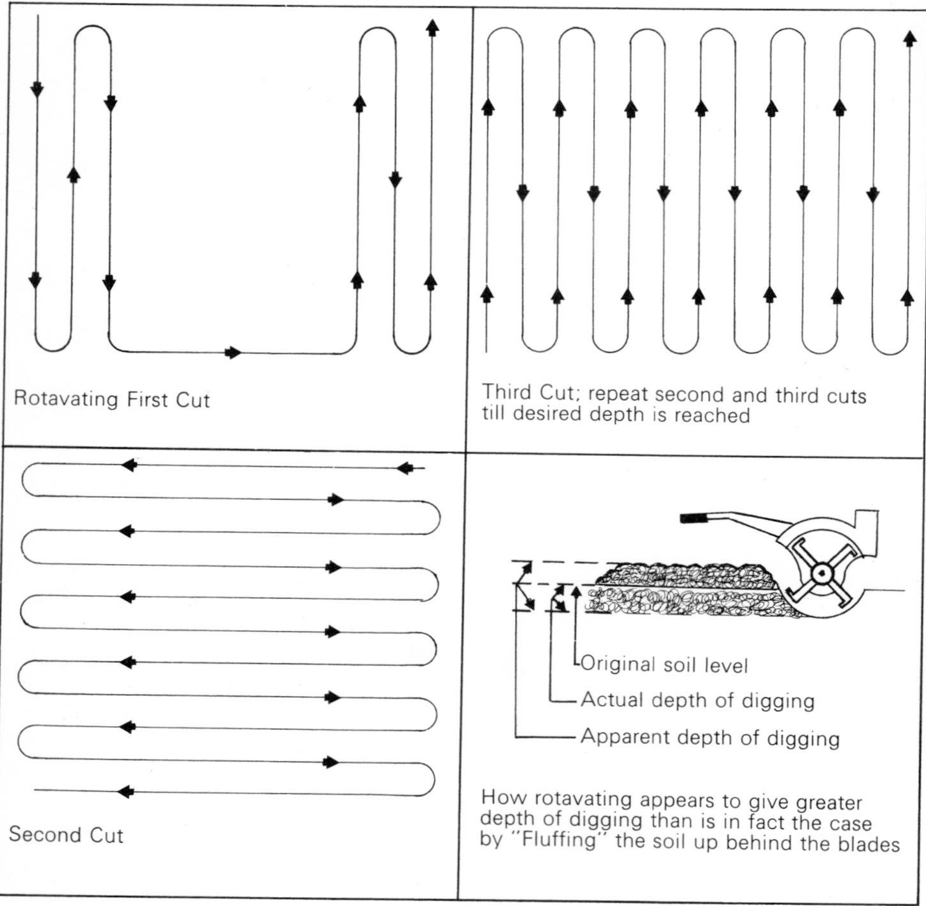

Rotavating First Cut

Third Cut; repeat second and third cuts till desired depth is reached

Second Cut

How rotavating appears to give greater depth of digging than is in fact the case by "Fluffing" the soil up behind the blades

Facts about fertilizers: chemical and natural, and testing the soil

There are two main sorts of fertilizers, the chemicals and the so-called natural fertilizers. The first are ordinary manufactured chemicals. The second are manures such as cow manure, stable manure, various composts, leaf moulds and peat.

The gardener's purpose in using fertilizers is to improve the soil and thereby feed his plants.

Plants live solely on *chemicals*. If 'natural' manures are given, the plant extracts the raw chemicals from the soil and the manures. If 'chemical' manures are given, the plant may feed off these directly. The result is the same though chemical fertilizers may be more swiftly absorbed.

It is not desirable, though, for the home gardener to rely solely on chemical fertilizers because plants need a wide range of foods, and many of them are not available commercially. Although such foods are often only used in tiny quantities they are quite vital to the plant, just as minute traces of vitamins are essential to human health.

The great advantage of 'natural' manures is that they tend to contain a wide range of plant foods and also supply the traces of minerals which the plant needs, and which may not easily be given in any other way.

Another reason for preferring 'natural' fertilizers is that they usually have secondary but important effects on the soil itself. They give it better 'structure' by encouraging beneficial bacteria to live in the soil and by improving its drainage or its water retaining properties. In clay, the straw in manure may open out the land and allow freer drainage; in sand, the same manure gives the soil extra bonding or 'sticking' power, thus preventing the water from running away so quickly.

Finally, due to certain compensating reactions that take place in the soil, it is practically impossible to *over*dose with natural manures, but it is all too easy to overdo the chemicals, which may only be needed in fractions of an ounce per square yard.

It is all very well to talk of the advantages of natural manures, but in many parts of the country they are very difficult to obtain. Chemicals are essential under such conditions. The best compromise might be to apply chemicals judiciously, being at the same time more generous with dressings of peat, and saving all domestic refuse for the compost heap.

Of course there are many gardens which are never treated with *any* fertilizer, chemical or natural, and the soil may have such deeply developed fertility that the plants grow well in it. But there is no doubt that plants—weeds or cultivated—do take food from the soil and unless there is some replacement then the goodness of the soil gradually declines. This may show itself by poorer growth of plants, greater difficulty with weeds, or even a slow change in the *kinds* of weeds present.

One fertilizer is almost universally known, even though it is not a plant food in the usual sense. This is lime. Most of our plants prefer the soil in which they grow not to be too *acid*. Yet in the course of nature, most soils get progressively *more* acid. Lime corrects this tendency. The exact amount that any particular soil may need varies a good deal and cannot be judged from the appearance of the ground. It is a question that can really only be decided by chemical tests.

Making up a compost heap

Fortunately this testing is very easy, calling simply for the placing of a pinch of soil in a glass tube, the pouring over it of a liquid which will change colour, and a comparison of the resulting colour with a printed chart. This will indicate how much lime should be scattered over the soil. The whole job takes only a minute or two. Kits to test soil for lime needs are sold at seedsman's shops everywhere now and are quite cheap, so this test can be made every year.

More complicated kits, working on the same principle but still quite easy to use, tell what amount of chemical fertilizer a soil needs. These kits are a good investment, especially where natural manures are scarce. No knowledge of chemistry is needed.

There is one sort of soil which will never need lime, and this is the strongly *alkaline* soil usually found near the great chalk hills of the South. Applying lime to this soil might in fact do it considerable harm. A test will usually show that no lime is called for, but occasionally, even in chalk country, a soil will be found, lying *above* the chalk, that is slightly acid.

Some firms of fertilizer manufacturers offer soil testing services and do these very well.

To sum up, then, all soils need fertilizers of some sort. Most need lime at times. Testing kits can be used to show how much lime or other chemicals are required.

Raw chemicals are powerful, simple to handle and easy to buy.

Natural manures have wide-ranging good effects as well as being more tolerant of error. Compost from house waste costs nothing and makes excellent manure.

Simply stacking up house refuse and garden waste will not make good compost. To rot down quickly and fully, a heap needs a proportion of soil and preferably a supply of nitrogen, given in raw chemical form.

Start by digging out a shallow, broad trench about 6 ins. deep. Many gardeners lay a criss-cross layer of sticks at the bottom of the heap to allow air access.

Spread the waste evenly about 6 ins. deep. Then scatter a layer of ordinary soil, 2 ins. or so deep, over all the waste and start another layer over the first. In this way soil and waste alternate in the heap. The rotting can be speeded up by spreading a handful of sulphate of ammonia evenly over the waste before the soil is spread on. A proprietary rotting medium, containing bacteria, is also helpful though not essential.

When the heap is finished it can be covered with soil and left for several months before use. Rotting can be speeded up by turning the heap over completely and re-stacking it, after two months. In most soils, a sprinkling of lime over each layer of soil will help to make good compost, of the correct acidity.

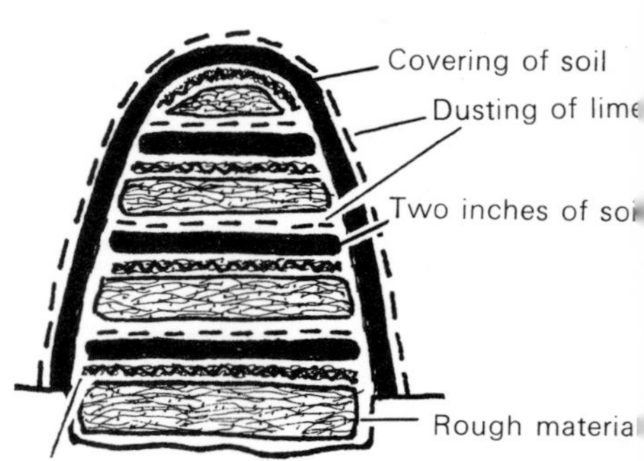

Note: On heavy or badly-drained land build heap at ground level; not in trench.

Drainage: why have a drain, and simple methods of installation

Not all gardens need full-scale drainage systems.

There are many, however, that lie waterlogged for large parts of the year. This is not only bad for the plants, but can be very uncomfortable for the house owner.

The part of the garden which suffers most from bad drainage is the lawn. Grass soon thins out if it is always wet, and mosses or even coarse, reedy grasses may get roothold. A lawn that is always wet is useless to walk, sit, or play on.

Yet it is very simple to instal drains, preferably *before* the lawn is laid out. If there is a suitable outlet nearby for the water, such as a ditch, this is fine, but the usual outlet in small gardens is the 'soakaway'.

This is merely a hole dug deep enough, 4 ft. is usually ample, to carry the water into the subsoil. The soakaway is filled up, not with soil, but with porous material, rocks, stones, broken bricks, gravel and coarse ash. The draining channels are led into the soakaway, sloping gently towards it and the water percolates downwards and away. Some people imagine that a soakaway in some way *holds* the water, like a catch pit. This is not so, for such a pit would soon be full to overflowing. But the ground below 4 ft. is nearly always rather porous and water can run away into it.

Although the photographs show pipes being installed, and these are certainly best, trenches filled with stones or even with tree branches laid lengthways and covered over with soil or shingle, will provide drains good enough for a few years service. It is usually enough to have drains 15 ft. apart at their widest. They may all flow directly into a pit, but in large gardens they should be arranged in a 'herringbone' pattern, with a number of branches running into a 'main drain' which in turn runs into a soakaway. See diagrams on p. 18.

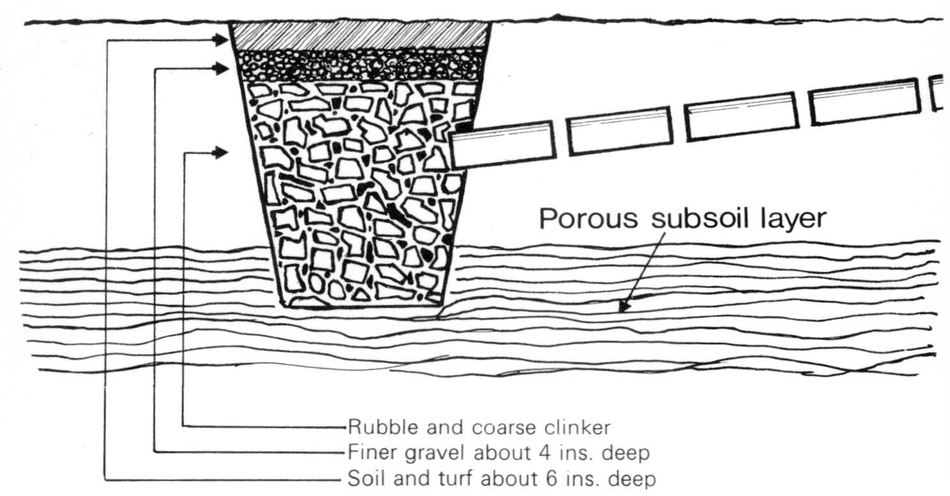

Diagram of a lawn soakaway

Fan-Plan drainage

Herring-bone drainage

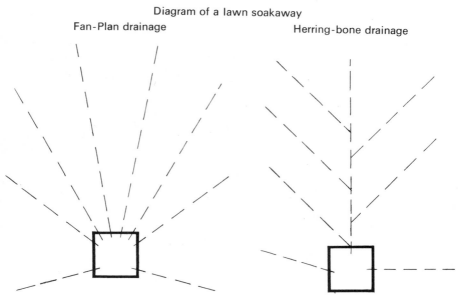

1 Pipe drains made with these 'land-tiles' are best. Simply lay the pipes end to end. They are not cemented together.
2 Check the pipes for even slope by sighting along the tops of three 'boning rods'. These are simple T-shaped wooden frames about three feet tall. Get assistance to hold the other two upright on the pipes. If the cross-pieces coincide then the pipe-run is even.

3 Pack the sides of the pipes with small stones to prevent them shifting and also to allow water to pass into them through the joints.
4 Spread a shallow layer of small stones or gravel over the pipes before refilling with soil. Leave the soil slightly mounded over the pipe, to settle naturally. Do not tread it back hard or the soil may be so compacted that water will not reach the drain beneath.

1

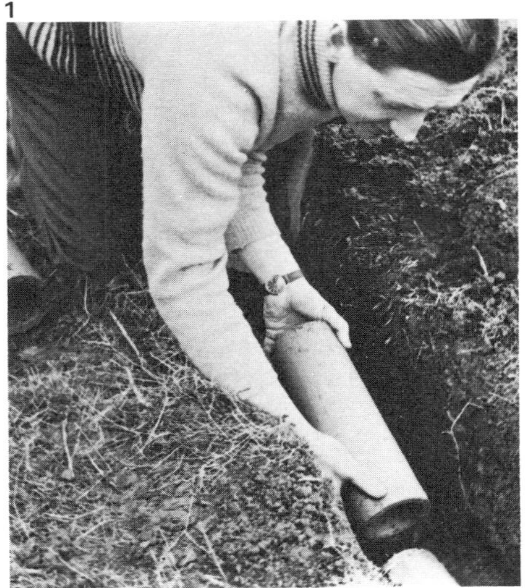

2

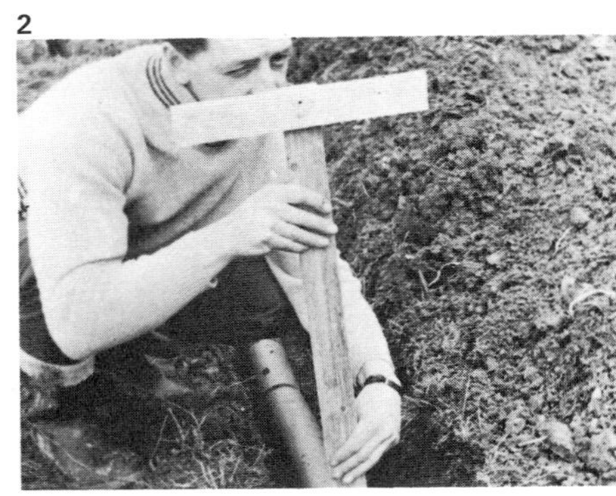

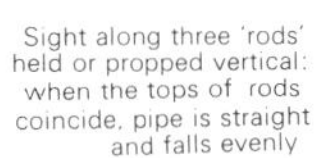

Sight along three 'rods' held or propped vertical: when the tops of rods coincide, pipe is straight and falls evenly

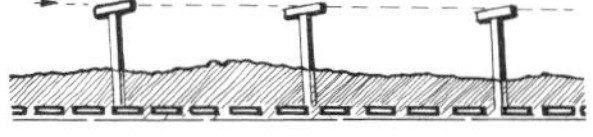

3

4

1 Making a lawn: what a lawn is, and the usefulness of weeds

Lawns are easy to make. In fact they sometimes make themselves, for if any land is left uncultivated for a year or two plenty of grass will be found amongst the growth of weeds.

Many lawns in Britain are in fact made up of common native grasses, carefully mowed every week. They may have been carefully sown with expensive seeds, but gradually, over the years, the natural varieties have crept in till, with their native vigour, they have quite eliminated their more cultivated cousins.

Yet the lawn seems to cause a great deal of work to many gardeners. They spend much time in soil preparation, go to great lengths first with the choice of seed, and later in the after-care of the sward.

Is all this trouble necessary?

It all depends on what you want. If you intend to cultivate a perfect, weed-free, rich, fine lawn like the finest of bowling greens, then certainly all this work, and more to follow, will be needed.

Even if you could be satisfied with a sward not quite so impeccable, but still of that smooth richness and evenness that the 'best' lawns show, then again a lot of work is needed. For the vast majority of us a lawn that does not approach such perfection will be quite suitable. We want a lawn that is green, neat, with few weeds, that takes little maintenance and that stands a little playing of children or neglect for a week or two at holiday time.

In this case, the making of a lawn can be very much simplified.

Starting with the ground preparation, grass does not need deep digging. In fact if the soil is free of weeds and relatively easy to rake, it need not be dug at all. Many new homes are provided with roughly spread out topsoil, which can be raked flat and sown with seed without more ado. If the surface is too hard for this, it may still be possible to dig very shallowly, 6 ins. or so, and then to break up the soil as finely as possible before scattering the seed.

Lawn preparation is a good job for rotavating digging because the very fine, fluffy result rakes down easily to a good seedbed.

If turves are to be used for the lawn then the preparation can be even simpler, as a really fine seedbed will not be called for. It is enough if the soil is firm and flat because the turf will soon root down. Stones and so on may be left in the ground with advantage, especially on heavy land, for they help the surface drainage.

Simplest of all is to put neither seed nor turves down, but simply to get the soil surface level by any convenient means, and then allow the weeds to grow! As these sprout upwards, mow them off with a rotary type

mower and carry on with this as frequently as possible. Of all British weeds, only the grasses and a few others such as clover, daisies and buttercups can tolerate frequent close mowing. The taller, more vigorous sorts soon get discouraged, leaving the field clear for the creeping types, and the grass.

Once these have all got a good hold, three or four sprayings with a selective hormone weedkiller (one that kills weeds but leaves all grasses unharmed) will result in a rapidly developing sward of grass. Wild grass, true, but perfectly serviceable for domestic lawns. This method is very useful where a large rear garden is to be put down to grass under orchard trees or as a play area.

We shall not be dealing with the making of ultra-perfect lawns, but we can say that of the other methods that seeding is relatively cheap, is light work, needs careful seedbed making and is rather slow; turfing is quick—you can use the lawn at once—rather heavy work and much more expensive, but nearly always successful; growing grass straight from the rough is quite practicable, costs nothing but the effort of mowing and applying a little weedkiller, and it does not take as long as you might think. We have made a good grass sward in this way, in a country district, inside three months.

A LAWN MADE FROM ROUGH GROUND

1 A vigorous growth of rampant weeds is a good sign of reasonable soil fertility. A small rotary mower will slash down a growth like this very rapidly indeed. It is best to rake off the cut-off weed leaves on the first few occasions. Later, they can be left on the ground.

2 After a week or two of close mowing the native grasses will start to thicken between the weeds. Broad leaved sorts may be dug out individually. . . .

3 but a really clean sweep can best be made by using a selective hormone weedkiller at intervals of three or four weeks.

4 The resulting grass may appear rather coarse at first but soon becomes much finer as the height of cutting is reduced. Constant mowing can transform grass like this into a respectable lawn without further attention. Any humps and hollows must be dealt with as described later.

A LAWN MADE WITH SEED

1 After shallow digging or rotary cultivating the ground should be well raked out to a fine, crumbly state. It should not, however, be *soft*.

2 Systematic treading of the whole area between rakings will ensure that at no place does one sink in when walking over the surface. Gradually, a perfectly flat, smooth and firm surface, with a fine top soil layer, will be formed. Never rake out in wet weather.

3 The actual sowing may be done in spring or autumn, with a slight balance in favour of September. To ensure easy and even distribution mix the required amount of seed (usually 2 oz. per sq. yd. for ordinary seed) with about double that volume of sand. Choose a sand that is coloured differently to the soil of the plot.

4 Very fine seed may be used at as little as 1 oz. to the sq. yd. but the sand gives 'bulk' and eases distribution. Make sure that the seeds are evenly mixed with the sand.

5 Scatter one quarter of the seed by hand, as evenly as possible. The sand will show up 'thin' parts. Work to and fro over the plot. Then take a second quarter of the seed and scatter it too, but working at right angles to the first sowing. The third and fourth quarters are done in diagonal pattern. It is advisable to save a little seed to fill in sparse patches later. (See over for diagram.)

1

2

3

4

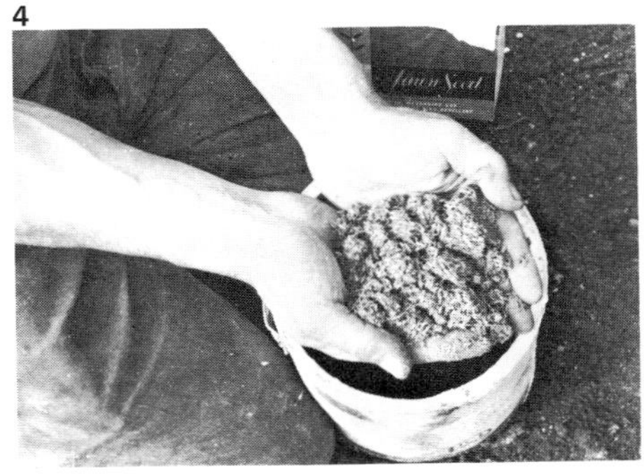

5

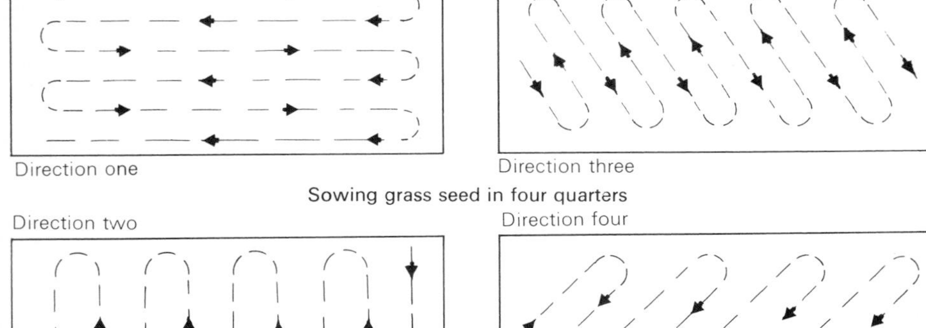

Sowing grass seed in four quarters

6 As each batch of seed is sown, rake the surface very lightly till the sand disappears. It will then be just below the surface.

A lawn made from turf: the importance of water and the importance of time

1 Turves may be delivered folded or in rolls. Make sure you have a strong and comfortable wheelbarrow ready when it is delivered, for delivery will usually be to the roadside.

2 Where the barrow has to pass over dug ground or newly laid turves, put down a few strong planks to ease the pushing and to prevent making unsightly ruts in the ground.

Winter is the best time to make a turf lawn as there is only one thing that will cause a turf lawn to fail—*drought*. Provided that turf has adequate water it is very unlikely to die. It is very difficult, though, to give it enough in summer, for new turf will absorb gallons of water per square yard.

The actual work is simple, calling only for making the ground flat and firm as described for a seeded lawn, but with less need to provide a very fine seed bed. Then the pieces of turf, usually 3 ft. long by 1 ft. wide, are placed on the ground and pressed gently down.

However, the sheer weight of a large area of turf has to be considered when planning the job. A lawn about 20 yds. by 10 yds. would need 600 turves, weighing anything up to about 7 *tons*. All this weight will have to be wheelbarrowed onto the site, lifted from the barrow, unfolded on the ground and beaten flat. Not a job that can be tackled single-handed at a weekend!

Although turves can in fact be left stacked for a week or more without suffering too much harm, they will certainly turn an unpleasant yellow and take several weeks to recover. Also, any weeds in the turf seem to withstand this treatment better than the grass itself!

If you have to keep turf for a day or two, try to open it out to the light. Better still, order your turf in several loads rather than in one lot.

Most lawn turves sold today are simply ordinary farm meadow, mown down and treated to discourage weeds. It is rarely grown specially. Meadow turf can be made into a good lawn, given time and patience.

1

2

3 In warm weather, and always in spring and summer laying, have a drum of water ready to soak each turf thoroughly just before laying it.
4 As each turf is laid, give its bed a final raking . . .
5 place it close up to the others . . .
6 and unfold it on to the soil.
7 Make sure that the ends are closely butted up to the next turf.
8 Heavy beating is not needed. Hand pressure followed by a light beating with the back of the spade, is adequate.
9 Turves are always laid 'bonded' like bricks in a wall. Sometimes if the weather becomes very dry after layout, the turves will shrink to leave gaps. Do not move the turves, but fill up the gaps with fine soil. Do not mix grass seed with this soil. The adjacent turf will soon grow out into the gap and seed is likely to be a different type to that in the turf, perhaps even of a slightly different colour.

3

4

5

6

7

8

9

Grass growing on slopes

There are several ways of dealing with a steep sloping part of the garden. These include providing supporting walls, rockeries, sloping beds and grass. All sorts of wall or rockwork are very expensive, and beds on slopes are subject to erosion, with the rains slowly washing the surface soil downwards. Grass, if well established on slopes, will hold the soil and the only maintenance required is mowing.

Although one can use an ordinary mower quite successfully here, the best is the air-supported Flymo machine which is so light and easy to control that it is even possible to lower it down a steep bank and swing it from side to side, thus mowing the grass without walking on the slope at all.

Establishing grass on slopes is not so easy if seed is used, as it takes some time to develop a good root-mat. Turf is ideal, and will soon knit together. In really steep parts this turf may also be reinforced with wire netting, or staples.

1 The slope is treated exactly as a flat bed until the area is raked perfectly flat. Then the turves are unfolded vertically on the slope.
2 'Staples' are desirable if the slope is greater than about 1 in 2. Take lengths of thick galvanised fencing wire, about 2 ft. long and fold them in the centre.

1

2

3 Press both legs of the staple into the turf. Each 3 ft. by 1 ft. turf will need three staples.
4 A hammer may be needed to drive the staple in the last few inches.

5 On really steep or unstable slopes, especially in wet areas, wire mesh can be unrolled over the surface and stapled down. The staples must be closely spaced to prevent upward bulging of the netting. Diamond-mesh 'chain-link' netting is even better, but more expensive. Close mowing should not be attempted on a netted slope.

3

4

5

Lawn maintenance: mowing and feeding, dealing with weeds, rolling and draining

For domestic lawns in normal use the most necessary maintenance is, of course, regular and frequent mowing. Where the ground is reasonably fertile it could well be said that the quality, fineness and richness of a grass sward will depend on the frequency of mowing.

When grass is sheared off at the tips of its blades, the plant's natural reaction is to throw out new blades from the base. This results in thickening of the individual grass clump and reduces the average age and size of the blades. Grass left unmown till reaching 3 ins. or more will not have this thickening tendency to the same degree and any small new blades that do develop will be over-shadowed by their taller neighbours. When such tall growth is finally cut down, the base of the grass is often found to be very sparse, each blade stump being broad and coarse.

The quantity of grass clippings removed from a lawn, even a small lawn, in the course of a season can be very large. Assuming 30 mowings, and an inch taken each time, makes 30 ins. of grass. Over ten years, then, 25 ft. of grass will have been removed, weighing several *tons*.

It is doubtful whether the average lawn receives anything like the amount of lawn fertilizer required to compensate for this large removal. It is this large and continuous removal of fertilizers that so often results in a gradual decline in the quality of lawns.

If mowing is continued, frequent and close, the recovery powers of the grass are reduced and fewer young grass blades grow to thicken the sward. This weakness of growth then opens the way to intruders such as clover, moss, daisies and so on.

Grass, well fed and watered and growing on fertile soil, is one of our very toughest garden plants. It is generally able to deal with weeds simply by smothering their seedlings and by not offering any vacant space for them to develop. The first requirement after frequent mowing, then, is adequate *feeding*.

Twice yearly dressings of fertilizer should be the minimum, and it is best perhaps to use proprietary mixed materials rather than raw chemicals, since it is not easy to strike a happy balance with these. Whatever the make purchased, always follow the maker's recommendations carefully (never giving more than the recommended dose) and aim for the most regular possible distribution. One maker offers the free loan of a small mechanical distributing tool with its fertilizers.

One chemical that may be stored in raw form for the lawn is sulphate of ammonia which is quite safe in use and can be given in very small doses of $\frac{1}{2}$ oz. per sq. yd., or even less. This can be done every month and will lead to a marked improvement in greenness and richness. Never allow thick patches of any chemical to lie on the grass. They will burn the blades. Brush the lawn over with a broom after every distribution of fertilizers.

Weeds are less of a problem these days for there are many special weedkillers that will remove the commoner weeds without harming the grass. These 'hormone' weedkillers act by causing the weeds to develop deformities, and often seem to stimulate the weeds rather than kill them. This effect soon disappears. It is important not to *exceed* the dosage recommended by the makers for sometimes a larger dose kills the weed leaves so rapidly that the poison has no time to find its way to the roots. These then survive to send out more leaves shortly afterwards.

These excellently effective weedkillers are often unjustly described as ineffective by gardeners who have not used them to best advantage. There is no magic in them and their proper use is a matter of common sense. Do not spray when rain is imminent for the rain will wash off the spray, or so dilute it as to weaken it. Do not, conversely, spray in blazing heat, for the spray will dry off in minutes and a plant can only easily absorb *liquids*. Do not spray at seasons when the weeds are *not* vigorously growing, for the killer's effect depends on acting on the plant's growth. The faster the weed is growing, the more devastating the effect.

With all this too, remember that these sprays will affect a large range of ordinary

LEVELLING HUMPS IN LAWNS
1 Dig a broad cross about 2 ins. deep over the centre of the hump.
2 Slide the spade roughly 2 ins. below the surface and lever the turf up between the cuts.

garden plants, even when the amount of the chemical is very small. Do not use sprays, then, when the wind can carry the fine wet mist onto nearby beds of plants.

Levelling humpy lawns is a fairly constant chore, for most ground moves a little through the years by the expansion and contraction of the soil itself. Hollows of up to 2 ins. deep can be dealt with most simply by filling them in with fine soil, applied in layers of an inch, through which the grass beneath will soon push its new growth.

Raised humps must be skimmed off, roughly an inch deep, a little soil beneath removed, and the turf replaced.

Worn patches can be replaced with new pieces of turf bought specially, or better, with pieces of the same lawn, trimmed from a suitable place, perhaps by widening a bed or taking off a corner. It is hard to make a perfect match with new turf or seed.

Rolling lawns is little done nowadays, for the average lawnmower, used frequently, will keep the ground flat enough. Hard, consolidated soil is very bad for grass, anyway. If the mowing is done entirely by a rotary mower, without a roller, then perhaps an *occasional* roll may be useful.

Drainage is most important for lawns for no grass except the very coarsest will survive long in waterlogged ground.

A most important part of good lawn care is spiking and sanding, especially if the pipe or rubble drains described earlier are not present.

This is simply driving a tool into the lawn surface to make holes several inches deep. The holes are filled up with coarse sand with perhaps a little fertilizer mixed in. These holes act as tiny drains to the lawn surface and give the grass roots adequate air. Making the holes *without* filling them with sand is a very partial job and hardly worth while because the holes soon squeeze together again. Sand keeps them open. Examining a spiked lawn usually shows markedly better root growth near and in the holes. Lawns deeply and frequently spiked are also less susceptible to 'burning off' in hot weather.

1

2

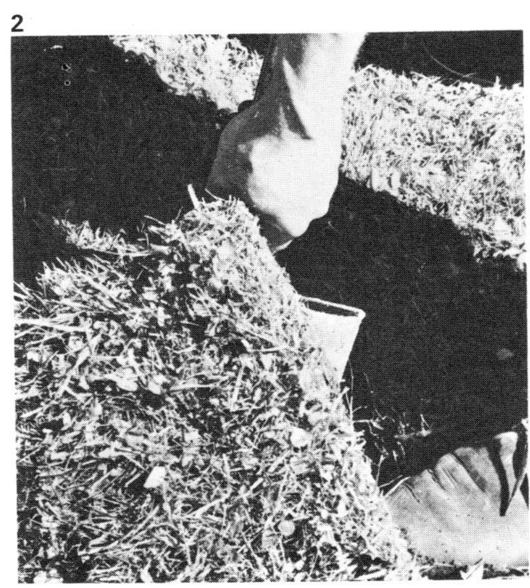

3 Scoop out the soil at the centre of the hump.
4 Replace the four quarters of turf, pressing them firmly down level. Lift them again and adjust the soil till they settle flat. Do not dig over the exposed soil.

3

4

REPLACING A WORN SECTION

1 Dig a cut 2 ins. deep round the worn section or hollow.

2 Slide the spade 2 ins. under the turf.

3 Scatter a layer of sharp sand or very fine soil into the turf bed.

4 Lay the new turf, or replace the old, and butt all corners well. Fill any gaps with fine soil well pressed into place. Drench the repair with water and keep it moist for at least 10 days in warm weather. Repairs done in winter will not call for this as the ground will be already moist.

1

2

3

4

SPIKING AND SANDING

1 An ordinary, preferably broad pronged, garden fork can be used to make the holes in rows about 6 ins. apart. There are special tools which actually remove a thin core of soil, leaving a clear hole. They are very good for this work. The removed soil is placed on compost heaps.

2 Coarse sand (not necessarily lawnsand; ordinary clean, washed sand will do and is much cheaper) is scattered generously over the lawn surface.

3 Brush all the sand into the holes and repeat the dressing until these are filled up to the brim. After a couple of days add more sand because the first filling is likely to have settled somewhat.

1

2

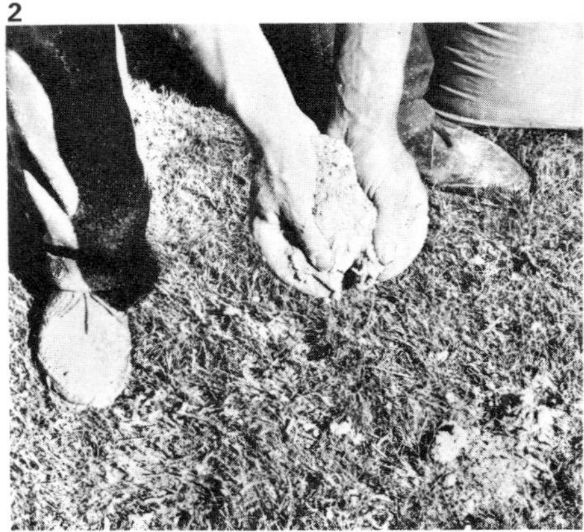

3

Grass under trees

No grass will grow happily in deep shade. There are certain species that will tolerate less light than usual, but even with these the first job to tackle is giving extra light. Cutting a few branches from an overhanging tree may greatly improve the light beneath without the shape and appearance of the tree being ruined.

Heavy drip after rain will also affect the grass and will also tend to consolidate the soil so that it becomes hard. The grass roots will then find it increasingly difficult to penetrate.

Perhaps most of all, a giant tree will certainly remove a good deal of the plant food chemicals from the soil around, so it is of great importance to replace them for the grass to use.

Spiking the ground beneath trees and filling the holes with a mixture of coarse sand and a general mixed fertilizer will do a lot for the grass. If the light is not too bad a reasonable sward should be obtained. Do not mow grass under trees as frequently or as short as that on open lawns. A rotary mower used fortnightly at 2 ins. high will often be about right.

Lifting and shifting turf

Few gardens remain permanently unaltered in design and a change in the lawn shape may call for the removal and replacement of part or all of the turf. This job is often a source of difficulty and the final result may be anything but neat. To be well laid turf must be perfectly even in thickness.

It is not possible to lift turf with a spade in perfectly regular pieces. Some will be 1 in. thick, some will be 3 ins. thick, and so on.

Sometimes one may find a farmer with a field which is to be ploughed, and where the turf is acceptable for lawnmaking. Again lifting must be done accurately to give turves which can be used with ease and speed.

1 Cut the surface of the turf into squares about 1 ft. each way, digging the spade 2 ins. deep.

2 To make the turves even in thickness you will need a 'box' which is simply a sheet of plywood or similar material, with strips of wood nailed round it. The box should be about 1 ft. sq. and exactly 1¼ ins. deep.

1

2

3 Lift each square of turf, more than $1\frac{1}{4}$ ins. thick, and lay it grass down in the box.
4 Press the turf firmly right to the bottom of the box.
5 Then with an old table knife or sharp scythe blade laid across the wooden sides of the box, slice away the soil.
6 This will leave a turf exactly $1\frac{1}{4}$ ins. thick, the depth of the box.
7 Stack the square turves grass blades to grass blades, soil to soil. Lay them again exactly as described under 'turf lawns'.

3

5

4

6

7

2 Fences and screens: some hints on buying materials

A fence may have more than one purpose. It may be intended simply to mark out an area. It may be to keep animals—or humans—out or in. It may be purely decorative. It may be designed as a screen to block off a view.

Which fence to choose in a given garden, then, will depend on which of these needs is the most important. Costs will come into the question too, as will ease of erection and maintenance.

Whatever the purpose, though, one consideration will be paramount; the need for secure posts. A fence that sags or falls down is an aggravation at all times and may be worse than no fence at all. In the following pages you will first find details of the most usual ways of erecting posts. Then details of the different types of fence that may be erected on those posts will be given.

The various indications of costs given are to be taken only as general guides, for much will depend on local conditions. In some areas it is possible to collect fencing direct from the maker's own yards, which will obviously save a good deal in transport charges. When buying from nationally known concerns the costs may be higher, but as a rule the standard of work is consistently high. It simply is not worth while for such firms to send out badly made goods, for they depend to a great extent on personal recommendations to maintain their sales. Because of large scale production, though, it does sometimes happen that an inferior fence panel slips through. If this does happen, our advice is to write a pleasant letter addressed to the Sales Director of the Company concerned, detailing what is wrong and asking for a replacement.

At least one major firm sells excellent

1 This is a post hole borer. The tip has a spiral digging screw.
2 Screw the tool into the soil, drawing it out after every 6 ins., bringing the soil with it. Holes up to about 3 ft. may be drilled easily, except of course if the borer strikes rock or very large stones.

1

2

ready-cut timber sets for all kinds of fence and they can be relied upon. They are exceptionally easy to erect and save a lot of time, though they are not cheap.

Fixing the posts

Any fence is only as strong as its posts. Not only must the wood, concrete or metal be suitable and adequate in thickness, but the post must be deeply and solidly planted in the ground.

Making the hole, especially on heavy ground, is the real labour of fence erection. If the work is to be done with a spade, do not try to make the hole too narrow. It is very difficult to dig a hole of say, 8 ins. diameter with an ordinary spade. It is quicker to start at once with a good sized hole, about as big as a bucket. Its sides can then slope a little, so that by the time that the usual depth of 18 ins. is reached, the bottom of the hole will be quite small in diameter. Such holes are ideal too when the posts are to be set in concrete, for the security of this method largely depends on the sheer weight and solidity of the concrete.

For posts that are only to be driven into the soil, a post hole borer costing a pound or two will save time and effort. It will take out holes only a few inches across with the minimum of fuss. It is easy to get adequate depth. The holes made are so narrow that a substantial post may almost fill them up, and little extra ramming is required. Such a tool would be a useful investment for a group of neighbours, all with fencing problems.

3 Every post, even those of supposedly rot-proof woods, will benefit by the protection of painting with a wood preservative. This must thoroughly cover the whole of the cut end of the post, for it is here that underground rot most frequently starts. Continue the paint up to a little above soil level. If time allows, stand the posts to soak in the liquid for some days.
4 It often pays to insert a half-brick or stone into the very bottom of the hole. This will prevent further direct contact between wood end and soil.

5 A baulk of timber makes a good rammer for consolidating the earth around the post base. Fill a little at a time, ramming each layer tightly before adding more filling soil.
6 Spade-dug holes are easiest made rather wide, roughly the size and shape of a bucket, but 18 ins. or more deep. They are very good where concrete is to be used to bed the posts. Place a generous shovelful in the hole.
7 Stand the post in place and tip more concrete around it, working it well down with the shovel.

8 Though a concrete layer only 1 ft. thick will hold the post base quite well, the upper part of the hole being filled with soil, it is certainly best to use concrete right up above ground level if possible. Then the top surface is smoothed over into a neat 'crown' to let water run away from the wood. Rot started by wet is commonest near this point, and cement rounded off like this will help to delay it.

9 End posts and gateposts, as well as posts along any long run of fencing, should have support struts attached. These are best concreted into the same hole. Dig a trench 18 ins. deep and spread a layer of concrete 8 ins. thick in it.

10 Place the post and its leaning strut into the trench and work more concrete round them.

11 Finally bring the concrete up the posts to give a post and strut that will withstand all likely strains for a lifetime.

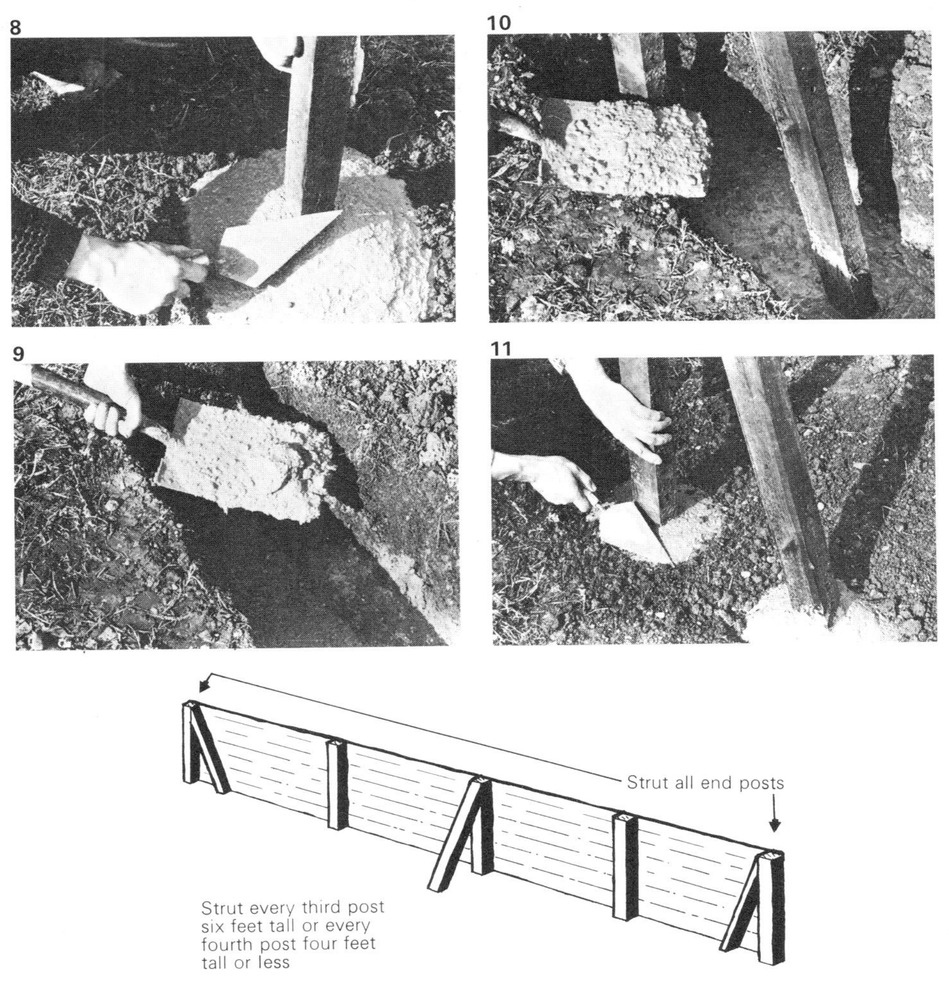
8
10
9
11
Strut all end posts
Strut every third post six feet tall or every fourth post four feet tall or less

Straining wires

Wire fences are usually only used to mark out boundaries of plots, but they also serve as a basis for other fencing such as netting. The posts are rammed or concreted in place and two or three thick galvanized wires stretched tightly between them. Wooden posts must be drilled but concrete ones will have holes provided in the casting.

1 Mark the height of the wire by a scratch on the post and bore through with a brace and bit or a power drill, a hole roughly ⅜ in. diameter.
2 You can buy these eyed straining bolts at any good hardware dealer. Remove the nut provided, then thread the bolt through the hole you have drilled.
3 Run the nut on to the thread. Then take the end of the straining wire and pass it through the loop.
4 Twist the wire end tightly around itself several times.
5 On the struts and other intervening posts, drive in large steel staples over the wire but not tightly. At the other end of the fence fit a second eye strainer and twist the wire into it.
6 Use a spanner on the nut to draw the wire taut. These eye strainers have a 'pull' of about 3 ins. each, enough for most short runs of fence.
7 For longer stretches of strainer, tensioners such as this are used. Cut the wire and twist its ends around the end-loops of the tensioner. Then twisting the centre portion will draw the wire ends together and so tauten the wire.

5

6

7

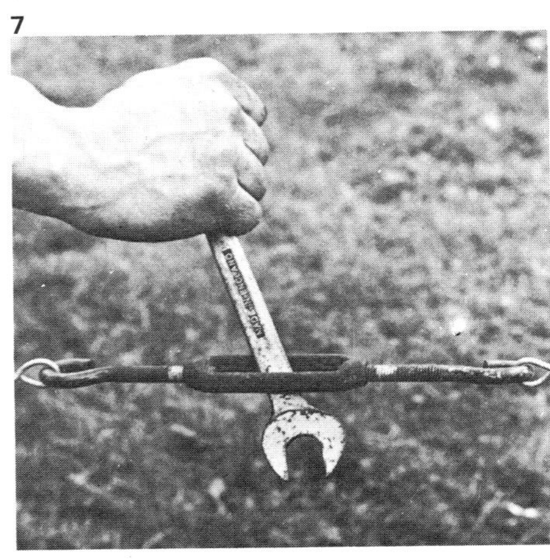

Chainlink Fencing: materials, cost and methods

The best netting fence to use is that known as 'chainlink' because it is considerably stronger than the conventional 'wire netting' and will not stretch or lose its shape. The diamond mesh is proof against dogs, cats and children.

Materials

Usually galvanised steel. There are some makes with a coloured plastic covering, which are certainly better for garden use. Although the size of the diamond mesh itself is usually the same, there are differences in the thickness (gauge) of the wire used. It is bought in rolls and is not willingly cut to short lengths by dealers.

Cost

Depends on height, which may be from 2 to 4 ft., thickness (gauge) and length bought. Three ft. high, galvanised, 14½ gauge is about 5/6 per yd. roll. Plastic coated in similar gauge about 7/6 per yd. run.

Methods

Erection may be on wooden or on concrete posts. On wooden ones, the essential point is that the netting must be nailed in place at *every* loop of wire at the roll end. Due to the manufacture of this netting, failure to do this will result in rapid sagging and collapse. Chain link is supported on two or three straining wires as in the last section.

On concrete posts, special attachments are made for the fitting of the netting. At the roll end, a steel strip is passed through all the loops of the netting, and then bolted to the end post. Straining wires, attached to the posts by wire loops or sometimes passed through specially provided holes in the posts themselves, support the netting.

Occasionally metal posts are used. Special attachment methods, roughly similar to those used with concrete posts, but often having spanner-tightened stretching devices are required. These should be examined at builders' merchants for there are several different types.

1 Apply the roll end to the post and staple it tightly. Note that every loop must be stapled.
2 The netting is unrolled against the straining wires, and attached to these with twists of fine galvanised wire at intervals of about 1 ft.
3 The netting is cut to length by withdrawing a single cross-wire, because in chain link the mesh is made up solely of zig-zag cross wires spiralled together.

1

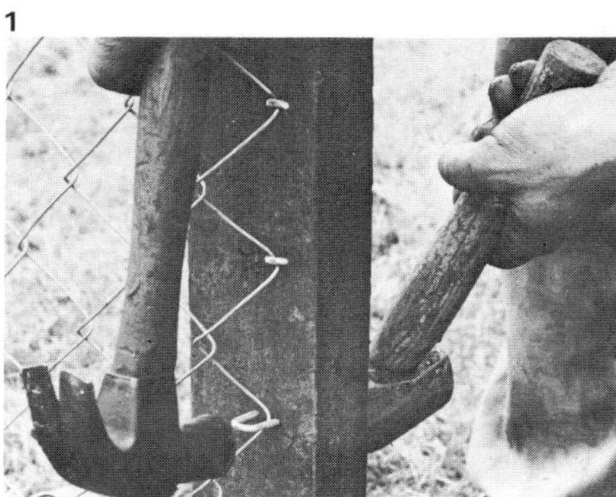

2

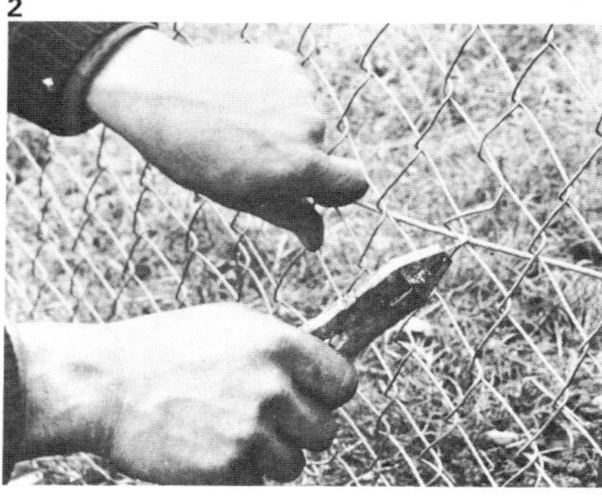

3

4 Concrete posts are precast with notches or slots in which supporting struts can be inserted.
5 Intermediate posts have holes through which wire is passed and looped around the straining wires before the netting is applied.
6 The netting is drawn taut by a steel strip thrust down through all the loops at the end of the roll.

7 These steel strips are bolted to angle-brackets which also carry the straining wire tensioners.

4

7

5

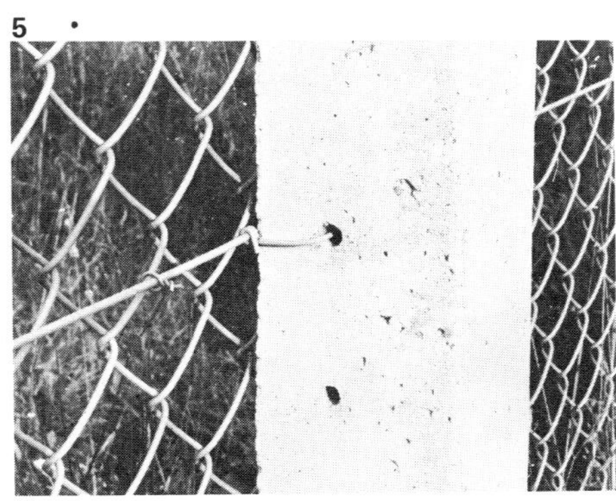

6

Wire Netting: materials, cost and methods

1 Attach the top edge of the netting to the upper straining wire by twists of thin galvanised wire.
2 A wooden cross rail in place of straining wires gives a more permanent job. If this type is maintained by regular painting it will give long service.

The conventional soft wire netting with its six-sided mesh is the cheapest and most generally used of all the netting fences. Available in a wide range of sizes and thicknesses of wire, it is proof against animals when new. It does not wear well, soon stretching out of shape or rusting, but is often used as a temporary boundary especially where a hedge is to be grown.

Materials
Always galvanised steel wire in various thicknesses. The size of mesh varies widely from less than 1 in. to several ins. In width, too, the rolls vary a good deal. Most dealers will cut off lengths shorter than a full roll of 50 yds.

Cost
Depends on the wire thickness (gauge) and the size of the mesh. The thicker the wire and the smaller the mesh, the higher the cost will be. Two in. mesh in 19 gauge 3 ft. wide will probably cost about 4s per yd.

Method
It is possible to mount wire netting without straining wires by simply nailing it directly to the posts. It is far better, though, to provide straining wires along the top edge and at least one other half-way down. The base of the wire netting may either be attached to a third straining wire or buried a few inches in the ground to discourage tunnelling animals. The netting is held to the straining wires by twists of thin wire. A more permanent fence is made by providing a wooden frame with cross rails to which the netting is nailed. This greatly increases the cost.

1

2

Wooden Trellis: materials, cost and methods

1 Cross rails are nailed securely to the posts, which must all be well painted. If the post timber is soft, use woodscrews instead of nails.
2 Tap the points of the nails with a hammer before use. The blunt point will break through the wood fibres without splitting the timber.
3 Top and bottom rails will be enough for fences up to 4 ft. tall. Over this height use a third rail in the middle as well.

More of a true garden fence than any of the nettings, trellis is not used a great deal today except where wear is not likely to be great. It cannot withstand strong wind pressure for long, and the thin wood means that children and animals may break parts off easily. It provides good support for climbing plants but if these are of the permanent variety then their presence can hinder the painting that is essential for long life. It is ideal where a light and decorative screen is needed, in an unexposed position, and on which annual climbers such as some types of nasturtiums can be grown. The strength depends almost entirely on the strength of the supporting posts and rails.

Materials
Softwood, in various widths. Some are already treated with preservative. If not, some sort of painting must certainly be given or the trellis will soon rot. All supporting timber, especially in the joints and the cut ends of the wood, must be treated with creosote or other preservative.

Cost
Not high for the actual trellis. A length of about 8 ft. (expanded) by 3 ft. tall would cost about 23/–. The supporting timbers are likely to cost much more than the trellis, if a sound structure is to be given. Posts should be 3 ins. by 3 ins. or 4 ins. by 2 ins., with cross rails about 2 ins. by 1 in. In softwood such timber is likely to reach an average of 12s. a yd. run of fencing.

Methods
Erection is simple, merely requiring nailing the trellis to the cross rails with oval steel nails. It pays to blunt the points of these before use to avoid splitting the thin wood.

1

2

3

Ranch Style Fencing: materials, cost and methods

For modern houses this type is excellent in appearance and will keep larger animals out (or in). It is far from child-proof, being singularly easy to climb! Its good appearance depends largely on proper maintenance of the paintwork. Though very strong and permanent it is expensive, especially in hardwoods.

Materials

Usually softwood rails fastened to hardwood posts, but sometimes also made all in hardwood or in cedar. There are manufacturers who have recently produced plastic extrusions for use in fencing. This material never needs painting and appears to withstand outdoor conditions very well indeed. Plastic is fairly expensive but may become cheaper as production increases.

Cost

Moderately high. The well-planed, smooth and straight planks needed are not cheap and, with oak posts, a 3 ft. high fence may cost about £2 per running yd. When considering costs remember that the wood will normally need three or even four coats of paint, one primer, two undercoats and a gloss. This may raise the cost to a point where plastic becomes cheaper, for this needs no painting at all. Fences more than about 4 ft. tall will also need extra thick posts and struts because the rails are heavy.

Methods

Erection is very straightforward. Erect the posts first, using concrete. Allow these to set thoroughly (about four weeks if possible) before mounting the rails. These are simply screwed to the front face of the posts. Use thick screws threaded through holes drilled in the rails. These holes should be large enough to accept the shank of the screw freely. Countersunk screws are commonest, the head being carefully painted. Joints in the rails are made at the posts.

Paling Fences: materials

As with Ranch Style, palings depend for their effect on the maintenance of the paintwork and on perfectly regular and even placing of the timbers. Plastic extrusions are used for this type too, and give good results. The commonest material is still timber.

Materials
Often entirely softwood, or with posts only in hardwoods. Plastic extrusions and mouldings are available in different styles and colours.

Vertical Closeboard: materials, cost and methods

This is certainly one of the most satisfactory of all fences, being strong, permanent, peep-proof, animal- and child-proof and good looking. Unfortunately it is also one of the most expensive. It is at its best in cedar, which requires no maintenance, but may be made in softwoods of other types, preferably with oak posts.

Materials
Any timber, but the posts must be substantial for this fence is heavy.

Cost
High. If a large fence is contemplated it is probably best to consult one or two different timber dealers to get quotations. Though the price per ft. run of wood is not likely to vary much, some merchants will give better service, to get the order, by sawing the various pieces exactly to length. This will save a great deal of labour.

Methods

Posts and two rails are erected in the usual way. The boards are simply nailed vertically in place, overlapping their neighbours by about $\frac{1}{2}$ in. A top rail over the cut ends of the vertical planks is quite essential to protect the cut-end grain, or rot and splitting will soon occur. All the timber should be treated with preservative before erection for it is impossible to do this correctly after completion.

Steel Mesh Panels: materials, cost and methods

Steel mesh such as is used for the reinforcement of concrete is on the market in panels several feet long, and covered in green or white plastic. These offer a very swift-erecting, modern style fence that wears very well. It is proof against large dogs but children can climb it. The posts should be secure but the weight of the panels is not great so their attachment can be very simple indeed. If the posts are simply in rammed earth this type of fence can be erected quicker than any other.

Materials
Steel mesh, plastic covered, in panels 8 ft. by 4 ft. and some other standard sizes. Cutting may be done with a hacksaw but should be kept to a minimum as the ends will rust if left unpainted. Otherwise, no maintenance is required. Posts may be in soft or hardwood.

Cost
Considering the very long life and versatility of these panels they are not dear. (They can be used for trellis on walls, and can be easily shifted later if need be.) An 8 ft. by 4 ft. sheet might cost about £2 10s.

Methods
Posts are erected the correct distance apart and the panels are attached by large galvanised staples. These should not be driven in so hard as to cut the plastic. Rather, use a larger number at intervals of about 6 ins. A capping of timber 2 in. by 1 in. improves the appearance a good deal. The mesh is stapled to this, too, underneath.

Panel Fencing: materials, cost and methods

Panels of thin wood, woven or overlapped, are probably the most used of all 'solid' fences today. They are simple to mount on soft or hardwood posts and withstand a fair amount of wear. They keep out animals, cannot easily be climbed and some sorts (not all) are peep-proof. In exposed positions they can suffer from high winds, the panels occasionally disintegrating, but the commonest faults arise from negligent erection or failure of the posts.

The panels are made in various sizes. There are quite marked differences in quality that are not always apparent at first glance. The 'weaving' boards should be straight-grained, free from splits and from too many knots, and properly held to the edge frames. All panels must be treated with preservative except those made of cedar.

Materials
Softwood or cedar throughout, with hardwood posts if possible. Some special makes are designed to suit concrete posts. Posts should enter the ground by at least one third of the panel height with a minimum of 18 ins. Flexing or shifting of the posts causes the panels to be pulled out of shape and these then collapse shortly afterwards.

Cost
Panels 3 ft. high and 6 ft. long may cost between £1 and £2 each, with oak posts priced at roughly 11s. for one 4 ft. 6 ins. long. Cedar will be dearer but is a much better material and needs no maintenance.

Methods
Panels are simply nailed to the posts. It is

best to blunt all nails as the framing is usually thin and may split if sharp-pointed nails are driven through. Screws can be used, but there is little advantage in this slower and more expensive method, for these fences rarely fail at this point. Many panels vary a little in length from their advertised sizes, making pre-erection of posts difficult, but this can be got over by using the erection method shown below.

1 Erect the first post and place the first panel against it along the proposed fence line.
2 Drive in a post hole borer or dig a narrow hole under the corner of the panel.
3 Drop the second post loosely into this hole, raise the panel and thrust it closely against the first post. Raise the panel on bricks clear of the ground if a space is to be left.
4 Now nail the panel to the first post.
5 At the other end of the panel, lift the second post up to meet it and check that it is aligned correctly.
6 Then nail the panel to the second post.

1

4

2

5

3

6

7 Finally ram the second post tightly and remove the supporting bricks. Then repeat the operation with the second and subsequent panels.
8 At corners, nail the panels to adjacent faces of the posts.
9 To make a fence with invisible posts, especially with the peep-proof 'overlap' types of panel, nail these to the front face of each post. First apply the panel half-way across the post face.
10 Then nail through at an angle through the rear panel frame only. (Nails thick and long enough to drive right through both front and rear panel frames will certainly split the wood.)
11 Similarly, apply the adjoining panel and finally nail the two panels' front frames to each other.
12 At corners, nail the panel frames to adjacent faces of the post, concealing this completely.

7

10

8

11

9

12

13 Posts may be cut off to a suitable height *after* erection. This is easier than trying to attain exact equality at the time of erection. Use a scrap of wood as a guide to get the heights equal.
14 Never leave the end-grain of the posts exposed to the rain. Nail capping pieces in place, or cover the tops with thin zinc sheet.
15 For a flush-capped fence, or to strengthen one that has sagged out of line, remove the upper capping from the panel frames.

16 Then saw the posts flush with the panel tops.
17 Pull the fence panels exactly into line.
18 Replace the capping strip but place its centre on the post top and nail it down. Then nail it along the panel tops, too. Thus the strip 'bridges' two adjacent panels and keeps them in line. You will need a short length of timber of similar shape to the capping strip to give the extra length needed to bridge the posts.

13

14

15

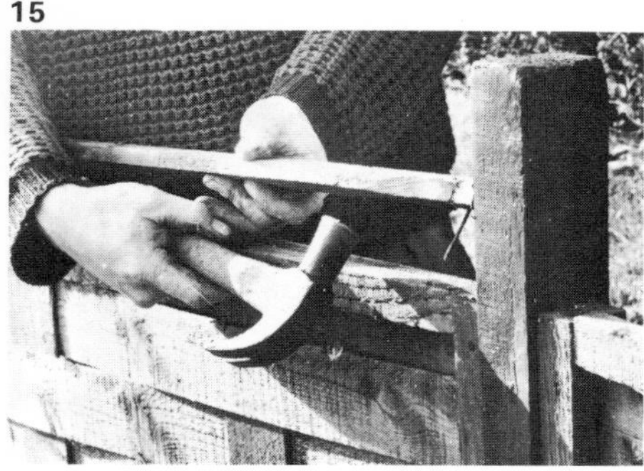

16

17

18

19 Special concrete posts are made in different designs. All must be strongly set in concrete, not rammed in earth. This design has side slots in which the panels slide, held by their own weight without any other attachment.
20 This type is simple to repair by inserting a new panel to replace an old one but requires precise placing of the posts or the panels will not fit tightly.

19

20

Fences on slopes

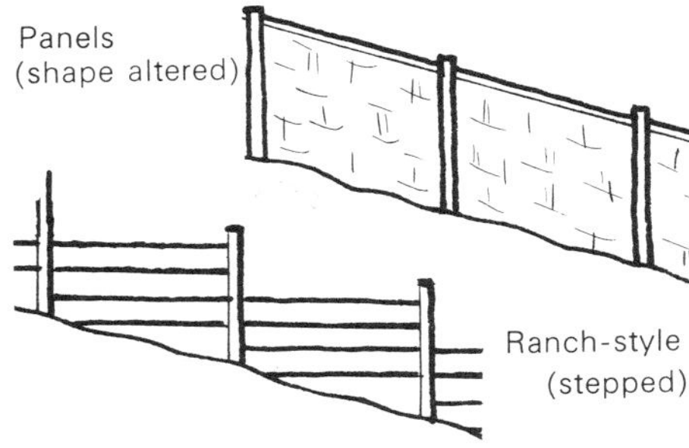

Any fence, especially the panel type, that has to pass up a slope poses problems. Any sort of netting can simply be unrolled up the slope and nailed to the posts, but these posts *must always be vertical.*

Ranch style, too, is easy, the rails being screwed in place on the vertical posts in the normal way. Palings should always have the upright strips vertical too.

It is not possible to erect the steel-mesh panels on a slope, except in 'stepped up' form with posts and panels rising in tiers.

Wooden fence panels may be erected in tiers, using shorter panels than normal. This will leave triangular spaces at the base of the fence to be filled with nailed-on footboards.

Woven wood panels can often be reshaped into a diamond pattern by loosening the frame attachments and sawing the plank-ends off neatly. In this shape they will fit to vertical posts up a slope without leaving any gaps at ground level.

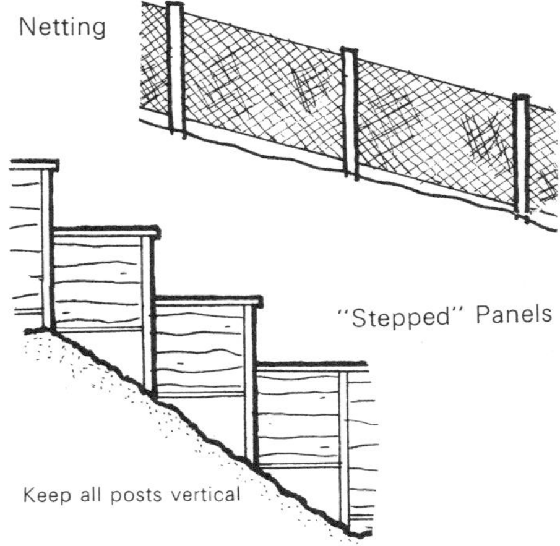

Clothing a fence: the choice of plants

Not all fences are things of beauty and one of the most attractive ways of dealing with this problem is to clothe them in flowers.

This solution has problems for it makes painting and repairs difficult, but occasionally the climber will take over so successfully that it serves adequately as a screen on its own.

The vigour of growth that a climber puts out comes from the soil, and it is essential that this is dug deeply, and given plenty of compost or manure when the planting is done. After this, an annual surface mulch of compost will keep the plant in trim.

Three examples show what can be done.

Honeysuckle can be trained to smother a fence in a riot of heavily perfumed blooms.

Climbing roses of many varieties are available, some, such as the old favourite Zephyrine Drouhin, being thornless. Always tell your supplier that you want the plant for a fence. He will then supply a vigorous grower, with prolific blooms.

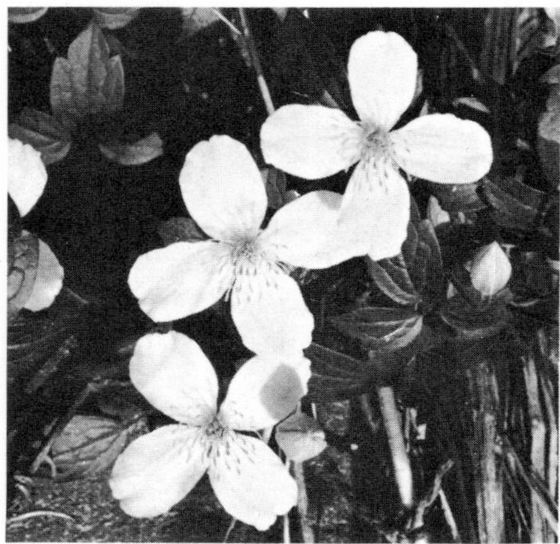

Clematis of the more vigorous sorts, especially the smaller-flowered Clematis montana rubens group, can be used for fence covering. They may need some work tying in, but established plants bloom profusely.

Other plants that might be grown are climbing Forsythia (yellow), some of the Cotoneasters, many with bright berries, Wisteria, Virginia Creeper etc. Avoid Russian Vine (Polygonum baldschuanicum) for its tremendously swift growth will soon get out of hand.

A SELECTION OF LESS USUAL FENCES

1 Plastic Netting (not wire covered in plastic, but plastic all through). It has much to commend it for garden work, being light, rot-proof, decorative in colour and very strong. At present it is too expensive for general use but the price may come down as more is produced.

2 Purely as a decorative boundary marker, a chain slung on posts can be attractive. Besides the original iron varieties, these chains are now made in plastic, needing no maintenance.

3 Imaginative fences may be made from many materials, such as this fine row of retired farm wagon wheels.

4 For a fence which is also a handrail, and can also be erected up slopes or at the sides of steps, use steel tubing as sold for builders' scaffolding, locked together by Kee Klamps. These joints are made without difficulty at home, and may be easily dismantled.

1

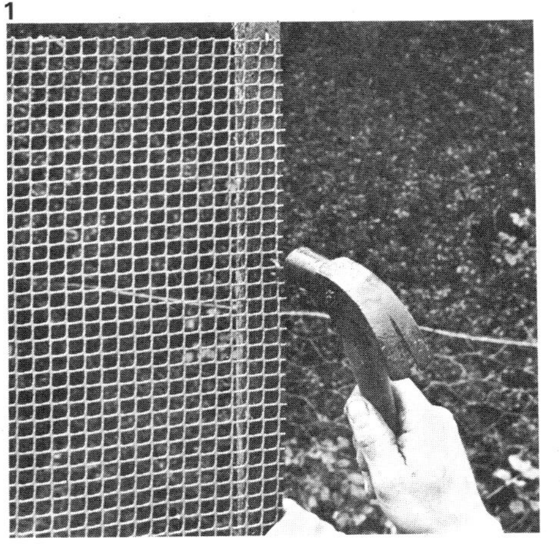

3

2

4

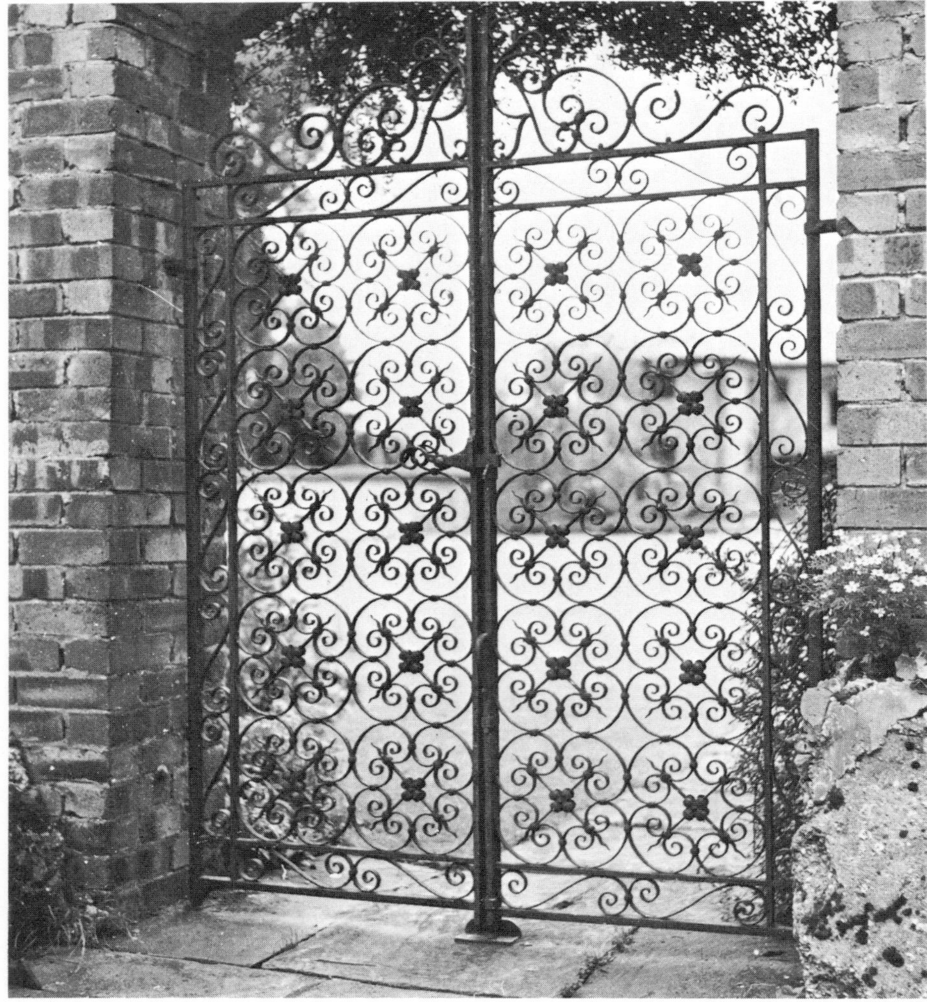

3 Garden Gates: the importance of fixing the posts correctly

Garden gates are made in innumerable designs in wood, iron or plastic. They are all hung in much the same way. Some are mounted into walls, or on brick pillars. For these, the larger Rawlplugs fixed into holes bored into the cementwork can be used for for attachment of the hinges. Since gates for such positions are usually 'made to measure' the job is usually quite simple, with the exact details differing with the make of gate.

For the usual garden gate mounted on posts, the problem is basically to get the two gateposts into the right place, at the right spacing from each other, and in such a way that they will stand up to a good deal of wear.

Simply driving in the posts, no matter how

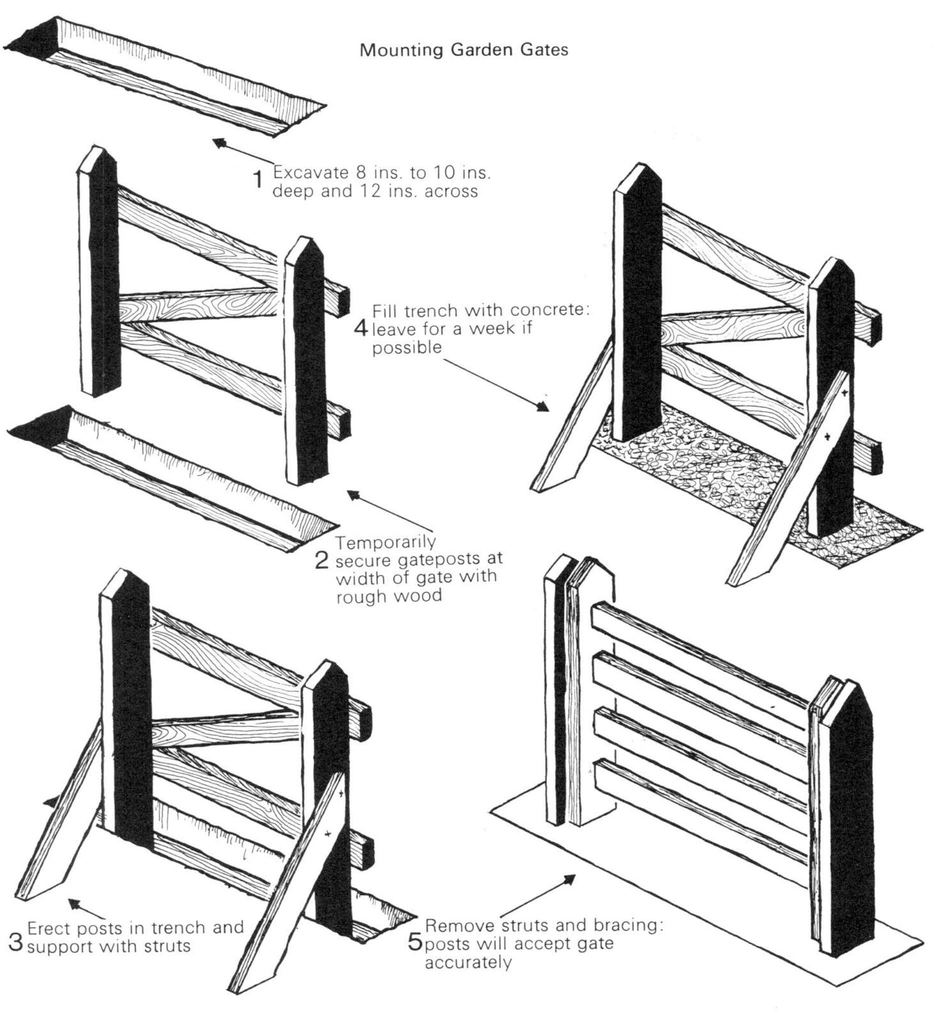
Mounting Garden Gates
1 Excavate 8 ins. to 10 ins. deep and 12 ins. across
2 Temporarily secure gateposts at width of gate with rough wood
3 Erect posts in trench and support with struts
4 Fill trench with concrete: leave for a week if possible
5 Remove struts and bracing: posts will accept gate accurately

well done, will in time lead to them sagging apart, making the gate askew.

The best method is to concrete *both* posts together in a trench dug across the gateway opening. The concrete beneath locks the posts so solidly that only an earthquake could shift them!

The sketches show how this may be done, with both posts fastened temporarily together while being erected. In some cases the gate itself may be mounted on its posts and fastened securely as the concreting is done.

Do not use the gate more than necessary in the four weeks after erection. Leave it propped open. This will allow the concrete to set properly.

Making a Garden Gate-Box

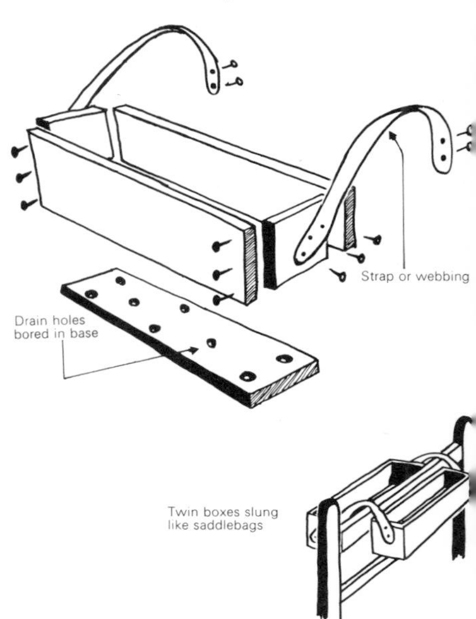

A charming and unusual feature can be made to suit any gate from a few old planks of wood nailed together in the shape of a long narrow box, about 6 ins. deep and across, and a little less wide than the gate.

Holes bored through the base will give adequate drainage (an important point), and the box can then be slung over the top rail of the gate by leather straps. If only one box is made, the straps can have holes made in them. These holes are arranged to fit over thick screws driven into the rear of the gate top rail.

Alternatively, and even more attractively, you can use *two* similar boxes, 'back to back' on the same gate, slung across the top rail like saddlebags on a horse.

1 Many plants fail through having poor drainage in their container. Spread a layer of clean stones or gravel over the box base, about an inch deep.
2 Fine soil, compost or peat can be used to fill the box. Peat alone has no food value for plants, but if kept moist will support pot-grown annual plants for some weeks. These can then be changed for new ones.

3 Knock the plants from their pots but do not disturb the root ball. Press the peat firmly round them.
4 If soil is mixed 50/50 with the peat, other plants such as the trailing Lobelia, Celosias, etc., can be grown, to make a very colourful display. In winter, put in pot-grown ivies, with spring bulbs thrust beneath for a March or April display.

4 Hedges: soil preparation, planting and the advantages of different types

As an alternative to a fence, or sometimes in addition to one, the hedge is widely popular. In fact few countries in the world have as many hedges as Britain, both in farms and gardens.

Since a hedge is merely a row of bushes placed in a continuous line so that they grow to touch each other, almost any shrub can be used to make one.

Usually, though, a hedge is also trimmed to a formal shape and some bushes do not thrive on this. Others make rapid growth after trimming and soon become thick impenetrable screens.

Over the years several species, each with their special virtues and defects, have become established as hedging plants. The choice will depend on the desired appearance, cost, speed of growth and ease of maintenance.

Preparation for hedges is the same in all cases, for the plants will remain in the same soil indefinitely and it is in the nature of things difficult to give fertilizers to an established hedge, except on the soil surface. Accordingly, as much deeply placed manure as possible must be incorporated along the hedge site before planting is done. Otherwise growth may be weak and irregular.

In the following pages the main hedge plants are shown and described in detail.

Good preparation of the soil is vital for all hedges. The plants will remain in the same spot for many years and it will be impossible to improve the soil later by deep digging in of manure and so on. Remember too the great amount of growth that will be removed over the years in the trimmings, all of which will have to come from the fertilizer resources of the soil beneath. Failure to give good deep cultivation and adequate manure may often result in the hedge plants' roots seeking food well away from the line of the hedge thus affecting plants in nearby beds.

Such care will also reduce the risk of odd losses among the plants, losses that are obviously more difficult to make good than if the shrubs were in open ground. Gaps appearing in a hedge ruin its entire purpose.

First take out a broad shallow trench, perhaps 2 ft. wide and 10 ins. deep, setting the soil aside.

Scatter all available compost, manure and so on, and a generous dressing of coarsly ground bone meal, within this trench. Then fork the trench base as deeply as possible.

Finally replace the original soil, incorporating bone meal here too.

PLANTING

Hedge plants are cheapest if bought from rows grown in the open ground of a nursery, though there are great advantages in buying more expensive plants grown in containers. The risk of loss is then almost eliminated.

For 'open ground' plants delivery is usually taken in late summer for evergreen types and during late autumn or winter for the deciduous varieties. Evergreen planting is also sometimes done in April.

Planting simply involves taking out a hole for each plant large enough to accommodate its whole root-spread without crushing. Hold the plant by its stem and fill in between the fine roots with soil, trying to ensure that this soil is evenly spread between the roots, and that these are pressed tightly to the soil. The result should be that the plant is at the same depth it was in the nursery as shown by the soil mark on its stem, or perhaps very slightly deeper. When all the soil has been replaced, tread it firmly with both feet, till it can be held even against a firm pull. Loose planting is the commonest cause of failure.

After the hedge is complete, spread a 1 to 2 in.-thick layer of compost or peat over the root area and soak this thoroughly in water. This mulch will maintain moist conditions around the roots during the first few weeks which are specially important with evergreens.

In windy, exposed areas it also pays to place a number of short posts at intervals along the hedge at both sides, with wire or tough cord stretched along them. This will help to restrain the new plants from whipping in the wind which would loosen the grip of the roots. Frost, too, may lift the ground and after the cold snap is over all the soil must be firmly trodden back.

When planting, it is important that all the fibrous roots are well spread out in a hole large enough to accept them comfortably. Work the soil closely around the roots. Plants only feed through the fine roots.

Evergreens in particular suffer from lack of water at or after planting. 'Puddling' is done by flooding the half-filled hole with water, with more given after the planting is complete Do not use this method in clay soil, though. Clay usually has more than enough moisture in it already. In hot weather, spray new evergreens occasionally with a garden hose. Plants absorb their water supplies through the leaves as well as through the roots.

PRIVET (Ligustrum)

Appearance

Too familiar to need description, privet has gone rather out of favour over the past few years. It is, however, certainly one of the hardiest and the easiest of all hedge plants to grow. Apart from its speed of growth, which makes frequent cutting necessary, it presents few problems as to soil, situation or disease.

The golden varieties are best to plant, but these are a little more tender and slower in growth when young. Also they tend to revert to plain green at times. Usually this only happens on one or two branches at first, and these reverting stems should be cut away completely.

Attempts are sometimes made to plant green and yellow forms alternately but this is rarely successful as the more vigorous green usually gets the upper hand.

Privet roots soon penetrate widely and flowers grown in beds adjoining the hedge will be unable to deal with this sort of competition. These roots can be cut off by digging a trench 18 ins. deep a foot away from the hedge. This will check them for a year or two. Often a better plan is to rearrange the garden to place a path or a lawn next to the hedge with the flower beds well away.

Cost

One of the cheapest hedge plants (in the green form) and so swift in growth that one can buy quite small plants. The usual spacing is about 1 ft. Price depends on height, being in the region of £15 per hundred plants 2 ft. tall.

Speed of growth

Privet grows very fast indeed and a tall hedge can be developed within three or four years. Height will be of little value, though, if the hedge is thin. Frequent clipping, including the cutting back of upward growth, will make a thick hedge. Plants allowed to develop upwards too quickly may be very sparse at the base.

Maintenance

Frequent clipping is needed to maintain a thick growth. At least six times a season, with the preference being for frequent light trimming rather than for infrequent severe attacks. Privet is very susceptible to growth-retarding sprays. These are applied in spring after the first trimming and the new growth will be much slower than normal. This applies to hedges which have attained the desired size. As with all hedges the trimming should leave the upper part narrower than the base so that the sides face upwards to the light. Power trimmers work well.

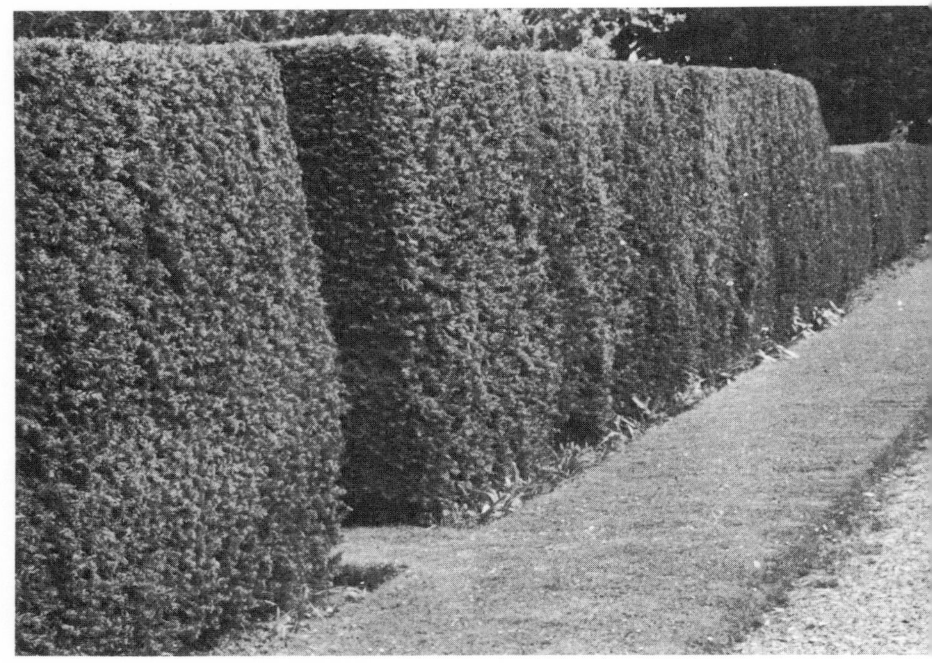

YEW (Taxus)

Appearance
Yew makes a very fine close-textured hedge which can be kept in perfect shape without heavy clipping.

It was often used for topiary work in which elaborate shapes were 'carved' from the bushes. Since growth is not rapid it is relatively easy to maintain in neat order. There are golden varieties which have an excellent appearance but they tend to be rather costly. Its greatest defect is that virtually all parts of the plant are very poisonous to animals, or indeed to humans, and certainly yew should never be planted at a roadside.

With holly, yew is one of the two best evergreen hedges in suitable situations. It will grow in any soil.

Cost
Expensive individually, but the plants, which should be bought fairly tall, about 3 ft., can be spaced rather further apart than other species. Twenty ins. is not too much and well-grown plants may even be adequately close at 30 ins. Each will cost in the region of 25s.

Speed of growth
Very slow when young (which accounts for the plants' high cost from the nurseries). Growth speeds up later and a substantial hedge 4 or 5 ft. tall may be had within six years. With strong plants there is a screening effect right from planting time.

Maintenance
Clipping even once a year will keep a yew hedge in bounds but the typical rich, thick leafage is only attained by fairly frequent but very light trims. It is most suitable for precise and decorative clipping and for topiary. The stems are rather wiry for power trimmers but younger growth is soft and readily cut. Growth retarding sprays do not seem to be suitable.

HOLLY (Ilex)

Appearance
Another very familiar plant. The holly is grown throughout Britain and gives one of the finest of hedges. It is tough, impenetrable, attractively coloured, evergreen, hardy and needs little maintenance. Its slowish growth means that it needs only infrequent trimming, though it follows that tall hedges take some time to grow. Yet even a low hedge looks attractive as a boundary and keeps out animals and children from the start. Holly should not be used where any rapid screening is needed. Though it will tolerate most soils it is slow to establish itself on chalk.

Cost
Expensive. It is slow in growing but if plants upwards of 3 ft. tall can be found, the planting spacing may be as much as 18 ins. This may work out at 50s. per yd., with the variegated varieties substantially more, if obtainable at all.

Speed of growth
Slow, especially when young and newly planted. After a year or two settling in, development may speed up a little but it never becomes really fast.

Maintenance
Easy. A single annual trim is usually enough. Power trimmers do not cut holly well, tending to slash the leaves. Do not trim severely, as cut stumps of branches commonly die back.

THORN (Crataegus)

Appearance

The hawthorn or May blossom is familiar to everybody, and 'Quickthorn' is probably the commonest of farm hedge plants. It is less common in gardens because of its thorns, its rapid growth calling for frequent trimming, and its loss of all leaves in winter.

For places such as the rear of large gardens where protection from intruders is important, thorn is very good indeed and exceptionally cheap. Usually, in fact, it is the cheapest of all hedge plants.

Flowering is less common in hedges than in individual bushes or trees because the trimming removes the buds, but when it does take place the sight is splendid.

Any soil will serve. Power trimmers work well, as do growth retarders.

Cost

Cheapest of all. Though planted fairly closely, 8 ins. or so apart in double staggered rows, the plants may be put in very small and cost only about £6 10s. per hundred, 18 ins. tall.

Speed of growth

Rapid. Even from small stock a good 4 or 5 ft tall hedge may be grown in five years. Rich soil speeds growth a good deal and there are fairly wide variations in the rapidity of development.

Maintenance

Frequent trimming is essential or the hedge will rapidly become straggly and thin at the base. Precise shaping can be done. The hedge is dull in winter as it is not an evergreen.

LAUREL (Prunus)

Appearance
The familiar large rounded leaves of the laurel make a good screen and there are several yellow variegated relatives that make rather more decorative hedges than the plain dark green. They do especially well in town atmospheres with soot or smoke prevailing, and in places where deep shade prevents other species from flourishing.

Cost
In the middle price range. Well grown 2 ft. bushes cost about 12s. each. A thick hedge needs two or three plants per yd. Since laurel grows fairly rapidly one may plant much smaller bushes without losing much time.

Growth
Fairly swift, and soon thickening well to make a good screen.

Maintenance
Clipping is not needed very frequently, perhaps two or three times per year. Laurel does not clip well with shears, for these slice across the large leaves which often then turn brown. Snipping the individual leaves is done best by using secateurs. This though is not as laborious as it sounds, for with laurel a little such work goes a long way. Power trimmers are unsuitable.

BOX (Buxus)

Appearance

The tiny leaves of evergreen box are familiar, especially in older gardens, and sometimes in the form of miniature hedges, only inches high, around flower beds or rose gardens. As a main hedge it serves very well, though it takes several years to reach any size.

As it is not poisonous it is to be preferred to yew at roadsides or where children have access. Like yew it is very suitable for close trimming and topiary work. Very good on chalky land.

Cost

Not cheap. Bushes 2 ft. high costing roughly 15s. each and being planted two or three per yd. It pays to buy bushes at least this tall, provided they have adequate leafage lower down their stems, as they are very slow to grow when young. For miniature hedges it is usual to buy by the yard, current cost being about 12s. per yd.

Speed of growth

Slow, especially when young, but soon thickening if frequently clipped.

Maintenance

Though once a year shearing, in late summer, is adequate for a mature hedge serving mainly as a screen, younger hedges do well with three trims annually. This promotes faster thickening at the base. Power tools work fairly well.

LONICERA (Lonicera)

Appearance
The tiny, closely set evergreen leaves, very dark when mature, give a well trimmed Lonicera hedge a smooth, solid texture. Tall hedges tend to become open and rather straggly at the base, with loss of leaves, but this is easily corrected by severe cutting back. In fact a large hedge can be cut almost to the ground without killing it, and the resulting young growth can be retrained into a compact, pleasing shape. This is not a good choice for hedges required to be over 5 ft. tall because its stems do not have the strength to support the height.

Cost
Moderate. The plants can be put in quite small, though rather close, say 10 ins. apart or 1 ft. apart in a double staggered row. Plants 18 ins. tall may cost around £15 per 100.

Speed of growth
Lonicera is one of the fastest growers of all, and a good hedge 3 to 4 ft. tall can be produced in three years or so. It is as well, though, to restrain upward growth at first to ensure adequate leafing at the base.

Maintenance
Frequent clipping is needed to keep this hedge in order and the stems are fairly wiry. They tend to jam in power tools, especially if trimming is infrequent. Ideally, a quick weekly trim after the lawn is mown saves time over the year by preventing long growths and making the surface close and leafy.

BEECH (Fagus)

Appearance

One of the very best of the non-evergreen hedge plants. Beech in fact often retains a number of leaves through the year, though these will be brown in winter. The range of colours offered by a beech really is splendid, ranging from the delicate yellow-green of the new leaves in spring, through the rich greens of summer to the yellows, golds and browns of autumn.

As a summer screen the beech is ideal and may be grown 8 ft. tall or even higher. The roots are not as demanding as privet but beds near such tall hedges will certainly suffer some loss of plant food. Grass right up to the hedge looks well and makes clipping easier.

Cost

Quite low. The beech is popular, and fairly quick to grow. Spaced 15 ins. apart the cost for a 2 ft. tall hedge might be 8s. per yd. *Copper Beech* is grown similarly but costs rather more. *Hornbeam* is very similar in habit and appearance to beech and does better on clay soil.

Speed of growth

Moderately quick, depending to some extent on the care taken in preparing the soil. Chalk is no drawback, but any waterlogging must be cured before planting.

Maintenance

One clipping a year, in August, is all that is required for a mature hedge though younger ones should be shaped in spring too. The rather large leaves are awkward to cut with a power tool, but not impossible. For such infrequent trimming, though, most gardeners would use hand shears.

;YPRESS (Chamaecyparis)

\ppearance
Лany plants that are not in fact cypresses are :ommonly called by that name, including ;hamaecyparis and Thuja. Their general ppearance is very similar, as is their reatment and care.

This group of plants may be placed as a creen, with spaces between them, or they nay be allowed to grow together to form a olid hedge. Chamaecyparis Lawsoniana, vhich grows naturally in a pleasing flame hape, is best planted separately, but ;upressus macrocarpa grows very rapidly nto a thick hedge. It may be clipped omewhat, but none of these plants really ike hard trimming.

The greatest risk is that of die-back due to rost or cold winds. This affects even quite vell established trees, and a hedge gap made ike this is almost impossible to fill.

The biggest advantage of this group, if planted as a screen, is that they can be put in quite tall, upwards of 6 ft. if need be. It is ital to keep them well watered, both when planting and afterwards, and for this reason puddling' is often the planting method hosen. (See page 64.)

Cost
Varies a good deal depending on the species chosen, the size of the plants and the district in which they are bought. The best plan is to visit local nurseries who will advise on the best types for the district and the costs. As a very rough guide, in the South of England 4 ft. tall Chamaecyparis Lawsoniana may cost about 21s. each and may be planted 2 ft. apart (as a hedge) or as separate specimens in screen.

BARBERRIES (Berberis)

Appearance
There are several members of the Berberis family that may be grown as hedges as well as separate shrubs. The two commonest may be Berberis Darwinii and Berberis stenophylla, with Berberis Thunbergii becoming also popular. All these have vigorous flowers as well as a compact growth of small leaves. They are all spiny and make impenetrable hedges. Thunbergii has a purple form that makes a striking hedge. None of them are really happy as tall hedges, more than 4 ft., say, but because of their prolific flowering they can make a very pleasing garden feature.

Cost
Moderate, with plants 2 ft. tall costing between 16s. and 18s. each. Plant about 15 ins or 18 ins. apart for vigorous growth. Do not buy larger bushes for they do not always transplant well.

Speed of growth
Moderate. Much will depend on the soil. Deep, rich loam will give the plants a flying start though they will do reasonably well almost everywhere.

Maintenance
Shearing once or twice every year will be adequate in many cases, with power trimmer being usable but tending to jam on older stems. Strong gloves are essential because the spines are very sharp and tough.

PRUNUS PISSARDII (Prunus Pissardii nigra)

Appearance
This plant has deep purple leaves and can be trimmed into a hedge of distinction. The leaves are lost in winter so it is often grown in conjunction with some form of fence. It has close relatives that are green-leaved. These rapidly make a fairly dense hedge. Trimming is not difficult for the stems are slim and cut easily. Power trimmers work well, as do some retarders.

Cost
Moderate in price. Depending on local demand many nurseries may now stock this in quantity, as it makes the easiest of the 'red' hedges. One can plant fairly wide, even up to 2 ft. as the growth is fast, but 18 ins. is better. Plants 3 ft. tall cost about 12s. each.

Speed of growth
Fairly quick to develop, but growth upwards should be restricted till the base of the hedge has thickened. Plants can be had several feet tall at times, but there is no real advantage in buying large ones. They can be a bit checked on transplanting and smaller ones may catch them up in a year or so.

Maintenance
This hedge survives a certain amount of neglect, merely becoming a little looser in appearance. But the strong upward growth of untrimmed plants may cause rapid thinning of the base. Trim lightly and often to get maximum screening for it is not, in its purple form at least, always a thick grower.

Light trimming may lead to flowering, with white or pinkish blooms appearing in early spring, before the leaves.

Shrubs for Screens: flowering shrubs and modern methods

Modern gardens have lost a good deal of the old formality and the close-cropped hedge is not seen quite so frequently. Yet the popularity of a living screen, rather than a simple fence, has led to the wide use of shrubs which are allowed to grow more or less naturally in size and shape yet so placed as to give screening. Protection of the actual boundary may still be left to a fence, perhaps a simple stretch of wire netting, but this is partly or completely concealed behind the shrubs.

Flowering shrubs are widely used, as are those having coloured leaves, and there is a very big range from which to choose.

For swiftest results and tolerance of a wide range of conditions, and of some neglect at times, we have selected fourteen shrubs. However, no two gardeners would choose the same ones, and before making a final choice for an important position in the garden it pays to visit some nursery or Garden Centre where the shrubs can be seen in leaf and flower.

With modern techniques of growing shrubs in containers for immediate sale, even in full flower, there is a great deal of interest in buying at these Centres. The owners are often willing to advise on plants especially suited to the area.

Success with container grown plants is uniformly high, provided that these are *genuinely* grown in the containers and are not merely field stock, hastily lifted and thrust into tins or polythene bags for sale.

This is not simple for an amateur to detect and the best thing is to deal with large and established nurseries, if possible, or with smaller ones where the plants can be seen in bulk, and under care.

Planting shrubs from containers: the modern Garden Centre

The modern Garden Centre has largely developed with the increasing use of containers, in which quite large plants are grown. The containers may be tins, pots, fibre cups or even tough polythene bags.

There is no transplanting problem because the plant develops all its roots inside the container rather than in the soil of a field.

Plants bought like this may be taken away at once, even in flower, and planted immediately in the buyer's garden.

Because the roots are not disturbed the plant suffers no check and continues to grow happily.

In the Garden Centre the containers will be stood on the ground but the buyer will bury the roots. Some sorts of container must obviously be removed. The tin can, for example! But some made of felt may be put in just as they are. Once underground, the pot can rot away and the roots will find their way out into the surrounding soil. Polythene coverings are simply torn away.

The commonest cause of failure with the larger plants is looseness of planting. After frost the soil may lift, so tread the soil back into place round all new shrubs, after the frost has passed.

1 Although felt pots like this need not be removed completely, it is helpful to pull away the base of the container as the plant is put in. The latest types, however, must be removed.

2 Stand the plant in its prepared hole.

1

2

3 Make certain that the plant is firmly held by pressing the soil at each side with the feet. Tear away any felt of the container still remaining above ground level.

4 Tin containers are still used by some nurseries. They should be cut apart before purchase.

5 *Wearing gloves*, thrust the tin apart to extract the plant.

3

4

5

Simple Shrubs: a survey of suitable types

1 DEUTZIA
Usual colours: white, pink, cream.
Flowers in early spring.
Pruning: remove old wood after flowering. Leave new growth to flower the following year.

2 BUDDLEIA
Usual colours: white, blue, purple, dark red.
Flowers in late summer.
Pruning: cut all branches right back hard in spring.
Flowers appear on current season's growth.

All these shrubs are familiar in our gardens today. They are popular for the best of reasons. They grow strongly into large bushes. They are hardy. They require no skilled attention. They flower profusely and reliably. They are not expensive.

There are others, of course, equally desirable. A visit to any nursery or Garden Centre will show many more, suiting special conditions. But those we show can be used for screening, without much effort beyond the original planting, in most parts of the country.

Other good shrubs to look for at nurseries or Garden Centres are azaleas (on acid soils only), camellias, cotoneasters, diervilla, euonymus, hamamelis, hibiscus, hydrangea, kerria, magnolia, rhododendrons (acid soils) rhus, ribes, spiraea and syringa (lilacs).

1

2

FORSYTHIA
sual colour: yellow.
lowers before the leaves appear in early pring.
runing: remove old wood after flowering. eave new growth to flower the following ear.

ACERS
sual colour, *of leaves*, may be yellow, reen, red or purple, and many change olour brilliantly in autumn.
hese are small trees or tall shrubs.
lowers: negligible.
runing: not usually required.
lote that Acer is a family name. The ones to uy are known as Japanese Acers or laples (*Acer japonicum*).

5 VIBURNUM OPULUS STERILE (Guelder Rose)
Usual colour: white.
Flowers in early summer.
Pruning: not essential.

6 PHILADELPHUS (Mock Orange Blossom)
Usual colour: white.
Flowers in summer.
Pruning: remove the stems that have flowered, in mid or late summer.

5

6

7 MALUS (Apple family)
Usual colours: white, pink.
Malus is a large group with many species, all fairly easy to grow. They like sunlight.
Flowers in late spring.
Pruning: to shape only; in late autumn or winter.

8 AUCUBA (*Aucuba japonica variegata*)
'Variegated Laurel'
Usual colours of leaves yellow/green.
Bright berries on female plants only.
Flowers: negligible.
Pruning: clip to shape if desired. This shrub will withstand deep shade.

9 CYTISUS (Broom)
Usual colours: white, yellow, orange, pink.
Flowers in spring.
Pruning: none. Likes sandy soils.
Low-growing.

10 DAPHNE
Usual colours: white, pink, red.
Flowers early winter or spring.
Pruning: none needed. Likes peaty soils.
Low-growing.

7 9 8 10

11 FIR (Family)
Usual colours: evergreen, pale or dark, some species almost golden. Many sorts.
Flowers: none.
Pruning: none. Tall evergreens give more height to shrubberies needed for screening.

12 POTENTILLA
Usual colour: white, yellow, orange.
Flowers in summer.
Pruning: none. Low-growing.

11

12

Questions and answers on lawns, hedges, fences and gates

My property is not fenced at present. Am I legally bound to provide one?
Not as a basic legal rule. But there may be a requirement in the deeds of your property under which you have to provide a fence. Of course if you have animals it is your duty to prevent them straying.

My neighbour claims that the fence between our two gardens belongs to him, because the the posts are on his side. Is this correct?
It is often the case that a fence's ownership will be shown by the position of the posts, being set on the owner's side. This is not however a legal requirement and cannot be relied upon as proof of ownership. Usually the house deeds will show the true owner. In the absence of hard and fast proof, it is often ruled that a fence is a joint property, maintained by both neighbours equally, and requiring the consent of both to any alteration.

Our house deeds show that one of our fences belongs to a neighbour. This is very unsightly and I would like to build a much taller one, inside our own boundary. But my neighbour will not allow this. What can I do?
Your neighbour has no power to stop you building any fence, in reason, within your own boundary, provided that you can do this without encroaching on his land at all. But you will have to do all the erection work, and all future maintenance such as painting, from your own side too, which may prove difficult. You have no legal right to enter your neighbour's land even to do essential repairs.

All the houses round us have 'Open-Plan' front gardens, which we dislike. Can we erect a fence round our open plot without getting planning permission?
Planning permission is not required for any normal garden fence. However, if *all* your neighbouring houses have Open Plan front gardens this suggests that there may be a restrictive Covenant on the houses preventing fences being erected. Consult your Solicitor or Building Society, or the house deeds, if you have them.

We have a large hedge that screens us from our neighbour's garden, but he claims that it is obstructing the light to his flower beds and insists that we must cut it down low. We like our privacy and wonder if he can, in Law, insist on this?
There is no 'Right to Light' for a garden, so your neighbour has no possible means of making you remove or cut your hedge. He could of course cut it back to the boundary if it overhangs his land. Could you not trim the hedge at his side at an angle, so as to let more light strike through, without affecting its screening power?

I have a large garden and have been told that the best plan for easy maintenance is to cover it with lawn. Is this correct?

Grass is certainly less troublesome to look after than, say, large flower beds, but a true lawn is more than just grass. If by a lawn you mean a close-mown, weed free, level sward in perfect order, then it certainly will not be very easy to keep in trim. But a grass area that is fairly rough, mowed perhaps every month with a rotary mower, can certainly look pleasant and needs little work. There is, for many people, a kind of pleasure in motor-mowing, especially with rotary types.

How do the modern selective weedkillers work?

These act by being absorbed by the plant and upsetting the natural balance of the growth-regulating hormones. They control the growth that a plant makes in its leaves, stems and so on. This type of weedkiller causes growth to become very rapid and irregular, so as to produce deformities and weaknesses that lead to injury or death.

Since straight leaved plants such as grass are very little affected by the hormones of broad leaved plants, they remain in normal, or very slightly retarded growth, whilst the others die.

What is a lawnsand?

Lawnsand is a mixture of chemical fertilizers and sharp sand which is scattered generously over the lawn surface. It provides chemical food, and the sand improves the general texture of the soil.

Also, it acts as a mild and safe weedkiller, because direct contact with chemicals, even fertilizers, will scorch leaves. Since the leaves of many weeds are broad and flat, the sand tends to rest on them, while falling *between* the vertical grass blades. This effect may also be increased by the inclusion of selective killers.

Our lawn is covered with the casts of worms. What is the best treatment for this?

Start by brushing the casts off the lawn surface on a dry day. If the number of casts appearing before the next weekly mow are not too great, simply make a practice of sweeping before mowing. Worms do so much good in the soil that they should only be destroyed in extreme cases.

To kill worms, buy Mowrah meal from a nurseryman or seedsman, and water the liquid over the surface. This will bring the worms up to the surface in hundreds and they can then be swept away to the compost heap. Most people find this a very unpleasant task!

I have a lot of moss appearing in my lawn. How can I remove this?
As a rule moss indicates bad drainage. Start by spiking and sanding the whole lawn, using plenty of coarse sand well brushed into the holes. Since mossy soil is often impoverished, improve it by giving a really heavy dressing of compost, well-sieved, till the whole area is covered about $\frac{1}{4}$ in. deep. After three or four weeks, when the grass is growing through, scatter a dressing of mercurised lawnsand. This will both discourage the moss and improve the grass. Continue to apply layers of fine soil or compost each year till you have added about $1\frac{1}{2}$ ins. to the original lawn surface.

For more rapid effect you can rake the moss vigorously with a spring-tined rake, giving a lawn fertilizer afterwards. This does work at times but some gardeners have claimed that it may also spread the moss further by scattering the spores.

In my garden there is a gigantic old laurel hedge which we would like to cut much lower. However, this would mean sawing right into very thick branches well below the leaves. Will this kill the plants?
Go right ahead and saw the branches off. Laurel will break out into new growth even from trunks several inches thick, as a rule. Saw the whole lot to about 9 ins. shorter than you wish the final hedge to be, to allow for the outward and upward growth of the new stems.

How do you make a rose hedge?
There are two sorts of rose hedge. The first and cheapest is to plant the wild Rugosa plants, or similar, which are often sold as 'Rose Hedging' through advertisements in the gardening or Sunday press. These will grow vigorously enough and make a large, tangled thicket of wild roses, which, if there is space enough, may be quite attractive.

The true rose hedge, though, is made by planting rows of tall-growing Polyantha (Floribunda) Roses such as Frensham, and pruning these off at a regular height to make a thick hedge. These look magnificent and do well in any reasonably rich soil, but naturally cost a good deal. The plants are commonly placed only 18 ins. apart and may cost six or seven shillings each.

What is a chamomile lawn?
Chamomile is a low growing and aromatic plant and it is not impossible to grow it as a continuous sward like grass.

There are several strains, some growing quite tall, but a low growing sort will give a green covering that rarely needs mowing, but which also cannot be used as a normal lawn. It will not stand walking on very well.

A normal compromise is to mix the chamomile seed with fine grass seed so that the lawn becomes partly grass. Mowing will then be needed but the lawn is unusual in texture and slightly perfumed. One or two firms specialise in this seed and their advice should be sought before going ahead.

1 A path inlaid in a lawn.
2 First lay out the slabs to a pattern or string guide on the lawn surface.
3 Cut down all round the slab with a spade to about 3 ins. deep.

We have to pass across our lawn to reach a side gate. This is wearing the grass away. What sort of simple path could we make here?

Inlay concrete or stone slabs into the turf. If these are set just below the grass level then the mower will easily pass over them when mowing.

1

2

3

4 Lift the turf within these cuts 2 ins. or so thick. Remove it and use for repairs to the lawn.
5 Spread a thin layer of fine soil or sand in the hollow.
6 Lower the slab into the sand bed.
7 Use *light* taps with a baulk of timber to bed the slab down.

4
6
5
7

Can Flowering Currant (Ribes) be used to form a hedge?

Yes, but the growth is never strong. Support it by straining wires on posts, at least for the first few years. Trim after the flowers have died away.

I have a large lawn. Suggest a decorative tree that might be planted as a specimen in its centre.

Magnolias. Either the very early white *stellata* (1) or the later pink Soulangeana (2) make good lawn specimens. Or use one of the flowering cherries (3). Some varieties grow straight upwards like poplars, and are good for smaller lawns.

1

3

I would like to try my hand at topiary. Which plant is best?
Box makes a good topiary plant for amateurs, also yew. (1, 2 and 3.)

2

1

How can I best prepare for daffodils, to be naturalised in part of our lawns?

Remember that the bulbs will be there a long time. Plant them as carefully as you would in a bed, giving deeply dug and well-fertilized planting places.

To do this well, you may have to lift and set aside the turf (see pages 36, 37). Without this careful preparation bulbs often make a good show the first season, then rapidly deteriorate in following years. Do not mow off their leaves. Wait for them to die down naturally. This means that turf having daffodils cannot be close mowed like a lawn. They are good in grass under trees, which is left rather long in any case.

I have been told that more modern wood preservatives are better than Creosote. Is this so?

No. Creosote remains one of the most effective of all preservatives. It is also relatively cheap. Indeed, a great number of experiments have been done to try to find *more* effective treatments, but without much success. The snag with raw Creosote for home use is that it is extremely irritating to the eyes. When using it on, say, fence posts it is very hard to avoid the occasional splash. Even the passing of a weary hand over the forehead will get Creosote dangerously near your eyes! And the very best treatment possible, using *hot* Creosote, could never be recommended for this reason and because Creosote is inflammable.

Always use Creosote out of doors, preferably by some sort of dipping method, not brushing, and never smoke while doing the job. And never let it get near your eyes, or severe pain will be inevitable. In fact it is worth while to improvise goggles for the job.